Where the Lost Dogs Go

Where
the
Lost
Dogs
Go

A STORY OF LOVE, SEARCH,
AND THE POWER OF REUNION

Susannah Charleson

Houghton Mifflin Harcourt   BOSTON   NEW YORK   2019

For information about permission to reproduce selections from this book, write to trade.permissions@hmhco.com or to Permissions, Houghton Mifflin Harcourt Publishing Company, 3 Park Avenue, 19th Floor, New York, New York 10016.

hmhco.com

Library of Congress Cataloging-in-Publication Data
Names: Charleson, Susannah, author.
Title: Where the lost dogs go : a story of love, search, and the power of reunion / Susannah Charleson.
Description: Boston : Houghton Mifflin Harcourt, 2019.
Identifiers: LCCN 2018046441 (print) | LCCN 2018052049 (ebook) |
ISBN 9781328995100 (ebook) | ISBN 9781328995056 (hardcover)
Subjects: LCSH: Lost dogs — Anecdotes. | Search and rescue operations. | Human-animal relationships.
Classification: LCC SF427.6 (ebook) | LCC SF427.6 .C43 2019 (print) |
DDC 636.7 — dc23
LC record available at https://lccn.loc.gov/2018046441

Book design by Martha Kennedy

Printed in the United States of America
DOC 10 9 8 7 6 5 4 3 2 1

All photographs provided courtesy of the author with the following exceptions: Chapter 2 opener photograph used with permission of Conroe Animal Shelter in Conroe, Texas; Chapter 4 opener (top) used with permission of The Retrievers.

For my parents, Peggy and Lynn,
who never turned away from any need on four paws

August 2015.

CONTENTS

1. Magnet Dog   1

2. The One in the Back of the Cage   15

3. In the Goodwill of Rescue   27

4. The Quality of Mercy   41

5. Welcome to the Clown Car   61

6. The Human Factor   73

7. Ghost in the Hall   83

8. A Boy and His Dog   93

9. Houdini   99

10. Survival Mode   109

11. Against the Wall   123

12. Safe Harbor   131

13. Thy Neighbor's Dog   143

14. A Little Ambition   151

15. Finding His Voice   161

16. The Bastard Search   167

17. Together and Apart   175

18. Cats in Tight Places   185

19. On Our Street Alone   195

20. Air and Ground   205

21. The Dog in Question   215

22. Good Fences   225

23. The Little Stranger   239

24. A Winter Storm   245

25. Bring Egg Home   259

26. Big Dog, Little Shadow   269

27. Love, Find Us   279

28. Next   285

    AFTERWORD   297

    ACKNOWLEDGMENTS   301

    APPENDIX   303

    SOURCES   310

Where the Lost Dogs Go

Puzzle off-duty,
at play beside our house.

1

MAGNET DOG

P UZZLE WAKES ME with her going. Somewhere in my sleep I must have felt her head lift first, before she rolled up onto her feet, but it is my hand in empty air, the stab of her absence, that truly wakes me. The golden retriever pads to the edge of the front porch, and I open my eyes, squinting into the afternoon haze. Puzzle moves a little stiffly, as though her hips are tired. She poises at the steps that lead down to the yard, turning her head toward the cross street and drawing her ears forward in question. In this light, I can see her silvered face.

Puzzle is an eleven-year-old search-and-rescue dog, and I'm the partner who runs beside her to find missing persons. A decade ago she was the bright spark of a puppy in training and I the human adult who had to keep up with her, but in the unfair way of dogs and time, Puzzle is senior to me now — her dog years equate seventy-two to my fifty-five. She wears it well. Puzzle's pretty face still lights up at the prospect of work — her favorite adventure — and she bounds across the search field with joy. But I've seen a change in her gait lately, and sometimes at the end of long days across rough terrain, her hips betray her.

The golden trained hard in the heat this morning. We both did. We came home ready for a late lunch followed by a nap together. It is an after-work ritual we've had for years: I lie in the porch swing, and Puzzle stretches out beneath me on the wood planks, where my fingertips graze her shoulders with each movement of the swing.

Something got her up now, though.

What's going on? I wonder, as Puzzle trots down the steps and rounds the corner of the house out of sight. I sit up fuzzily, thick and stupid with nap sleep, more curious than worried. Puz works with me off-leash, sometimes searching a long way away before communicating back to me. She's a faithful dog with a solid recall. The invisible line forged between us means I could call her now and she would return from wherever she's gone, for whatever reason. But part of the deal is that I pay attention to what she shows me at any time.

I find her standing in the dry grass at the edge of the front yard. She's concentrating there, her head cocked, gazing down the street. Puzzle has always paid attention to change near her territory. Her tail waves idly as she marks my approach, but she doesn't turn her head.

Something is happening a few houses north of us. From where we stand I hear the long bleat of a horn, the slam of a car door, and faint voices raised. Then a battered white car speeds past us, followed by anxious, escalating cries. Louder now, I hear the unsteady slap of feet running toward us. A young woman hurtles into view, so awkwardly I'm afraid she'll fall. She's got on black yoga pants and a sweat-soaked pink tank top, and she's trying to run along the uneven sidewalk in flip-flops. Her expression is panicked. Her short light hair is wild.

"My dog," she says. "My dog is gone." She's breathless and hoarse. "A lady . . . back there says you, says your dog . . . says you can . . ." She looks at me blankly, like she doesn't know what to ask for. "His heart is bad," she says. "Please."

Puzzle can sense the tension. She steps forward to the young woman at the fence, scenting her hand and quivering with adrenaline. *We'll come,* I tell the young woman. When I bring out Puzzle's long lead, the golden pops up on her forepaws, ready for anything.

Whether she's searching for a single lost person or multiple victims of catastrophe, search and rescue (SAR) is work that Puzzle is good at and a job beside me that she passionately loves. But Puzzle's search work has always been human-specific; part of her training involved proofing her *against* finding animals. This is a standard for many K9 search-and-rescue teams, who must assure fire, law enforcement, and disaster agencies that the dogs deployed to find a missing child won't alert, that is, signal to the handler, on every pet they pass. But it's confusing to neighbors, who often believe a search dog finds anything at any time. I can never ask Puzzle to find missing pets.

Here's the twist. Lost pets find *her*. She's got that reputation in the neighborhood, too. There's something about my golden retriever that attracts stray animals. Friendly, spooked, or simply confused, they seek her out. It's not something Puzzle does; it's something she is, something I don't understand and can't explain. *Magnet dogs,* I've lately learned such creatures are called. But now is no time to lecture my neighbor about the distinction.

His name is Odie, the young woman tells us as we jog back to her house. And he is very old. Black all over except for gray on his face. She was in the shower. She was in the shower and Odie was there in the bathroom with her, because when she gets out of the shower he likes to lick her wet feet. But someone else in the house was going in and out the front door, and maybe the screen didn't close or something, and Odie must've slipped past it, because when she got out of the shower he wasn't there, and he was always there, and she knew right away that something was wrong. That was noon or maybe a little later. She's been searching since then. He never goes out the door. Never. Except he must have. The young woman pauses, says her friend—and she hesitates on the word—is out driving around looking for Odie in his car. She's tried to ask the neighbors. She's knocked on every door for three blocks. People don't answer their doors here, she says. Why don't people answer their doors? Odie is a very old sort of dachshund. He's fuzzy, and he has a spine thing and a heart murmur and a deformed windpipe, but he is the sweetest dog, the best dog, and this heat will kill him. And there are coyotes. She has seen them. Could a coyote have gotten him this fast? Jesus. He weighs only nine pounds. He's been with her since he was six weeks old. She searched the house and the yard and around the block, and she's called and called, but he hasn't come. And Odie always comes when she calls him. He couldn't have gotten far, right? Unless a coyote got him. Or someone took him. Would someone take him? His name is Odie, she repeats, Odie for the cartoon dog in *Garfield,* and he is shy.

She says all of this in the four and a half blocks between her house and mine — a tangled narrative charged with the same pain I've heard from others who've lost someone they love. Words on words, they claw their way back to the moment when things went wrong, when they made a choice they would change, if they could, and everything would be okay.

If Puzzle was tired when she got up from the porch, she's shaken it off now. She trots easily ahead on her long lead. I explain to the young woman that Puzzle doesn't search for other dogs the way she would search for humans but that strays sometimes come out for her. I'm glad to take Puz through the house and the neighborhood in the hope that Odie will do the same. The young woman stops. I see her face change. We're not the miracle she was hoping for. *Okay,* she says after a beat or two. *I'll take any help at all.*

I recognize her little corner house. I've passed this 1920s box cottage on walks. There was a party here back in November — I remember feeling a little envious as the passing outsider — the house bright, bursting with guests and laughter, figures shadowed beneath the porch light, crowded on the stoop with their red cups, spilling out onto the front lawn.

It's a different house now. A neighbor's dog barks furiously as we hurry onto the tiny porch and through a paint-flaked screen door. The place looks like it's been ransacked. From where we stand I can see the living room, dining room, and kitchen and, around the corner, the closed door to a bedroom. Bare walls are riddled with nail holes. The floor is a jumble of boxes. Some of them are open, full of random items — there's a juicer, a pair of sunglasses, and a hard drive. A few boxes have their leaves folded shut. BEDRM, reads the label on one. KITCHEN, another.

The young woman says Odie likes to tunnel under things, but he can't climb or jump. He couldn't get in a box, and there's nothing much to tunnel under here in the house. Not a couch, not even a bed. She'd hoped my search dog might find him squeezed into some tiny place she had overlooked.

"So you're moving, and . . . ," I begin.

"*I'm* not," she says, wrapping her arms around herself, and that sums up the sense I get from her, standing in this uneasy space, that the only thing she's got left that matters is Odie. She looks exhausted as she gestures us freedom of the house and leaves us to change her shoes.

Moving quickly, Puz and I wind through the disarray. A book stack tilting against a milk crate of record albums. A framed high school diploma lying flat, a coffee cup ring on the glass. Two fat wine bottles with candle wax melted down the sides. There's a striped sheet in the middle of the dining room, tied up at the corners around what looks like laundry. An empty closet stands open; a plaid shirt droops from its doorknob. I've seen houses like this before: abandoned houses on search deployments; estate sales after the pickers have come; my own home at the edge of divorce, when I got to a point that I was tempted to give everything left away rather than fill another box marked MISCELLANEOUS — things no longer ours, things painful as mine.

Puzzle hops over a slid stack of magazines, where a steady-eyed Willie Nelson gazes up from a *Rolling Stone*. As we move, I'm thinking hard about Odie. In a disrupted house, this anxious, elderly, disabled dog, who comes when his person calls, goes missing in the heat of the day. He might be hiding. He might be running—hobbling, more likely. I can't think a dog like Odie could go far on his own. I peer into the closet, open the bathroom cabinets, and gently roll over the striped bundle of laundry. Dachshunds like to tunnel, don't they?

No sign of the little dog here. Puzzle has picked her way across the last of the space. She thrills in the kitchen, where a green-eyed cat stares down at her from the top of the refrigerator. Puz likes cats, and she beams up at this one, her tail swaying. But the cat is having none of it. The tabby shrinks himself by a third, and his eyes dilate wider.

The young woman meets us at the back door. She glances up at the fridge. Neighbor's cat, she tells us. He visits. She has just searched the tiny backyard again, where I can see burned grass cut short to a chain-link fence. There's nowhere for a dog to hide there. No tree for shade, no porch to duck under. She's looked everywhere she can think of twice, she says. She even crawled behind the bushes in front of the house. She has no idea what to do now.

We've got to head out, but we need to be smart about it.

I'm wrestling lost-person strategies on behalf of a missing dog. In human search and rescue, we consider three factors in the plan for the wandering lost: *direction of travel* determines which way someone went from the place last seen, helping us figure out where to put searchers first; *containment* creates barriers in an area to prevent that someone from wandering out of it; and *attraction* uses things like lights, siren pips, music, balloons, which might draw a lost person to those searching for him or her. These factors are just as relevant to lost Odie as they would be to a missing child, but now I need to think like a skittish, low-slung black dog with a heart condition, so small that he is able to fall into gutters, who can't recognize human help when it comes for him and who's not going to be interested in music and balloons at all.

Puzzle looks up at me, ready for whatever is next.

The young woman says the back door was locked before Odie went missing. She's pretty sure he went out the front door. It had been open a lot with her friend going in and out, and the screen door didn't always close. I have to wonder—and I have to ask—about the friend. Strange things happen in the search for lost humans, and the people closest to the missing person are often involved—a spite move, a joke gone wrong, even something accidental and unknown. In all the confusion, is it possible that Odie jumped in the car with her friend? The young woman shakes her head. Odie wouldn't jump in the car. He's scared of cars. Besides, it was gone before Odie went missing, and she's been in that car, searching with her friend, since then.

Though we're pretty sure Odie went out the front door, we don't know which way he went from there. There's a huge dog at the house to the right, whose savage, teeth-clicking barks sound like he could eat the fence between us. He rages at the young woman and at me as we stand on the porch, softening only a little bit at the sight of Puzzle. I think his noise would have kept Odie from turning that direction. The hot asphalt would probably have discouraged the little dog from crossing the street in front of the house. *Containment,* I think: a scary dog to the right; a steep slope down to the pavement, hot asphalt, and traffic straight ahead. Wanderers often choose the path of least resistance. I think Odie went left.

We turn left and separate. The young woman follows her street, crossing the shaded intersection, but Puzzle and I turn left again, around the side of her house. Its bare little yard butts up to another fenced lot owned by the same landlord, who did not answer his phone when the young woman called. She has searched along that scruffy lot and called there, but she's found nothing. I peer through a weathered privacy fence at the ugly, unpromising space, so overgrown it's almost impassable. NO TRESPASSING, a sign says. I don't think many people would want to. The owner stores a trailer, a truck, and some sheds here, half hidden in weeds behind the fence. The gate looks like it hasn't been opened in a long time, its latch held shut with a knotted twist of rusted wire.

Little old dog, where are you?

There's a natural urge to call a lost dog, but I don't call to this one. I know this about canine behavior: if shy Odie is not responding even to his young owner, he is certainly not going to come to me when I call—and a stranger's calls could scare him farther away. So I look for places where he might duck out of the heat, seeing, or thinking I see, a little black dog in every pool of shadow we pass.

Gentle Puzzle is all I've got for attraction. I tell her to *wander*, a cue that lets her know she's at will on her lead. She walks ahead, skirting the fence, sniffing the recent history of the road we travel. Behind her, I peer beneath cars and into runoff drains. I've seen dogs curl up in some of the most unexpected places to get cool.

Heat roars up from the asphalt. Puzzle and I hug the shade to spare her paws. This is a far cry from the pace we use to search, and I fight the impulse to give her a *find* cue and hurry. Odie's situation is dire—even healthy dogs can die in this heat—but with the best intentions, it would be easy for us to make things worse now. We just need to be nonthreatening, a nice woman on a walk with her nice magnet dog.

Not a human in sight. The neighbors have all wisely withdrawn. We pass 1930s wood-frame cottages rumbling with window air conditioners. I can see a few TVs flickering from shaded rooms. I'm thinking that if we don't find Odie quickly, a next step might be another round of knocking and signs and hand flyers for the neighbors who don't open doors. Maybe some kind person has carried the little found dog into the cool.

A blue jay flaps from tree to tree above us, shrieking its warning call. Puz pays no attention to the bird, but as she rounds a corner she pauses and pricks her ears. I stop with her. I hear nothing unusual, and

I can't make out what she heard. Even she doesn't seem sure. She turns her head a couple of times as though to pick it up again. Nothing. We stand for a long moment before moving on.

At two blocks away, I think we're moving too far for a disabled dog in hundred-degree heat. I pour bottled water onto my hands and give Puzzle a drink, then smooth a little more water down the length of her. We double back toward Odie's house. We are passing the empty lot a second time, on the sunny side right next to the fence, when she stops again and pricks her ears. This time I hear what must have paused Puzzle before: an odd rasp, almost like the sound of a Styrofoam lid being removed from a cooler. Animal? Mechanical? I can't tell. There it is again—a dry, drawn-out scrape.

Puzzle's head snaps toward the fence. We move board to board along it. Peering through the wooden slats, I see nothing but deep weeds, drooping hackberry branches, the derelict truck, the trailer, and the rusty, tilting sheds. But Puz is so curious now that I think we must go in.

NO TRESPASSING. *Same landlord,* I rationalize, calculating that by the time we could finally reach whomever for permission, Odie might be in a very bad way.

I could really use a pair of pliers to untwist the stiff, rusted wire holding the latch closed. But it takes an even harder pull to prize open the warped gate. Runoff dirt and gravel prevent it from swinging open more than a foot or so. I gesture Puzzle through the opening, wider at the bottom than it is for me at the top, then turn sideways and squeeze myself through after her, feeling the scrape of old wood and the poke of the latch on my back.

We stop just inside. On a search we'd call this moment a *size-up,* a time to evaluate the terrain, its hazards, and any "hot spots" likely to attract someone lost. Puzzle lifts her nose and brings her ears forward, making dog sense of the space. She had wanted to come in here, but she's cautious now, thoughtful and alert. I need to make my own sense of it, too. The property is more neglected than it appeared from the other side of the fence, peppered with enough junk metal that it's just shy of a dumping ground, the Wonderland Alice might have got to if she'd sipped from the wrong bottle. This is no place for a nice woman and a nice dog on a casual walk.

The lot seems huge. Maybe it was once one of those historic plats from the earliest days of this old town, when front yards were gracious and backyards generous enough to hold a stable, a chicken coop, and room for children to play — a century ago or longer. A sort of pergola still stands at one end. However trashed the place might be, nature is struggling to reclaim it. There's a derelict purple martin house on a high, leaning pole; I can see some determined bird has made a nest in what is left. Insects hover over flowering weeds that are taller than Puzzle in some places, waist-high to me in others. A human would have to fight his way in to get to that truck and those sheds. But the trailer is visible from where we stand, braided with vegetation and resting on what must have been old driveway gravel.

He likes to get under things. So many lost behaviors are rooted in choices at home. There are plenty of places to hide here, but getting into them wouldn't be easy for a disabled old dog, a space that even for humans deserves boots, gloves, and a machete. My human mind is almost ready to dismiss the area when Puzzle stiffens, shudders at the end of her lead, and gives a low, warning woof.

Something moves in my peripheral vision, and I twitch. A snake. A fair-sized one. Three foot, as they say in Texas. Maybe four. I might not have seen it if Puzzle hadn't woofed. Struck on the throat by a copperhead when she was young, she is snakewise now. I hold very still. Puzzle, too, freezes where she stands — good girl. The snake wants no part of us either. When we don't move, it retreats, the tall grass tracing its liquid, easy motion. I'm guessing a rat snake by the flash of pattern, but we'll give it a wide berth anyway. As I urge Puzzle toward the gate, we hear the raw rasping sound again. And again, louder. What is this? It's like nothing I have ever heard. *Another snake? I wonder. Are we hearing another snake killing something?*

But now my snake-averse golden retriever turns back, stretching toward the sound. Then the grass shifts, a cloud of insects lift, and out from beneath the trailer a small black dog slides toward her, rasping a desperate cry and dragging his spent back legs behind him.

There is a car in front of the house and two figures on the porch, their postures tense. The young woman turns as I round the corner with Odie in my arms and Puzzle beside me. She and a young man both shout his name. The little dog is trembling and sunken-eyed, but when his person rushes to us and he sees her, Odie struggles in my arms to get to her, vocalizing his odd scrape. She bundles him to her chest, bows her head, and presses his name into the fur of his neck. In her tumbling way, she tells him how scared she was, how she never thought she'd see him again. She'd imagined cars and mean kids and coyotes. The overjoyed little dog licks her ears. He is young again with reunion, tapping his forepaws on her shoulders.

The young woman tells me that Odie is so much more than a dog to her—a best friend since she was in elementary school. She says I'd never believe how important he is. I understand, I tell her, and I do, cradling the dome of Puzzle's fair head beneath my palm.

When she hears where we found him, Odie's owner can't quite believe it. She had passed that weeded lot several times; she had called over the back fence into it, and her dog hadn't come when she called. How had he even gotten in there? *Why wouldn't you let me find you?* She kisses the flap of Odie's ear and whispers. *Why didn't you come when I called?*

The young man watches from the porch. He had started down the steps when he first saw Odie, then checked himself, his expression uncertain. He and the young woman could be twins: similar build, same spiked platinum-blond hair. The young man has keys in his hand. He glances toward the old white car I'd seen earlier, which is loaded, front and back, with boxes. But he doesn't interrupt, and he waits for the young woman, twisting his key fob as if there is something unfinished between them. Murmuring thanks and something about water for Odie, the young woman cradles the little dog back toward the house. The young man meets her halfway across the brown grass. I hear him say, *I'm sorry. God, I'm so sorry.* The young woman lifts her head from her dog and puts a hand to the young man's arm. It is a gesture I recognize from my childhood, signaling something gentle and spent between them as they disappear through the front door.

Puzzle laps water from my cupped hand before we head for home. She looks up at me when she's had enough, her eyes alight, blond muzzle beaded with droplets. The familiar tug of search urgency has begun to relax. It feels no different from the aftermath of a human search, when every sense, stretching out, calms. Three hours ago I didn't even know the little dog or his young woman, but for a time their cause was mine. That sensation is familiar, too. I know what it is to lose love.

The relief I feel for both must be palpable to my own dog. I can't know exactly what Puzzle makes of the experience: a walk that was not quite a walk, a search that was not quite a search, and a distressed little dog at the end of it. But this was a save nonetheless, and she's an old hand at that kind of joy. I'm sure she could sense the human happiness around her, and frightened Odie's relief. Dogs know when their people are pleased with them. Puzzle's jaunty ahead of me now across the cooling street, sidewalk, and grass. *Wrooo-wrooooo,* she croons back to me over her shoulder. I think I could not love her more.

Afternoon light gives way to evening. Cicadas sing out the first stars. Somewhere in the neighborhood a grill is firing up. Though there's a shortcut she knows well, Puzzle leads me home the long way, yearning, lifting her nose to the scent of steak. The old white car passes us on the road that leaves town.

*The shelter intake photo for a
rescued Maltipoo designated
A006140.*

2

THE ONE IN THE BACK OF THE CAGE

A NOTHER ONE?" my father asks over the phone. "Do you really need another dog?"

Dad is teasing, sort of. We have this long history of second guesses, where he asks what I'm doing these days, then responds, "Another one?" or "Again?" no matter what my answer. It used to bug me when I was a prickly teenager — this notion that all my choices were questionable, that I was a repeat offender at whatever — but now I chalk it up to quintessential Dad. And it's a versatile schtick, applying equally well to jobs, head colds, new loves and exes, fender benders, books in progress, and homeless dogs taken in.

I am standing in my study — actually, pacing in the study — looking out a window to the road Odie's young man took out of town. Puzzle is sleeping belly up beneath the ceiling fan on the cool wood floor. She's snoring deeply. I step over her, walking back and forth while Dad and I talk on the phone. I've told him the story of Puzzle and lost-and-found Odie, and the conversation has now shifted to a shelter stray needing a home.

Dad has caught me on a morning already fractured by earlier calls. This dog is out of time in a shelter 250 miles to the south of me, and have I looked at Facebook this morning? Have I seen him? Have I given this dog any thought at all? Too many phone calls, too many social media posts to respond to individually, all about the same wounded Maltese-poodle mix headed for euthanasia just outside Houston. I have seen a photo of the little creature, and he has wrung my heart so terribly that when my father asks what I have going on today, this dog is the only thing I can talk about. I am uncertain until our conversation convinces me to go.

"Another dog. Well, okay then," Dad says, trailing off. He's been sick this year, and his tired voice sounds disapproving, like he knows it's pointless to argue. But then he says gently, "Go get the one in the back of the cage." It's a phrase we once shared, a secret bridge across the divide of us, and I know he loves me and is proud.

My parents made me a rescuer. I credit them, blame them affectionately if I sometimes get *a little over the top* (this is also Dad's phrase). From the time I was a toddler I had the urge to save living things, sparing spiders on the windowsill and downed birds from playmates in the schoolyard. No doubt I got this from my folks, who were rescuers in an age when I don't remember other adults having that mission. We were always saving something. Mom would bring in a skinny puppy she found after night class and Dad would fry it a hamburger, first thing. Dad would find a dying kitten in a gutter and Mom would bottle-feed it back to life. I grew up with strays from the roadside and pets from the local shelter and learned to believe, as my parents did, that too much animal suffering can be placed at the feet of haphazard humans.

Most often in the places where I grew up, dogs and cats existed as accessories to families rather than a part of them, somewhere in the nether region between livestock, property, and pet. The neighbor dogs I remember from childhood never went inside the house. They were yard animals beneath home-built shelters, maybe chained, maybe not, and fences were often slipshod at best. Those dogs had been puppy playmates for my friends once, but then the puppies got big and their kids got older, and the dogs were left to run fence lines or lie in bare dirt at the end of long chains. Sometimes they got loose and made trouble. Sometimes they got loose and never came back.

In those days the pet-care industry had not yet exploded with all the ways to mark pets as owned. Dogs and cats have had tagged collars for centuries, and most of the dogs (and some of the cats) I knew as a child wore them, but we would never have imagined pet tattoos, embedded microchips, and GPS trackers. Those would have been science fiction in the 1960s — and the stuff of ridiculous excess. In those days you put the dog or the cat out at night and left it to chance. So pets got lost — and often stayed lost — with little hope of return.

When your dog or cat went missing, you asked the neighbors. You walked the streets for a little while, calling. No computers to make signs, no photocopying then. You thumbtacked notices written in Magic Marker on a few phone poles, sad signs that drooped, unreadable, after the first rain. With the exception of my mother, who once sat out every night for two weeks beside a can of tuna to lure a neighbor's shy cat from a collapsed crawlspace (it worked!), if a pet went missing, I don't remember anyone searching for more than a few days.

Many adults made those lost pets into life lessons. Kids had to learn about loss sometime, grownups said. *Probably got hit by a car* was the writeoff I remember hearing most often as a child, when the adults were fed up with searching.

"Where?" I asked one mother, who'd said my best friend's dog, Brownie, missing for two days, *had probably got hit by a car.* I remember the sharp silence that followed, and being told not to sass, that I should shut my smart mouth.

I wasn't trying to sass, but I kept talking. I knew mistakes could happen. My dad thought one of our cats got hit by a car once. No probably about it. Smokey had been missing for days when my father found a furry gray-and-white mass in the road at the base of the hill below our house. Dad got out of the car and knelt to it and was sure. I remember him coming home and telling me with tears in his eyes, and I remember walking with him down the hill to get her. We scraped up what was left of the fluff with a shovel, put it in a paper grocery bag, and buried it in the backyard, where Dad, Mom, and I all stood weeping, because we really loved that cat. Two days later my father woke me and said, "Go look out on the patio," and there was Smokey, very much alive, beside an empty food bowl, stretched out on tiles and winking sleepily in the sun. Dad had found her. For whatever reason, he'd had second thoughts about the fluff we'd buried and decided to walk the alley behind the house. He'd heard Smokey crying from a neighbor's toolshed, where she had been stuck for days.

So when I asked my friend's mother "Where?" about their missing dog, the question was genuine. The need for evidence was real.

How many of those lost, probably-hit-by-a-car animals were still alive? If modern numbers suggest anything about the past, quite a few. We saw wandering pets often enough in those days—I remember skinny cats slipping out of trashcans that skinny dogs had knocked over, kittens huddled beneath bushes and ribby pups following us home from school, ears down, tails trembling. These weren't feral animals. They were well socialized; they'd likely once been somebody's pets. Displaced from their owners, they became someone else's problem. Passersby in the city had few choices: ignore them, harass them away, take them in, or turn them over to the shelter. Country folk shot them sometimes. The outcome could be grim for those untagged pets. In those days, city pounds were also often the end of the line.

My dad found a lost Labrador retriever named Sonny more than once. The Lab was a genial, slightly goofy chocolate dog with a red collar and a signature cat-notched ear. Despite his age, this athletic old fellow could take your average chain-link fence in a single bound, and he did so almost daily. Sonny was the local nuisance, a digger of flower beds, a tipper of trashcans. But he had cataracts and ran into things, and at night he cornered himself in unexpected places, unable to see his way out.

Sonny was three miles from home in the middle of the freeway the last time my father found him. Dad somehow fashioned booster cables into a kind of slip lead and lured the half-blind dog into the car with (my) Nutter Butters. I remember the dog's huge, slobbery head leaning over from the backseat, huffing cookie breath into my ear, and I remember Dad walking Sonny to his owners' front door as if the dog were wired for a jump start and pleading with the woman to Sonny-proof the fence. He offered to help. *A good boy,* I heard my father say, *but how much luck has one dog got?*

Why was pet ownership so cavalier? When a pet went missing, did people not care enough to search for it, or did they not know how?

Perhaps overpopulation encouraged it. Lose a dog? It was easy enough to get another one. Pet spaying and neutering were not yet common practice. Backyard breeding was the standard. Indeed, when children were of a certain age, it was often thought a good thing to let the family dog or cat have at least one litter, the better to teach youngsters about the Cycle of Life. Enough dogs jumped fences that the Cycle of Life rarely stopped at just one litter, so we kids saw quite a few goopy puppies slide out of shuddering females onto the grass. Those backyard litters could be an ugly instruction in supply versus demand, too. I remember the Saturday boxes of free puppies at the gas station, friends' parents pitching pets to neighbors and office mates, and I remember darker moments, when I would go home with a play-mate and find fresh kitten graves in the backyard or a dog and her little ones mysteriously gone.

That casual cruelty infuriated my parents, who stirred from their shy natures and said so. Particularly my mother. Troubled by a loose and ever-pregnant dog and her disappearing litters, she advised a neighbor who did not welcome it, *You could prevent her from having puppies, you know.* I can see Mom so clearly then, all five-foot-three and ninety-three pounds of her, standing at that chain-link fence in her Capri pants and seersucker blouse—a beautiful brunette who looked enough like Natalie Wood that people sometimes did double takes—telling a man who did not welcome it how to care for his dog.

You could prevent her having puppies, you know. My folks were early advocates of pet birth control. They knew there were more animals than there were homes. They also knew that in-season animals were more likely to chase and be chased, to get injured or stray. Mom and Dad kept our cats inside when the females were in heat, which could be maddeningly often. Red embroidery thread tied around the door-knob: I remember learning early which days the cats couldn't go out. I learned a lot about the Cycle of Life from that—the queens in heat sidewinding and rolling and piteously yowling at the windows and the round-eyed tomcats fighting deep in the night, their terrible screams raising me straight up from sleep with ice in my veins. Eventually I understood enough about the Cycle of Life to give a speech about the process in elementary school—I may have described genitalia —which got me sent home with a note from the teacher about inap-propriate subject matter for a nine-year-old in her third-grade class.

When we had room for a new pet, I remember my parents checking the newspaper want ads for pound notices, cryptic because they were priced per word: "Many kittens available" or "Variety of unclaimed dogs." We couldn't save every animal, my mother said; we couldn't fix it all, but if we could do something for even one, we should. Then off we'd go to get another one. We put our heads down and went into those hard places, usually choosing the unloveliest ani-mal—the one in the back of the cage—to bring home.

Another one? Again? Madness, the in-laws, my grandparents, said every time a new pet came in. And they had a point. Mom and Dad didn't have much money. Even so, I remember the priority they gave those rescued animals. The little creatures were family members as surely as I was. When our shelter kitten Rosie became terribly ill, I remember the juggling my parents did to save her, pawning trifles and hosting yard sales and holding their breath and floating checks. *Robbing Peter to pay Paul,* they called it. It was the first time I ever heard that phrase. It would not be the last. I remember that my soft-spoken father was furious when our vet shrugged away heroic effort because Rosie was "just a cat." Dad swept the dying kitten up in his arms and stormed out, with me trotting beside him, intent on finding a new vet who would give the little tabby a chance. We had to drive a long way.

Some other vet in some other town saved her. How my parents paid for it I have no idea at all.

Rescue the hungry wanderers, adopt the homeless, reunite the wandering lost. We were a fragile family but for this shared mission. Even in childhood I could sense my parents' unease. Raised in the twin shadows of family discord and mental illness, my parents had married early to escape and rocketed themselves into hardship, which they did not always handle well. Lost jobs, never enough money, poor health, contentious in-laws, and a kid—me—way too adventurous for her own good—my folks struggled with all of it. Dad's panic attacks made him pace at night, and some weekends my mother never came out of the bedroom, her hard tears echoing down the staircase.

But they loved their animals. That was the one thing that did not divide them and perhaps part of what held us together for so long. My parents were the first people I ever knew who talked about saving animals and being saved by them, the first I ever saw turning to their pets for solace. I carry a few mental snapshots: Dad in the living room with Rosie on his lap, Mom with her perpetual cigarette talking to them from the couch; Mom on the front steps coaxing some shy dog forward with an open can of Underwood deviled ham while Dad fried bacon as a backup. My father showed me how to calm the skittish ones. The thing was not to pressure them. Dad was a big fan of humming and looking away. My mother said, *Let them think it's their idea.* Even when we'd brought them in and they were safe with us, Mom celebrated silently. A basketball fan, she would make this funny little gesture as if she'd sunk a basket from the free throw and then raise her hands while the imaginary crowd went wild.

It took me years to realize how my parents' saving impulse shaped me. I was drawn to emergency response. As a commercial pilot in my early thirties, I flew my first support flights for disaster relief after violent storms, which ultimately led me to join a ground K9 search-and-rescue team early in the new century, training and partnering a search-and-rescue dog of my own to find missing people.

But SAR wasn't enough. I was my mother's daughter, Dad said, without admitting that I was equally his. I went back to the animal shelters I knew from childhood, pulling animals facing euthanasia, fostering dogs or cats that needed a little time to be adopted, and flying or driving homeless animals to new families. Too many dogs were passed over for adoption, so I pursued formal dog training and earned professional credentials, hoping to better their chances. It was — and is — my parents' mission, translated to this modern life: we can't fix it all, but if we can do something for even one, we should.

Sometimes my father worries. He hopes I won't repeat the mistakes he and my mother made. All is well, I tell him. He maybe half believes me. Forty-five years after Rosie, without the troubles my parents knew, I, too, have a shifting houseful of rescued animals, dog and cat. Dad says, *Another one?* every time, an echo of his parents said more fondly to his relentless child. Whenever he adds that *over-the-top* comment about my life in rescue, I resurrect the treasured story of him saving kitten Rosie — and I remind him of the chubby, bossy cat Rosie became, sleeping across Dad's face while he tried to watch *Get Smart*.

Usually I know the histories of the dogs I pull from shelters. I have a soft spot for disabled or terminally ill hospice dogs — still able to have quality of life, but too impaired, too old, or too ugly, for whatever reason, to be attractive to the average adopter. These frail rescues that come to me have usually been turned in to shelters by their owners. Money may be the issue, or lack of ability to care for the disabled animal. Sometimes an owner has simply grown bored with an old dog that used to be healthy and cute. Whatever the reason they arrived there, *owner surrenders* often have very little time in shelters, because the staff know that no one will come looking for them. If an animal impound has run out of space, surrendered animals usually need to find homes — or a rescue group that will save them — quickly.

Now I have a crew of little aged animals — some blind, some

deaf, some blind *and* deaf, most with one chronic disease or another that will eventually take them. These special-needs rescues lead rich, loved lives in my house, but my time with them is often painfully short. A single season. A year, if we're lucky. In 2010, I lost six senior dogs in as many months, comforted only by the knowledge that they were loved to their last hour.

Friends grieve each loss with me, but they waste no time suggesting another homeless dog to fill the space. They're not heartless. They know one dog can never replace another. But they are rescuers themselves, awash in the stream of last-chance images on Facebook and Twitter and Instagram, and they're committed to getting euthanasia candidates to any safe harbor they trust.

So I woke this morning to find a Maltese-poodle cross in Conroe, Texas, peppered across my Facebook page. At-risk A006140 had been photographed by a shelter volunteer and advertised widely. This dog was not an owner surrender but a stray in terrible shape. Lost? Abandoned? He has no backstory. No collar. No microchip. He'd been picked up on a Tuesday and had seventy-two hours for his owner to claim him. Now, in an overfull shelter, his chances are poor.

In the intake photo, the image before me is troubling — A006140 is a ragged, whitish, half-bald mop pressed into the corner of his kennel, eyes terrified, one paw tentatively raised. His fur is matted, his skin bloody and raw. This dog has been through hell. This dog looks like big vet bills. Most adopters would never consider him, and even rescues are turning away. But friends of friends have met the battered little creature, and despite his state, they are moved by his gentle intelligence.

One has written: *Every local rescue has said no to him. Can you do anything at all?*

I get nudges like this on social media almost every day, and I've had to learn to let most of them go. My friends mean well, but they don't know how many dogs get sent my way. Every dog tugs at me. But the line between rescue and hoarding can be slim, and crossing that line is no good for anyone involved. So I've learned to trust my instincts, and I've come to believe that any rescue move I need to make will be made clear. Even as I'm messaged with other pleas for other dogs, I've been watching the A006140 posts. *For God's sake someone help this dog*, someone posts. But no one in South Texas has moved for him. No one anywhere has moved for him. He has never left my thoughts.

Dad's random call seems like a benediction. "A nine-hour drive, he says. "Give you this: you're willing."

After hanging up with my father, I sit cross-legged on the floor with sleepy Puzzle's head on my knee. I call the Conroe shelter volunteer who knows A006140 best. He is a sweet little thing, she tells me, a timid dog, kind of a train wreck. She guesses about eight years old. Maybe older. It's hard to tell. An animal control officer found him in a drainage ditch. The dog looked feral, but the story is that he came to the officer, crept out of the ditch on his ragged belly. He will lick the hand that feeds him, but huddled in the back of his kennel, A006140 doesn't look good. He smells even worse. And he shakes. But under all the mess is a dog who deserves a chance. He has only a day left on his stray hold. His space will better serve a more adoptable dog. He needs a commitment soon.

I tag A006140 for rescue. If no owner or adopter comes forward for him in Conroe by Saturday, I'm his fail-safe. But the volunteer stresses that I will have to come get him quickly. The shelter is so beyond capacity that they've run out of foster homes, too. His stray hold is up on Saturday afternoon. The shelter won't put him down on Sunday, the volunteer says, but *Monday* . . . She trails off. We make plans for getting him to Dallas on Monday. The rescue tag will buy him time, and the transport will save his life.

"Another one," I tell Puzzle, stroking her soft ears. She squints at me through one open eye and goes back to sleep.

Those plans should have been enough, but that Conroe dog keeps me up at night. There is something unsettling about him, something I can't explain. Early Saturday morning I juggle my schedule and start asking friends to make the drive with me to get him. Longtime fellow rescuer Ellen agrees, giving up her own weekend plans. After twenty-five years of this, she doesn't question my reasons—and I couldn't give them to her if she did. I just know this dog needs out of the shelter before Monday.

Something the volunteer said still echoes. "We're trying to give him every chance, but he just looks . . . so bad," she said on the phone. "Unexpected things happen in shelters. Decisions get made."

I know she's right. One of my earliest rescue efforts involved a Pomeranian in a Nevada pound. The Pom was tagged for rescue, a pull deadline was given, and in the time it took the rescue volunteer to miss an exit and make a U-turn to go back to the right one, the dog—who had a home waiting—was euthanized.

That is not going to happen to this one. And so we make a hasty trip from Dallas on a summer Saturday at the end of a hot, dry month. As Ellen drives, I study the intake photograph and try to imagine what recent life must've been like for this dog we are saving. Is this a case of terrible neglect or long-time lost? Whatever the story, A006140 looks like he's been on his own for a while. With no protection from the elements, he would have been exposed to so much disease. If he doesn't come with heartworm, it will be a miracle. Too many southern dogs do.

A last-chance dog leaves the shelter.

3

IN THE GOODWILL OF RESCUE

THE LADY AT THE DESK has got patience. She's got compassion. She's got a lobby in motion and a phone that won't stop ringing, and—roughing a sort of first-come, first-served justice—she's managing it somehow. She's on the phone trying to help a desperate someone on the other end. Despite the din of countless dogs in the containment area beyond the wall, those of us pressed together in line at the desk can hear the frantic buzz of the caller's panicked voice, and we can't help but hear the young woman before us calmly reply. It's not hard to parse what's going on.

A couple of days ago, while traveling, the caller lost a dog in another state. She had to keep going. She couldn't stay where the dog disappeared. Now she's turning to her local shelter for advice. She is pouring out her heart. *Help me.* The receptionist opens her mouth to speak several times. Her expression is kind. In what seems like a pause on the other end, she makes some suggestions for services on the Internet that can help with lost pets, spread the word to distant shelters and vet clinics and that kind of thing. "Was Mitzi wearing tags? Does she have a microchip?" the receptionist asks, and the caller falters.

"Okay. I understand," the receptionist says quietly, shaking her head. No microchip. The young woman has both elbows propped up on the counter. She's rubbing her forehead with an index finger. She tries again, recommending things to try for a dog lost so far away. *Photos,* we overhear. *A clear description. Contact information.* Somehow she manages to close the conversation with some hope. Call finished, she makes a flat little gesture at the phone, like telling a dog to *stay*, takes a deep breath, and looks up at us.

The man who's first in line at the desk seems to feel bad for her. "Sorry," he says, as if apologizing for the call. Or maybe he's sorry for the new trouble he's about to bring her. He's got a pissed-off tabby in a carrier. He plops it on the counter. We can hear a growl rising and smell the contained cat's hot pee.

The receptionist's eyebrows raise, and she scoots back just a hair. "Okay," she says to him kindly. "Who's this?"

A summer Saturday afternoon at the Conroe Animal Shelter, just north of Houston, Texas, and the place is full. Hot, stuffy, and loud—the small lobby is crammed with people. Some, like me, are in line at the desk. A few are milling about with bewildered animals they seem to plan on leaving there, holding them at a sort of "Not mine! Not mine!" arm's length. Volunteers walk winsome, adoptable dogs through the crowd and outside to visit on the front porch. Some people are in family huddles. They have printed flyers in their hands, but they look overwhelmed by the crowd and confusion, the riot of sound coming from the animal area.

It's an uneasy room. Standing there, I feel my gut clench. Though this modern shelter is bright and the volunteers in rocking chairs outside are welcoming, there's no denying that this is a place where some animals get second chances and others come to die. There's an anxious edge to the cheer. My own impulse is to grab every animal in here and run.

One pale young mother looks closer to running than I am. Her husband is in line behind me, and occasionally I see her mouth messages to him across the din. She stands by the door with her arms folded and her right foot turned out, ballet-style, but she's white-faced, as if she has a migraine, and she winces every time the barking escalates. Her expression suggests that she'd really like to get out of here, if she hadn't committed to this, if her three kids didn't have fist-fuls of dog flyers and a whole lot of restless anticipation.

The kids don't seem to be bothered by the noise, but it's probably ramped them up a little. Every time someone walks out of the kennel area with a dog, all three push through the crowd to see. Maybe they have their hearts set on adopting a particular dog, one they are afraid someone else will get to first. "Ohhhh," they say every time, in a ragged little chorus.

"You guys adopting this morning?" I ask the father behind me. I'm eager for some good word. Apparently the man at the desk with the angry cat has a lot of explaining to do.

The father shakes his head. Not adopting. They're here to look for their own dog, lost two weeks ago. When he says her name — Bella — the children's heads all snap toward their father, and now I make sense of what they're doing. They are asking people in the lobby if they've seen her. It's Bella's picture they have on flyers they made themselves, and it's obvious that, from the preteen down to the kindergartner, they really love their dog.

Bella's a beagle mutt of some kind, the father says, describing her big eyes, a brown spotted body over white paws, and dangle-down ears that are very soft. There's affection in his description. Sadness, too. She's a rescue from South Texas that they've had a little while, but they've never been able to get ahead of her digging. One day they came home to find her gone from the backyard. Bella has a collar and tags she wore out on walks, but they never left them on her otherwise, because they'd always feared she'd strangle herself trying to break out under the fence.

When Bella went missing, the whole family hit the streets right away, knocking on neighbors' doors. They put up signs on phone poles the same day, too, but it was an HOA violation or something, because someone came through and took them down again. They called the closest vets. They posted flyers at grocery stores. So far no one has responded. Now they are checking the shelters again. They come about three times a week, the father says. They come so often because the animal shelters hold strays only a few days, and they know if they don't come in soon enough, Bella could be adopted out. Or worse. Right now the two shelters in Conroe have more dogs than space to put them.

I understand. Those grim stats are the reason I'm here.

So the man and his family are driving in every other day or so to walk through this place "where the lost dogs go," as his littlest daughter calls it. But they don't live close, and this is wearing them all out, and they're crushed every time they don't find Bella. Two weeks. How long, he says, do you do that to your kids? The father's vacation is over. He's back overseas on Monday, and his wife is back to work in Houston, and he isn't sure how she can check the shelters again during the week, because both close before she can get there. They'll have to trust the pictures on the websites, and they hope some of the shelter volunteers will keep an eye out for Bella.

Microchip, he says, nodding his head toward the receptionist who had asked that important question of someone else. They are kicking themselves because they always meant to get her one. Now they're looking for their sweet lost dog without a microchip. She carries nothing to signal to a finder that she is theirs. "We played the odds," he says ruefully.

"Yes, ma'am?" the receptionist calls to me over the shoulder of the man with the angry tabby. He's had a change of heart about leaving it, and I feel a flash of gratitude, because things would probably not end well for that cat in the shelter. He trundles the dribbling carrier back out the door.

I step to the desk and hold out a flyer. "I'm here to pick up this little guy."

"Oh," she says, looking down at the dog in the picture. Her face shifts a little. "That one." She pulls out some papers for me to sign, then gets up from the desk, slips down a hallway, and disappears. Moments later she's back. She bundles the bony tangle that is intake A006140 into my arms, her expression apologetic. The little dog is filthy. The overwhelming smell of infected wounds and urine causes the father behind me to step back involuntarily and whisper *Jesus*.

"I'm sorry," says the young woman, stroking the dog's ear.

"Awwww," murmur Bella's kids.

The trembling creature looks up at me. I can see dark, frightened eyes through a sticky tangle of fur. I can feel his heart pounding against my hand. He doesn't struggle.

"Hello, sweetheart," I say to the little dog. He lowers his head to the crook of my arm, giving the inside of my elbow a tentative lick.

Awkwardly gathering up purse and papers, I turn to the man behind me. "You might try posting on social media for Bella, if you haven't. And check to see if someone has posted about her. Craigslist? NextDoor? Facebook?"

He looks at me blankly. "Craigslist," he repeats. "I don't have a Facebook," he says. He glances at his wife.

"*Next*," calls the receptionist. Her expression is kind, but she's got a full lobby, and she's on her own.

"Good luck," I say to the family.

"Good luck," says the mother at the door doubtfully. She looks at the dog in my arms and shakes her head, as if luck for the pair of us has long since run out.

The dog in my arms lifts his head as we leave the building. Curiosity? Reprieve? I don't know what he can sense from me, but literally things are looking up. He must hurt everywhere. I carry him the way I'd hold spun glass, but there's no good purchase on that terrible skin. I regret even the thud of my feet on the pavement. He looks unreasonably brighter nevertheless.

We never know how rescues will take to the car. An animal control truck may have been the first experience for some dogs—an isolated, frightening journey—and on a rescue car trip later they may panic, whine, or bark the entire way. Freedom Rides, they are called in the rescue community, but some dogs have no idea that this car trip leads to better things. Some throw themselves against the walls of their crates. Some shake nonstop. I've seen dogs fold themselves into a little ball of misery, turning away from the light as though this is just another in a long string of horrors. But a fair number of dogs like it. We've seen more than one perk up at the prospect of a trip. We hope for the best, and we come prepared for anything. Today we have a crate and a soft carrier, a harness and a leash, puppy wipes, poop bags, disinfectant, water and food and soft bedding and almost anything else the dog we're bringing back to Dallas might need.

A006140 likes cars. The moment we get into ours, he squeaks with excitement. He seems more confident, less defeated, and his trembling stops. He first puts his forefeet on the dash to peer out the front window. Then, though he's watchful and clearly uncertain, the little dog settles with me on the passenger side, tucking onto my lap with his paws folded over my right arm, positioned to look out the window. It's a practiced move.

"Look at that," says Ellen, nodding at his ready, set, ride position.

Sometime in his past, with someone from his past, Ace had been an accomplished car traveler. And somewhere he'd been socialized enough to accept a kind stranger. He's just as dirty as he was when he was handed over five minutes ago, but here in the car A006140 looks better already.

He loses his number and gains a name. Maybe it's just my imagination that shedding the shelter intake number jump-starts a dog's healing. Friends have already suggested "Ace," and I try that out straightaway—Ace, Ace for the win. He deserves one.

"Hey, kiddo," I say, very softly. "Hey, Ace."

The dog turns at the sound of my voice, his eyes pensive. The raw curl of his tail twitches a wag.

We sit for a moment to let him adjust. I can't speak for Ace, but my head is still ringing from the noise of the shelter, and the silent car is welcome. The dog sighs and yawns, shaking off stress. He looks up at me again. Lots of soft, inquisitive eye contact from this one—he wants to engage. For the briefest moment, we connect with something like a mutual sigh of relief.

"Whew," I say to him, stroking one shoulder lightly. "Sweetheart, that place was loud."

I cup my palm beneath his face, and Ace chuffs gently into it, scenting. He is gray with road dust, ribs and hipbones protruding. He streaks dirt where he touches. Ace smells like grease and old blood and urine and he seems uncomfortable, but he leans slightly into my hand anyway, seeking affection.

When his eyes go uneasy at the sight of the crate and the shaking starts up again, I get the sense that Ace has been shoved into too many small spaces recently. So even though I think he'd be more comfortable in a crate with room to stretch out, travel harness it is. That's not going to be easy. I have to be careful of all his raw skin. The little dog is patient with the process, lifting his paws when I slip on the harness. I seatbelt myself up and make a cocoon of cushions around him for additional protection. We've got a long ride ahead of us.

Ace pricks his ears and cranes his neck to watch the shelter door open. Bella's family comes out. The kids are quiet, squinting uncomfortably into the light, their postures disappointed. Both parents, their heads ducked against the glare, walk behind them across the steaming sidewalk. Curious Ace puts his nose to the edge of the car window and huffs scent as they pass us. The father catches sight of me as he pips their vehicle unlocked. He pauses just for a moment to shake his head.

"They didn't find a dog they want?" Ellen asks.

"They were looking for one they lost."

We leave the shelter at the same time, down the long drive to the street. The family's Escalade pulls out onto the crossroad ahead of us, turning one way as we head out the other, and my thoughts go with them. Bella went missing two weeks ago. Certainly they'd done a lot of things right by combing the neighborhood, putting out signs, checking shelters and vet clinics and pet stores. But short of time travel back to a better fence and a microchip for their dog, what else could they have done? Social media, yes. Maybe another canvas of the neighbors when the signs came down. They could have used some help. As hard as they were working, I got the sense that they were searching alone. I wonder how long they'll continue for Bella. *Out of options*, the young father had said, which had the sound of giving up. The last I see of them is the little sticker family across the back window of the SUV: husband, wife, three kids, and a dog.

I've never lost a dog in the way that Odie and Bella so thoroughly disappeared. I have no experience with a dog wandering through a gate kids left open or bolting from backyard contractors or jerking a leash out of my hand and vanishing around a corner in a cartoon puff of smoke—gone for hours or days, sometimes gone for good. Those are the stories owners tell me when Puzzle and I walk some dog she's attracted back home. Good caution or dumb luck that I've never lost one? I don't know. I do know I've had nightmares about it. Protection dreams, I've been told they're called, these dreams of doors ajar and loved dogs disappeared, and in the way of dreams and symbols, theoretically they represent my vulnerability as well. Fair enough. I *am* vulnerable. I've known plenty of heartbreak. Twenty years in search and rescue, driven by loss, have only made me more aware of how easy it is to look up and someone cherished is gone.

I've had a couple of close calls. Our most ancient Pomeranian, tiny Mr. Sprits'l, was early an escape artist looking for a chance to bolt out the door. Very small, very fast, and very sly, when he was a youngster he once made it out the door and two houses down in the dark, me in hot barefooted pursuit. I didn't know he could run that fast. I didn't know that I could. I had no dog-training experience yet. I was all wrong-headed impulse until some memory of my mother paused me on the sidewalk—*don't make this a chase or a game.* When I stopped running, Mr. Sprits'l stopped running, too. That was a big lesson. A chased dog often runs faster.

We trained hard to discourage Mr. Sprits'l's flight risk and build his return when called, and I thought we had done a pretty good job until recently, when I opened the front door to feed one of the community cats. Just in the time it took to get the door open, Sprits saw the orange tabby and skipped between my ankles to chase him into the front yard and almost through the low fence that separates yard from street. I would have never guessed Sprits still had it in him. Mr. Sprits'l is now fifteen, deaf, and milky-eyed with cataracts. Apparently he is also undeterred. He would never hear me call him now. I had to drop to my knees to attract him. He teaches me still.

Rescued pit-bull-mix Jake Piper also slipped through the door once, when a friend was coming through it. Starveling Jake was skinny for a long time as a puppy, and he somehow managed to get out without her even feeling the brush of him against her. Jake was one of a crowd of other dogs in the house at the time, and we hadn't missed him yet in the head count when a woman called and said, "Am I speaking to Jake Piper's owner? We have this very nice puppy here, and he wants to go home." He didn't have to go far. Jake had made it only across the narrow drive separating our house from a school, where he'd wagged his way up to a couple of teachers, who read his tags and made the call. We could literally see him from the front door. I always buy a collar and tags for my dogs the first day they join us—a welcome-to-the-family ritual as much as anything—but it was the tag that brought Jake home just minutes after he left.

Some dogs get more lost than others. In the goodwill of rescue, I'm now driving someone's once-loved dog to Dallas. I'm sure of it. It's a mercy move for this dog out of time, but beneath the wounds and starvation is a lapdog that once knew care. The longer we ride, the more his head lifts, as though with every mile he lets go of a little more fear. He's no longer the terrified stray that cowered in the back of the kennel. He's clearly gone hungry for a long time, but Ace's good manners run deep. When I offer him food, he takes it politely, without growling or guarding it, without snapping at the hand that feeds him. We stop to give him a break halfway through the trip. Ace is leash-trained. He steps forward away from my feet and obliges at the end of a loose lead, lifting his leg absently.

He's a funny little soul. There's a dignified, shabby gentility about him, and his expression increases the effect. One ear up, one ear down, he peers into my face with his left eyebrow in a slight squint, as if he's wearing a monocle. Ace is like a figure Dickens might have written, or Conan Doyle—like that character in "The Blue Carbuncle" deduced by Holmes from his lost hat: a good fellow, once elegant, now fallen on hard times, whose wife has ceased to love him.

Despite his frailties, this dog is acute. Ace misses nothing, watching all that passes as we travel. He tilts his head at squeaky brakes on the truck ahead. He puts his nose to the window when two people cross the street. *Hmmph,* he mutters at an inflatable man waving wildly from a car wash—not a bark, not quite a growl, speculative. Frequently he turns to make searching eye contact with me, as if wondering what I mean to him, what possibility, what threat.

We drive out of the city onto a long stretch of summer freeway, and after an hour of hypervigilance, the exhausted dog finally dozes off in my arms, succumbing to the rhythm of the car like a baby might. Now I can have a good look without making him anxious. It's an ugly view. New and old, Ace's injuries are written plainly across him, a map of his misfortune. The shelter volunteer said that when he arrived, the staff tried to clip off that matted fur to give him some relief, but he cried at every touch and shook so violently they had to stop. The mats that remain are thick as a horse's saddle blanket, bound tightly to the skin. He doesn't have much healthy coat left; the fur he still has is curly and coarse. This could be owner neglect, but weeks or months on the street could also have caused it. Ace is not a dog that could go without grooming very long. I see curled, overlong nails, palm-sized abrasions, hot spots and flea marks across his terrible skin. He has chewed his tail bald.

Worse, the large purple crescent of a bite arcs over one hip. It's not a fresh wound; the scabs have healed, but somewhere in Ace's past he was attacked by a much larger, round-muzzled animal. How had an eight-pound Maltese mix escaped that? Whatever his history, Ace has suffered awhile. Somehow he's gone from car rides and leash walks and polite sits to this.

In the face of such misery, it's easy to get angry at an imagined owner who didn't give a damn. There are horror stories out there; bad owners do exist. Many rescuers have seen the worst far too often, and the abuse judgment becomes the reflex response. But not every stray dog has neglect behind him, and something doesn't make sense with this one. Nothing about Ace's behavior suggests that he was mistreated. I lift a limp paw and inspect his worn, dirty pads. In Ace's ways I see hints of affection, training, and companionship—and then something happened, a series of somethings, misadventure that he somehow survived. Ace is a lesson in stamina. He's a lesson in trust, too, this battered dog that crawled out of his hiding place for help.

As the car rockets northward, I look out the window and think again about Bella, whose owners were trying so hard to find her. At two weeks gone, a little "mostly beagle" could be anywhere—as close as one street over or five states away, farther now than we would have ever imagined before the Internet age. Maybe someone did take her in. Maybe she died. She, too, could be in a car, bound for a new family somewhere else. Perhaps Bella is still wandering, another dog in rough shape waiting to be found. It is at this moment in the car that I realize every lost animal falls into one of three categories: deceased, in transit, or absorbed. Found or unfound, the deceased dog has succumbed. It is an easy conclusion to jump to, but not the only one. A loose dog in motion is an in-transit dog, as is a

wandering dog picked up by a Samaritan, or a dog in a shelter waiting to be reclaimed, adopted, or put down. An absorbed dog is one
that has been rehomed. A searching owner has to consider all these
possibilities and appeal to others for information or help.

If Ace or Bella were my own lost dog, what would I have done? I've
never been easy about this, but—*you play the odds*—I know I haven't
thought about it enough. If another neighbor with another Odie came
to me, beyond a double handful of lost-pet recoveries I made beside
my parents, some makeshift human search strategy, and my cheerful,
willing magnet dog Puzzle, I have no solid help to offer, no insight, no
thoughtful search plan at all. And it could happen. A contractor leaves
a gate open. A nervous rescue slips his leash. The young dog that yesterday could jump only this high clears the fence today.

Challenged by Odie and Bella and Ace, I'd like to be better able to
help my neighbors. And I myself need to be better prepared. I've met
a few lost-pet specialists, often called *pet detectives*. Some were former
SAR volunteers who switched focus. Some were associated with animal rescues that worked to bring wandering and injured animals into
care. Some once lost an animal themselves and came forward to help
others in ways they had needed most. I assisted a search across the
rubble of a burned apartment building beside one of them once—a
sterling young woman and her clever Aussie shepherd, doing a follow-
up search for a resident's cat, feared lost in the fire. The cat was found.
She had not survived the blaze, but now the owner knew her fate and
could lay to rest the nagging possibility that the animal was wandering injured and abandoned in the ruins of an apartment complex.

Like SAR, lost-pet search is a difficult and much-needed service
to others. Search and rescue has shown me that good intentions are
not enough. Any kind of search requires you to be grounded in its
demands. I can sense that this work is no less difficult than that for
missing persons, and it will have challenges all its own. The wounded
dog in hiding. The wandering dog taken up by a passerby and transported to the place the driver was headed. The pitied stray adopted

immediately by a compassionate finder, who never looks back to an original owner at all. Any one of these conditions is possible. Every one of these requires different search strategies. I can see at once two search landscapes: the physical terrain where an animal went missing and the psychological terrain of the animal making choices and the humans who determine its fate.

"Back to school," I murmur to Ace, who still sleeps. He's a grubby little motivator stretched out across my lap, dreaming deeply, flexing and twitching his raw toes when I reach for my tablet computer. He doesn't wake when I swipe the screen to open it, or tap the browser, or with one hand awkwardly mistype in the search field: *Mising pets help.*

Showing results for missing pets help, corrects Google, and brings up pages and pages of links. It is my first real glimpse into the remarkable world of missing-animal response (MAR). Sister to SAR and a movement that took off in this new century, missing-animal response is peopled by volunteers and specialists of every stripe. Even a quick scroll reveals neighborhood lost-pet networks, K9 pet trackers, humane capture teams, drone flyers, social media strategists, and shelter volunteers who actively try to make reunion happen. I'm encouraged by what I find, bookmarking pages to come back to and taking car-shaky notes by hand. Whether served by paid professionals or professional volunteers, MAR is no casual effort. Vigorous, strategic, resourceful, and passionate, some MAR workers teach formal classes in lost-pet recovery; many have a wealth of information to share. For missing-animal responders, reuniting lost pets is a service against suffering — dog and human alike. Willing, my father would call them. Odie's young woman might say they were neighbors opening doors.

Caught on the trail cam: Devon Thomas Treadwell, of the Minnesota lost-pet team The Retrievers, calls a family to let them know their missing dog is safe.

Search volunteer Ellen Sanchez places a sign that can be read by car and foot traffic.

4

THE QUALITY OF MERCY

O PIE TAYLOR FINDS a lost dog in "Dogs, Dogs, Dogs," a 1963 episode of *The Andy Griffith Show*, a TV series my father and I watched religiously.

On the day of an important visit from a state investigator to determine if Sheriff Andy Taylor's department deserves more funds, Opie walks into the station leading a trembling black-and-tan terrier on a rope. Opie claims the dog followed him, followed him everywhere he went, and that he put on a rope just to give the dog a little help. The scruffy dog is an appealing creature with a whimper and a tilting head.

Opie and Sheriff Taylor agree that the dog looks hungry, and they ransack frustrated Deputy Barney Fife's packed lunch to feed him. The terrier wins no affection from the deputy when he gobbles Barney's sandwich and his beloved cookie, but the dog thoroughly charms Opie in the process. The boy wants to keep him. He promises his father he'll care for the dog. Sheriff Taylor is skeptical. Opie has not always lived up to his promises. But his pleading son and the winsome dog are too much for Andy Taylor, who agrees that Opie can take the dog home. Opie, ecstatic, rushes to the house with his new pet, only to have the terrier slip away when his back is turned. A relieved Sheriff Taylor tells the boy that the dog probably went back home.

Not long afterward the dog returns to the station with three others in tow—he is smart enough, apparently, to communicate that there are handouts to be had. Opie is thrilled, Sheriff Taylor worried, and Barney adamant that the dogs have to go somewhere before the state investigator arrives. Andy is firm with Opie—one dog might have been okay, but four dogs are not. They cannot come home with him.

Barney eyes Otis, the town drunk. Otis has spent another night at the jail and owes the department a favor. Otis reluctantly agrees to take the dogs, luring them out with another of Barney's sandwiches. Minutes later, those four dogs escape from his house as well.

The problem multiplies. Dog word has spread about the free food handouts at the station. Four dogs abandoned Otis, but those dogs come back to the station with seven more. Barney is beside himself. The state investigator is due at any minute, and he worries that the department's request for funds will be denied because the investigator will assume they just want money for dog food.

Otis has a bright idea: why not take the dogs to the local pound? An uncertain Opie asks what they do with the dogs there, and Otis tells him that they feed the dogs and take care of them until their owners arrive. When Opie asks what happens if the owners don't come, Otis replies confidently that the pound probably gasses them. Tone-deaf to Opie's horror, Otis begins to describe the process. The frightened boy begs his father not to take the dogs to the pound. Sheriff Taylor agrees. But Barney is more worried about the state investigator. When the sheriff and Opie are away from the station, Barney secretly loads all the dogs into his car and dumps them in the country. Opie is dismayed, but Sheriff Taylor and Barney console him, saying the dogs will be fine. They are relieved to have their problem solved.

A sudden storm rolls into Mayberry, its thunder and lightning so violent that Sheriff Taylor tells his son to stay at the station and not get caught in it. Opie, alone, is worried about the dumped dogs, despite repeated faltering assurances from an increasingly worried Barney, who is struggling with his conscience. As thunder crashes louder over Mayberry, Opie and the sheriff listen silently to Barney's worried babble, but they jump up when he finally demands that they help him go get the dogs. They return with the eleven soaked animals, and Barney moans about his decision, saying the sheriff's department can kiss the needed state funds goodbye.

But no. Sheriff Taylor tells him he did a good thing, an act of mercy.

Barney loves praise. He preens.

But now, what to do with eleven wet dogs? The sheriff and deputy hide the dogs from the state investigator, whose forbidding interview isn't going well for the sheriff's department — until the hidden dogs burst in on him, bringing out unexpected goodwill. The investigator surprises the sheriff and the deputy when he cheerfully agrees to every request for funds. Afterward, Andy and Barney look at each other in wonder. Mercy, it seems, was inspired by eleven stray dogs, who warmed up a chilly investigator.

Hours later, Sheriff Taylor and Deputy Fife return to the station. They are footsore and tired from a long day of finding eleven dogs new homes. Barney is surprised by how many people will take a dog if they're just asked. Satisfied that they've done the right thing, the two are wearily leaning against the door of the station when a turn of the latch forces them to open it. In strides a rough-voiced, unkempt man in overalls. He has come to the station after learning that his dogs were seen in the back of a sheriff's vehicle. He wants them home again. He lost eleven dogs in total; he describes them in detail.

Sheriff Taylor sighs, tells Barney to get some rope, and the two head out to bring eleven dogs back to the one who lost them.

How great is the problem of lost pets? A quick social media search can show us how many are lost on any given day in our area, our town, our neighborhood. The American Humane Association reports that roughly 10 million dogs and cats are lost or stolen every year, in roughly equal measure. Home Again, the microchip company, has asserted that one in three pets is lost in its lifetime, and without help, only one in ten ever comes home. A 2012 ASPCA study suggests that reunion is most likely when an immediate active search is made for the lost animal—including a visual canvass of the neighborhood, awareness outreach with signs and social media posts, and shelter searches from the first day the pet is lost—rather than after the owner expects the pet to find its own way back.

What happens to dogs displaced from their owners? What improves their chances of coming home? Much depends on three factors, according to Kat Albrecht, head of the Missing Animal Response Network and an experienced SAR K9 handler who went on to develop some of the earliest lost-pet search strategy in the late 1990s. The behavior of the dog, the behavior of searchers, and the behavior of owners all influence reunion outcome. (Based on my own experiences in animal rescue, I here add the behavior of rescuers and bystanders to the searchers category. Any human encounter puts a spin on a lost dog's direction of travel, and searchers need to keep those actions in mind.)

Those factors show up in that *Andy Griffith* episode: the wandering dog who follows a child, the boy who wants to keep him, the compassionate parent willing to take in the dog and indulge the child, the reluctant caretaker wanting trouble off his hands, and the owner, late to the situation but determined to get back what is his. Reunion is a near-run thing in that episode: Sheriff Taylor's first response to the lost dog is to let his son keep it. That an owner might be searching for him is very much an afterthought.

When we search for lost dogs, reunion depends on our understanding of canine behavior, of human nature, and of ourselves.

The Behavior of the Dog

Dogs stray for many reasons. A dog that slips through a gate or digs out from under a fence may go because she's seen a squirrel for two minutes or been bored in a backyard for months. Fear of neighboring construction or approaching storms may urge another dog to flee. One dog might be enticed by friendly children passing by, while a second dog might simply be curious about the world beyond his yard. Any loose dog is now a dog making choices—selecting what to pay attention to, making sense of what she perceives, and interpreting what those new things mean to her in order to respond. 1) There's a movement. 2) It's a squirrel. 3) This is something to chase! Or perhaps 1) There's a loud noise. 2) It's coming closer. 3) It's scary—better run!

For the curious, adventurous, or frightened dog, every new stimulus can lead him to wander farther. Some uncertain dogs get loose and hug their home turf. Others travel a little way and then go back. But some dogs go and keep going, either unable to orient back home or so endlessly engaged—or terrified—by the wider world that they don't think to.

Albrecht classifies dogs into three temperament categories: gregarious, aloof, and xenophobic. Those temperaments not only reflect how individual dogs respond to others but also suggest how they will roam as loose dogs and, depending on the location and nature of the place where they disappear, suggest how humans should search for them. SAR has similar behavior profiles. In the search for lost persons, we talk about impulses, perceptual frames, travel traits, and "hot spots"—places a type of lost person might be attracted to. A wandering child, for example, might seek out a playground. A lost hiker might head for high ground. The concept applies to lost dogs as well. Their individual natures suggest how they could behave at large, creating hot spots for searchers to check.

The gregarious dog is friendly and outgoing. These are the well-socialized dogs that by nature enjoy the company of people. A gregarious dog lost in wilderness may actively seek human scent; a gregarious dog lost in the city may not go very far, wagging right up to the first person he sees. I've known some of these party animals: a loopy Lab down the street with a fetch obsession and kisses for everybody; a little tricolored Pomeranian with crippled back legs who scooched over to every stranger on her round little backside, beaming; a clutch of golden retrievers who met me at the dog park and were certain I loved them as much as they loved me, ten seconds after we met.

If the humans who encounter them are not threatening, recovering this kind of lost dog by hand can be simple. Often the dogs come right to them! Gregarious dogs will follow strangers or settle themselves on an unfamiliar front porch, waiting to connect with any friendly human. Opie Taylor's little black-and-tan opportunist is a model of the type. My own puppy Jake Piper made a beeline from my front door to the first pair of humans he saw. Since they may go right up to their rescuers, gregarious dogs wearing collars and tags and having microchips have a much better chance of coming home than those same dogs without them. (That said, all this bonhomie brings other issues—these dogs' friendly dispositions can tempt finders to keep them. Gregarious dogs, particularly untagged ones, may be quickly absorbed into new homes.)

The aloof dog is far more reserved. Hesitant with strangers, these dogs lack the buoyant, universal sociability of the gregarious dog. Nonconfrontational human body language and the thoughtful use of attraction can play a key role in recovering an aloof dog. When lost, such dogs may be tempted into humane traps with food or quiet kindness from solitary rescuers, but it's a cautious business. Dr. Patricia McConnell, animal behaviorist, has noted how critical it is for humans to understand the differences between a primate's way of communicating friendliness and a canine's. Making direct eye contact, stretching forward, and reaching out a hand—those are monkey moves and human, too. They don't always translate well. A gregarious dog on the loose might forgive these blunders, but an aloof dog may perceive them as a threat. I think of my mother telling me to *let them think it's their idea* and my father intuitively standing sideways to let a wandering dog choose the approach. Because aloof dogs are shy and easily overwhelmed by strangers, they may also be easily provoked into greater levels of fear and flight. Aloof dogs that are wandering often skirt the edges of populated areas, ducking behind buildings and traveling down alleys. They can wander widely for a long time. When they are recovered, that shyness can lead rescuers to assume that these dogs have been abused.

Curiously, my search dog Puzzle is an aloof dog. Though she has every confidence in the search field and bounds to the people she finds with joy, search is a context she commands. She initiates that interaction with strangers. Off-duty, Puzzle has always been more socially reserved. *My Jane Austen dog*, I call her. Puz likes a genteel introduction. She hates to be crowded, to be stared at, to have an immediate fuss made over her by a group of people she doesn't know. Puzzle socializes better with individuals. She prefers to meet calmly and be left to make first overtures, giving her the chance to accept newcomers and to petition for petting on her own terms. When she has made the choice to meet a stranger, her acceptance can be quick and her affection deep and lasting, but I think that Puzzle as a lost dog would be wary, resourceful, and might take some patience for a stranger to bring in. It is startling to think of Puzzle this way—the dog whose off-lead confidence I know so thoroughly at home and in the field. Without the certainty of our partnership, without the mission, separated from me, wandering lost, she could be a different dog, I think.

The xenophobic dog is highly reactive and can be fearful of almost everything. Genetics, lack of early socialization, past experiences, or all of these may play a part in this behavior. These dogs startle easily and panic severely, and as lost dogs they may run and keep running—often called *flight mode*—too heedless to even recognize danger. When captured, their cowering terror or defensive behaviors can lead rescuers to believe they are feral or abused. Recovering xenophobic dogs is a conundrum. Their mad flight resists containment. Attraction is also difficult. Even half-starved xenophobic dogs may stay too wary to approach a food lure. One failed catch in a humane trap can teach them never to approach a trap again. These dogs learn quickly and remember well. Xenophobic dogs can become so deeply traumatized by fear that when lost, they bolt from any human and do not recognize even their owners. Shy little Odie was likely one of these. Loving and bonded with his person, in his youth he might have raced away from the things that frightened him, but lost as a very elderly dog, he simply hid, too fearful and overcome to even respond to the person he knew best.

Albrecht notes that many owners are surprised by their dogs' reactions when lost. It's a new context for them both. The aloof dog that loves his family may not have had much chance to show how he interacts alone with strangers. A xenophobic, "small world" dog that has led a sheltered life may never have demonstrated how anxious he is to the owner who has known him only within four walls. That timid, routine-secure house dog may reveal an unexpected side of himself when wandering alone, making impulsive, reactive choices the owner has no way to predict.

Trauma can overwrite any lost dog's inherent nature. The gregarious dog escaping a car crash, the aloof dog pelted by rocks from a group of troublemakers, the already twitchy xenophobic dog hiding in a quiet spot and becoming terrified when the place erupts into life as a construction site—all dogs can suffer from critical incident stress. As trainer Ali Brown notes, the production of stress hormones, glucocorticoids, is an ancient biochemistry that ramps up the impulse to fight, flee, or hide. Stress hormones, provoked again and again, can transform a dog, who never comes down from them, negatively spiraling with every new bad experience that comes along.

What happens to lost dogs that are not returned to human care? Traffic, predators, starvation and thirst, entrapment, drowning —many lost dogs meet misadventure and perish alone. Lacking human help, some resourceful lost dogs do manage to live in the wild. Conflicted, often traumatized, these lost dogs wander in *survival mode* and remain strays, half starved and evasive despite known sightings, sometimes across years. Some stabilize enough to eventually petition for human help. A very few make their own way home.

The Behavior of Searchers, Rescuers, and Bystanders

The people who cross paths with lost dogs are even harder to predict. Searchers want to find them; rescuers want to bring them to safety; bystanders may ignore them, take them, or harass them away. Every human engagement makes an impression on the dog.

Compassionate searchers and rescuers may try to bring lost dogs in—sometimes skillfully, sometimes not. There are many well-meaning but wrong choices at this. As our understanding of canine behavior evolves, old tactics of whistling, calling, chasing a lost dog by foot or in cars should be replaced by better strategy. While that gregarious dog may respond cheerfully to a kind stranger reaching out, other temperaments are less likely to do so. With the best intentions, many people instinctively run after a loose dog, perhaps calling her name at the same time. Such moves can be serious mistakes for the aloof or xenophobic dog, ramping up the dog's fear and need to evade. Even a gregarious dog can get spooked enough by a chasing crowd to have his own natural impulses overcome, the shouts of his name somehow translating to his confused mind as threat.

The case of a lost golden retriever in Massachusetts illustrates this. The beautiful four-year-old show dog was being groomed on a table at a dog show when a falling canopy startled him. The dog leaped from the table and ran. Well-meaning bystanders ran after him, calling his name, which only escalated his fear. The golden disappeared at 1:30 in the afternoon on a Saturday in June 2014. He was sighted once near a dog park later that day and then never again. Did he perish, unfound? Was he taken in by someone when he finally stopped running?

Run and catch him was the clumsy loose-dog strategy I remember witnessing as a child, but these can be wiser days. Many lost dog notices now have REPORT SIGHTINGS / DO NOT CHASE emblazoned across them for just this reason. It is a strategy slowly taking hold.

Rescuers who manage to recover lost dogs face other difficult choices. It's easier if the dog's recovery began with an owner asking for help, but people who find a random wandering animal now have that dog's fate in their hands. What to do next is a dilemma. Search for the owner? Take to the shelter? Keep or rehome?

A tag with current information gives the person who finds a lost dog the easiest solution. Pick up the dog, make the call, arrange for reunion, and shelter the dog in the meanwhile—ideally, it's a quick process. Dogs with collars and tags still seem to have the greatest rate of return, offering quick proof of ownership.

With or without a collar, a dog may be microchipped, and most shelters and many vet clinics routinely check for them when examining a found dog. Microchips have become a standard protection against the possibility of loss (some nations, like the U.K., and some U.S. cities require them), but checking for a microchip involves a trip to a shelter or a vet, and for some finders that inconvenience is greater than doing something else with the dog. (A troubling myth making the rounds these days is that microchips are GPS tracking devices, and that if an owner really wants to find his chipped dog, all he has to do is look on a GPS.)

While there is no legal obligation for a finder to actively search for a lost dog's owner, in many states the law is clear about making lost dogs available for the owner to find. Finders of lost dogs should take the dog to the shelter or, in the case of shelters that offer this option, notify the shelter where the dog is being kept and provide contact information for searching owners. There is usually a legal hold period for owners to find their lost animals, and only after that may a dog be lawfully rehomed. Many finders admit they didn't know the law when they made another choice for a stray they found, a situation that has sometimes ended up in court.

Shelter phobia is real. Old perceptions are tough to change. And while some shelters have demonstrated lifesaving care for the animals that come to them and have low euthanasia rates, other facilities are hard-pressed to do little more than cage for a short time, then put down. Some finders, certain that a dog they take to any shelter will die, make other choices. They may ignore the law — and any notion of past owners — entirely. Others creatively try to find those owners.

I have seen some desperate workarounds. While traveling through East Texas several years ago, I remember, I passed an infamous, underfunded country pound known for putting down animals the day they arrived. Too many strays, not enough money. No microchip scanner in the house. Compassionate locals and pound employees had an unofficial rescue system going. Their strategy: if you find a stray dog, foster the dog and put up a sign on the road to the pound — anything to keep the dog from landing there. So the narrow road leading to the gray cinder-block facility was lined with signs for searching owners: FOUND BRN DOG WITH WHITE FOOT, ASK BOB AT DOLLAR STORE, FOUND BLK CHIWAWA [sic], CALL _____, 2 FOUND WHT PIT BULL PUPS AT COUNTY FEED. I have a lot of respect for those rural neighbors in a struggling area, caring for strays and reaching out to the owners who lost them. The word around town was that anyone who lost a dog knew to drive that road, and owners and their dogs were frequently reunited. After a month or so, thanks to "some hard-headed, big-hearted women," any unclaimed dogs went north to a rescue able to find them homes.

Often lost dogs are adopted by the finder without a backward glance. Or the urge to save translates to immediately finding the dog a new home somewhere else. A stray is an urgent figure for many dog lovers, who may see a loose dog and, because he is stray, jump to the conclusion that he's homeless, abused, or has been dumped. If the dog has waded through mud or slept on the greasy spot under a car, that impression gets reinforced. The speed of social media can place a lost dog with a distant new owner within hours. In modern America you don't just lose a dog in a neighborhood. In modern America it's possible for a lost dog to disappear into the very system designed to save her.

Thousands of social media shares show us how quickly a lost dog can become someone else's pet. This is particularly true of puppies, small dogs, and popular purebreds. A 2016 Facebook post discussing a healthy, well-groomed, wandering border collie reveals how it happens:

> **Facebook Member A** (May 17): Looking for the owners of this beautiful dog. He was at our home this morning. Our neighbors said he was at their house this weekend. We aren't sure if he ran away or someone dropped him off. He's staying by our barn. He's very playful. Please share this post. If you know who he belongs to, please PM me.
>
> **Facebook Member B** (May 17): Looks like a border collie, they are the BEST dogs ever! Truly are the smartest dogs.
>
> **Facebook Member C** (May 17): He might have a chip, *if possible, unless you want to keep him, take him to the vet, if he/ she has a chip, they can locate the owner with the information on the chip* . . . [emphasis mine]
>
> **Facebook Member A**: UPDATE!!!! We found a good home for this puppy.

The Behavior of the Owner

For those of us who consider our dogs members of the family (and 95 percent of us do, according to a 2015 Harris poll), the prospect of losing loved companions and never finding them again is gut-wrenching. That 2012 ASPCA study suggests that owners have a good chance of finding their lost dog if the search starts quickly, but delay and poor strategy diminish those chances with each passing day.

What influences how an owner responds when a pet is lost?

Emotional Attachment

Lost-pet specialist Kat Albrecht notes that while many factors affect an owner's search for a missing pet, all those factors can be influenced by the connection existing between the two. An owner with only a casual relationship to a lost pet may search very little, if at all, while an owner who shares a deep connection with the animal is driven harder at an emotional level. Owners who are closely bonded to their lost pets—or who value them for reasons of property or income—may search more widely, employ more resources, and continue the search much longer.

Awareness

Owners may not search quickly because they don't know their dog is missing in the first place. A dog that jumps the fence ten minutes after an owner leaves for work has a full day to wander before the owner has any idea at all. Dogs that are lost from a pet-sitting or boarding situation may be lost across days before those caregivers inform the owners. This is particularly true during holiday and vacation periods, when traveling owners may be difficult to reach, or caregivers may attempt to search for and find the dog themselves before notifying them.

Physical Ability and Circumstance

Age, illness, strength, and stamina also affect how an owner is able to search. Some owners have the strength to do the footwork. I think of

Bella's family and Odie's athletic young woman, who hit the streets for their dogs and stayed out there for hours. And I think of a lady I know a few streets over from my house, living alone with her two beloved cocker spaniels and pulling an oxygen tank behind her. A walk to the end of her own block might be more than she could manage. While able-bodied owners may be able to search a neighborhood, others are unable to do much more than call from their own front yards. Without the help of family, friends, or neighbors, a disabled owner's limited search ends quickly. Similarly, an owner bound by work and family obligations, unable to leave her responsibilities as a caregiver or miss a day on the job, is forced to squeeze any search for a missing pet into the margins, if there are any margins at all.

Resources

Many owners have no idea where to turn for help. They may not know where to find lost-pet assistance. While social media like Facebook and NextDoor are a way to spread the news about a missing pet to people who live nearby, and there are free (and paid) online lost-pet services that get the word out widely, a surprising number of pet owners don't know about those resources or how to use them. That Internet inexperience also prevents some owners from connecting with trained lost-pet consultants or search teams, many of whom advertise exclusively online.

Of course, some search resources come at a price. Though there are owners able to afford billboards and postcard mailer campaigns for their lost pets, for others the cost of paid services is impossible and even the price of sign-making materials and photocopied flyers is far too high, forcing owners to resort to whatever they can manage—often handwritten signs on scraps at hand. Creative thinking can overcome some of these problems, but it's a stretch that worried owners often struggle to make. I remember seeing a family at a Dallas park a few years back, wisely advertising their lost dog to locals on a

Sunday afternoon. The young mother had a LOST DOG sign taped to her baby's stroller. The father, traveling the other way, pulled his older son in a red wagon, the little boy holding a matching sign — just the word LOST, a photo, and a phone number. Something about that effort caught attention and aroused compassion. Strangers paused on that lakeside walkway. I was not the only person who stopped and asked for more details about their missing terrier pup.

Knowledge of Strategy

What to do when a pet goes missing, and what to do first? Torn between running around the neighborhood, posting online, and making signs, an owner can be paralyzed by indecision. How do you get awareness out to an area and search at the same time? A family may be able to divide tasks; a solo searcher takes on everything alone, an overwhelming job. I have seen some online lost-dog posts that reflected this struggle. Almost indecipherable — a recent post titled Law Dig Hell [Lost Dog Help] was the product of one owner's panicked neighborhood run and failed cell-phone voice-to-text.

The search for a lost pet has so many variables — the circumstance of loss, the terrain of travel, the temperament of the dog, the behavior of encountering humans, the capability of the owner. How does someone who's lost a loved pet manage all the what-ifs? This is when trained lost-pet assistance can make a real difference. A direction-of-travel K9 unit can provide focus. A search support team, experienced with signs, flyers, and online posting, can help spread word. But when there are no local responders to assist in the search field, owners can still connect with remote consultants by phone or online and apply many of the search techniques these specialists have developed.

Most missing-pet strategists seem to agree. *Working outward from the place the pet was last seen, do whatever is needed online and off- to get sight-*

ing reports on your dog. Online *and* off-. Public awareness creates a kind of net.

Eyes on—or witness sightings—are critical to every search. Sightings update the place a dog was last seen and suggest the dog's direction of travel. But how to get those sightings? A hound missing from a hike in winter wilderness needs a different search strategy from a Pekingese missing from a burglarized apartment in the Bronx. In the woodland wilderness case, large signs at trailheads and on nearby roads for passing drivers, a quick phone call to park ranger stations and nearby vets, and the calm, considered use of a magnet dog or pet-trailing K9 might be effective early moves to get *eyes on* a lost dog, while in the city situation, neighborhood awareness and an immediate sweep of online lost/found pets and selling sites become quickly critical. A dog lost in a thousand acres of woodland is not likely to be up for sale in an hour; a dog that disappears after an urban burglary might be.

Those large signs that work near wilderness might be quickly torn down in a city, so in the urban situation, online social networking, notices posted and signs held in areas with high foot traffic, and hand flyers passed from the sidewalk might be the better choice. Even here, *eyes on* could suggest a city dog's direction of travel. A report of barking from the van implicated in the Bronx burglary and two calls about a similar dog for sale on a local classified page give that owner very different next moves to make.

Direction of travel. Containment. Attraction. These are values shared with the search for missing persons. Once we have an idea which way a pet went, what do we have to do to keep him in a known area and to attract his return? We can learn from SAR procedures, which have had a longer time to evolve. Missing-persons searches are coordinated efforts, typically involving an incident commander who deploys personnel in specific roles. On such a search, a K9 team works the scent dogs; a dive team might sweep local waters; grid searchers look for evidence across terrain; the law-enforcement public information officer spreads word online and through broadcast media.

Lost-pet searches rarely have that extensive professional support, but when help *is* available, the same thoughtful division of tasks is needed. Family and friends can take on important roles, one managing social media posts and responses, for example, while others make and put up signs and flyers and still others work the area, talking to neighbors face-to-face.

The search for lost pets has some significant differences from the search for missing persons. In most cases, lost humans welcome being found. Many lost dogs, however, flee from their would-be saviors. Sound strategy can help owners and volunteers avoid serious mistakes. I remember the case of a lost show hound years ago, owned by a man popular in his hometown. A hundred or more of the man's well-meaning friends deployed across the night woods to find the hound, waving flashlights, calling and whistling for him on foot. That disruption frightened the dog, driving him out of the woods well ahead of them, where he was hit and killed on a freeway.

A strategic search for a dog lost in Vermont had a much better outcome.

He was a loving family couch potato, handsome Murphy the golden retriever, who disappeared after a car accident in Stowe, Vermont, in June 2014. When a family member opened the car door to check on him after the crash, the frightened dog bolted from the car and disappeared into the summer woods. Traumatized Murphy became a different dog from that moment. Foraging across the wilderness for months, he made his way to Waterbury, ten miles away, hugging civilization and at the same time shying from it. His slim figure was seen often, poised like a ghost against the treeline, there and gone.

Murphy's searching owner, Ed Hamel, needed help. According to the *Waterbury Record*, one Waterbury resident, Lisa Lovelett, stepped up to be point person for Hamel, who lived seventeen miles away. Lovelett distributed Murphy posters throughout Waterbury. She reported sightings to Hamel, who was no less committed to his lost dog. He made repeated trips to Waterbury and, based on sightings and consultation, tried everything from net guns and humane traps to animal communicators to reunite with his dazed dog before the coming winter. Murphy no longer seemed to know him. The cheerful family dog now fled any human approach, owner and stranger alike.

There were some heartbreakingly close calls. On one trip to Waterbury, Hamel and his wife saw their dog sleeping under a tree near a local hotel. They had no leash, net, or anything else to capture the dog, no prospect of getting help quickly. But how do you leave this dog you've been searching so hard for? Ed Hamel succumbed to temptation; he slipped out of the car and moved toward Murphy, hoping that the sleepy dog would shake off his fear and recognize him if he approached quietly. Hamel called gently to the dog, rousing Murphy, who bolted in panic.

Struggling against temperatures as cold as minus nineteen degrees that winter, the golden retriever was sheltering randomly, living, apparently, on garbage and horse grain. But there was hope. Murphy repeatedly returned to property owned by Wilson Ring, a Vermont correspondent for the Associated Press. Ring knew Murphy's story, and he and the dog's dedicated owner concentrated recovery efforts there, baiting humane traps with meat donated by citizens and businesses of Waterbury. The dog and those traps were an education. Intelligent, resourceful, and strong, on one occasion Murphy was caught in the trap but managed to chew through the wire securing it and escape. He entered the trap again, on another night so cold that the frozen mechanism malfunctioned and the trap failed to close. Wary Murphy grew trap-savvy very quickly, learning how to snatch the meat while sidestepping the pressure mechanism that closed the trap.

Murphy's troubling, elusive figure became famous; his story was shared on local and national news. *Report sightings, don't chase*, reporters pleaded. Bringing in the dog would take patience. But after a time many local supporters gave up. Hamel and Ring did not, baiting the trap with cat food and Alpo when meat donations dwindled. It was a friend of Ring's on Facebook, animal control officer Erika Holm from Middlesex, Vermont, who brought in the different trap, tripped by a laser rather than a pressure plate, that would ultimately catch the dog. Strategy, commitment, and a collective holding of breath. On a January night in 2016, Wilson Ring woke a sleeping Ed Hamel with a phone call. "I'm here with Murphy," Ring said. "He's in the trap, and he's licking my hand."

Ring said he'd been cautious when he first approached the trap, uncertain how Murphy would respond to him. Who was this dog now? Had he become so fearful that he'd turned feral or mean? To Ring's surprise, the agitated dog came right up to him from within the trap, anxious, confused, and yet somehow relieved.

Humane trap recoveries can fail when it's time to bring out a captured animal. Hamel, Ring, and Holm were taking no chances with this one. They were extremely cautious with Murphy, clipping on leashes before they opened the trap, setting up a containment perimeter in case the dog tried to bolt when they opened it. Murphy didn't try to bolt. Nightmare over, the bewildered dog seemed caught between the world he'd survived and the world he had left long before, making slow sense of the people around him and the harness and double leashes they'd clipped on. He was the Murphy Ed Hamel knew, and he was not. The three took the dog to Ring's barn to warm up, and it was there that Murphy emerged from survival mode and recognized his owner. A short time later the dog happily jumped into Hamel's truck on cue, and he dragged his owner into the house when the two returned home. The dog seemed to know immediately where he was, recognized his family — dog and human — and settled onto the couch. Some mysterious internal switch had flipped, and a family dog had returned from the wild.

But what had it taken? Strategy, an owner who kept the faith, and willing strangers who came forward to help.

Murphy wandered lost for 559 days.

A little big dog joins the pack.

5

WELCOME TO THE CLOWN CAR

EVERY ONE OF MY DOGS is curious when I bring Ace home. Attuned to my normal rhythms and way too smart about these things, they ramp up with excitement. Something is up! And they can smell it! They spark at the scent of the shelter on my shoes and the essence of unfamiliar canine all over my hands and clothes. They have a sense of the new dog long before they will ever see him.

My protocol with rescues rarely changes. Newcomers have a private rest period in a one-room quarantine before they join the furry horde in the rest of the house. A few people have asked me about that—why wouldn't I want to let a homeless dog know the nightmare was over straightaway? I answer, *Would you want to go to a party straight off a sinking ship?* Now there's a nightmare for a dog already shattered—suddenly surrounded by a pack of canine strangers, full of curiosity and exuberant goodwill, all grinning faces and waving tails. No—too many rescued dogs come in exhausted and sick. They need some space and quiet, and I need some time to assess them. It's a safeguard for the home dogs, too. The family hospice dogs already have wonky immune systems, so we have double the reason to be careful.

The home dogs know the routine. Tonight they go in my bedroom on cue, but they have much to say about it anyway. I hear the mutters, the pointed thump of their elbows and hips as they flop down on the floor. Then the newcomer is slipped into a room of his own, my study. It's quiet there. Three of the home dogs give loud, expert sighs I can hear even in the hallway. For a while they will hear him and smell him without ever seeing his face. Ace will be the object of much curiosity. The home dogs, big and small, will sit outside the study door in a ring, fascinated by the mystery of him, like a family huddled around an old-time radio play.

As I carry him in, Ace droops in my arms, exhausted with change. His ears twitch slightly at the sound of the dogs in my bedroom. He remarks the passing cat without much interest at all. When I put him down on the hardwood floor of the study, he stands frozen, as though it's all too much to manage. He starts shaking again, overwhelmed. What can be trusted? What cannot? I talk softly to the dog, but I give him some choices, some control. These first moments are always tough.

I look at Ace's abraded skin and wince, reconsidering everything I set up before heading out to get him. Even the new dog bed I bought has too much texture for a dog with a skin infection, and so I start digging in the linen closet and pull out a washable silk duvet cover, the softest thing I know, to drape over it. The yellow-and-blue silk settles on the dog bed with a puff, like a parachute. Ace's ears perk, and he stares with round-eyed wonder. He is curious, a little more relaxed. But when I come back with a small bowl of water, he is still standing on the floor where I left him. I remember what they said about Ace at the shelter: that he seemed to hurt so much that he couldn't lie down. I pat his skin gently with a damp cloth, removing the worst of the dirt and urine.

I'm eager for Ace to know comfort, but I'm not going to push. When I sit cross-legged on the floor beside him, he gives the slightest twitch of his tail, takes a step toward me, and sniffs my extended fingers. I'm holding a chunk of canned chicken. Ace takes it gently, drops it to the floor, and nibbles it into fragments, then turns away, leaving half there. Not very hungry. Okay. He takes another couple of wobbly steps to the water bowl and drinks. I expect a quick lap or two, but instead Ace drinks and drinks, closing his eyes and working over the bowl as if he hasn't had water for days. I know this isn't true. He had water at the shelter and took some water in the car. He stops drinking, raises his head a minute, chin dribbling, then drinks again. He finishes all the water in the bowl. Fortified by his good drink, Ace seems brighter now.

"Why don't you lie down, buddy?" I ask him. I give the bed with the silky cover a little push toward him, a little *try this* pat, the way you'd beckon a dog onto your knee. He understands the gesture. He cautiously climbs onto the bed, circles a couple of times, scruffing the silk into a kind of nest, and settles into the soft balloon of it.

Ace can hardly keep his head up, he's so tired. With his chin on his paws, he watches me move through the room and dim the lamps. I kneel to stroke his neck with a fingertip. Sometimes it's so hard to leave dogs you've saved in the nick of time. I had to learn that the thousand reassurances I want to give them are better saved for later, said in other ways. Now Ace needs quiet, and he needs sleep. By the time I leave the room, his eyes are already closed.

The home dogs are aware, aware of the little stranger in the house. When I let them out of my bedroom, they race everywhere I have walked carrying Ace. The scent must be that specific to them: *our person and this dog we don't know*. They circle the mudroom, the kitchen, and the hallway, stopping short at the door of the office. Jake Piper, the pit-bull-mix service dog, sniffs lightly at the door handle while the two SAR dogs, Puzzle and Gambit (a young golden retriever in training), lie as low as they can to the space under the door, pressing their black noses into the space and chuffing up as much scent of the newcomer as they can draw.

Four-pound Pomeranians JiffyPop and MoonPie have much to say from a distance. Tiny and inseparable, the orange-and-white and chocolate-and-white dogs skitter to the study door and away from it, spin in the corridor, and mutter—they know all about this change and aren't so sure they like it. Or they smell chicken and didn't get any and don't like that much either. It's difficult to tell what they're on about. The family hospice dogs—creaky, blind, and mostly deaf—also toddle into the corridor. Like pensioners at a parade, they want to see what's up but wisely stay out of the way. Do they remember that once upon a time each of them was the new dog behind the door?

I let the home dogs have their moment of great curiosity—that's part of our rescue routine, too—and then it's time for a distraction. We head into the kitchen for a snack. Every one of them prefers a snack to a stranger. I'm standing in the kitchen with a ring of eager faces around me when I realize that Puzzle hasn't followed us all to the treat jar. I find the golden still in the corridor, lying quietly, her nose stretched to the space beneath the study door.

"You . . . missed out," I tell her, offering her the cheese cookie she didn't get in the kitchen. Puzzle takes it absentmindedly, her tail thumping briefly on the floor. It's a little odd, her staying there, but sometimes these strange affinities happen. I can never predict which dog will have a special interest in a rescue that comes in.

Puzzle is still outside the office when the other dogs go for an evening sit on the back porch, and she's still there when I lock the doors and shut the house down for bed. Later I hear her get up for a late-night drink and wander through the house as she always does, checking on everyone else before putting herself to bed with me. The other dogs are in their usual sleep spots. Golden Gambit snores loudly on his back on the floor of the kitchen, his paws going straight up the wall. Later he and Jake will hop up to sleep on the foot of my bed, after starting out in some dark, cool corner.

But Puzzle never comes to bed. I hear her flop down in the corridor instead. Around midnight I get up and step over her to peek in on Ace. He doesn't rouse when the door creaks open. He's sleeping well. She looks at me mildly. She has no intention of moving unless I ask her to. Perhaps she can smell the hard history that led him here. Maybe his scent is curious, troubling. Certainly he's the most wounded dog I've ever brought home.

"It's okay, Puz," I assure her before heading back to bed.

But somehow she knows it's not. Later, much later, Puzzle wakes me to trouble. She is panting and pacing back and forth between my room and the study. At first I think something is amiss with her, but no, she doesn't need water and no, she doesn't want to go out.

I open the door to check on Ace. I can't really see the small dog sunk into his bed at the other end of the dim room, but then I hear what Puzzle must have already heard: an erratic scrape, scrape across silk. I'd think it was a rat in the walls if the sound weren't so loud and so right here. I find Ace rigid with seizure, his legs blindly paddling and his head drawn back, mouth open in a soundless cry. He must have been at this awhile for Puzzle to have had time to wake me. He is far gone, eyes rolling, puddled with urine, and dying, I think, when I touch him. He's burning up with a fever hotter than I've ever felt in any dog. I throw on a jacket over my pajamas, grab keys, wallet, and a damp towel to cool him down. One minute, maybe two — it seems like forever before I can get back to him. Expecting that he has already died, I bend down to the slight shadows of his breathing. The worst of the seizure is over. He is still alive. Ace does not respond when I touch him, and his head lolls as I lift him, but his trip-hammer heart has steadied against my palm.

Ace is awake when I carry him into the all-night clinic. He is confused now, trembling and damp with urine from the seizure, but he seems to look at me with glassy-eyed recognition. He is subdued at the check-in, head resting on my shoulder while I awkwardly fill out paperwork and push a credit card across before he can see a vet. The receptionist glances at him and reflexively shakes her head.

When we get to the exam room, Ace doesn't struggle on the cold stainless steel of the table. He's still disoriented and a little wobbly, but he can stand. Without thinking about it, I give him a *sit* cue, and he surprises me with a sit. A sleepy-eyed young vet begins the examination—temperature, lungs, heart, eyes, ears, mouth—and Ace wearily offers her his paw every time she touches his chest.

"Aren't you a little gentleman?" the vet says. She shakes his paw gently after he offers it several times.

Again the gracious manners. Ace resigns himself to the thermometer and turns away from the blood draw, bowing his head and licking his lips.

"What a nice dog." The vet squints at Ace's paperwork. "Now, what's his story?"

It's a short one. There is so much about Ace I do not know. And so I tell her what I do—about his four unclaimed days in a shelter, that he was slated for euthanasia there, about my hurried trip to get him the moment his stray hold was up. I show her the bite scar from his attack. No microchip. The shelter staff guessed he was six to eight years old or so.

"Really," says the vet. She draws back Ace's unprotesting lip and says, "Look at these good teeth. This boy is younger than that. Maybe as young as two or three. Or he's had some very good care."

When she looks at the thermometer, the vet pushes her lips forward thoughtfully. She doesn't like his high temperature, and she really doesn't like the sound of his lungs. Kennel cough she might have expected, but this is something more. She's not surprised when his bloodwork reveals pneumonia, but I'm taken aback by how very sick the tests show he is. Infection all over: lungs, troubled kidneys, and that raging skin.

I realize that if I'd left him until Monday at the shelter, all this might have killed him before euthanasia ever could.

The vet cautions that his condition is going to be touch-and-go, and treatment isn't going to be cheap. She is kind when she says this, but emergency vets must give all kinds of bad news often, including a care plan that could strip a bank account. She strokes Ace's neck and shakes his paw when he offers it again.

He is taken from me then, and for the first time I feel his reluctance, the little clutch of kinship and need Ace seems to feel for me now. He looks very small as he disappears behind double doors to a kennel area, where he'll be set up on IV fluid and medication. I can go or I can stay, they tell me, but I'll have to be back to get him by the time they close at 8 a.m. I stay. I pull up some saved websites on my tablet and study lost-dog behavior theory until the words blur. Four hours later, after I've drunk two large Dr Peppers and flipped through every *People* magazine in the lobby twice, Ace is discharged to go home. He smells like rubbing alcohol and has pink vet wrap on a leg from the IV line. He buries his face in my neck.

"You'd think you'd had him forever," says the vet tech, who holds the door open for us to go out. "The nicest little dog."

Meds for fever, meds for infection, instructions for feeding and hydration. Ace returns to a rigorous schedule for home nursing. He's not much interested in eating. I make a whole array of little liquid dishes, trying to tempt him. The home dogs watch eagerly in the kitchen, expressions wistful. They lack human speech, but their poignant dog thoughts are easy to translate. *Whoa—is that chicken stock and rice? Chicken and rice is our favorite. We'll take it if he doesn't want it,* they seem to say. They have bright, eager faces, quivering good manners. *No, seriously, we'll take it.* Literally dogging my heels, the pack follows me to the study and then mutters as I encourage Ace to try whatever I've made. The home dogs know exactly what's going on. I can hear them chuffing beneath the door. *Little dude's not eating that.*

He's not eating anything.

Ace accepts the medicine I've got to give him, but it's a clumsy affair. Pink liquid antibiotic dribbles down his face, spotting the silk duvet cover and me. We'll be pink together for several nights, sleeping upright in a chair. I read about canine wandering patterns deep into the night, holding Ace propped on a pillow so that he can breathe more easily. He feels like a steaming hot water bottle against me. He is still exhausted and sleeps hard, slow to rouse.

Across the following days of Ace's care, Puzzle stations herself outside the study door. She doesn't need the smell of food to be there. I hear her chuffing beneath it every so often, scenting to confirm my presence and his and just what might be going on with each of us. Does she smell my fatigue and Ace's illness? Does she smell us winning? I wish I could ask her. Dogs know what they know, and I wish she could tell me what she makes of him on day three, when Ace rises shakily from his silk bed and toddles to the food dish on his own.

I leave the study from time to time. Puzzle rarely moves from her position in the hallway.

A week later, a welcome sight. I find her playing footsie with Ace beneath the door. The golden retriever is spread flat on the hardwood, frog-legged like a puppy, bobbing her head playfully and nattering at Ace's curly little paws peeking out from his quarantine. I hear him squeaking back to her from the study. The other dogs are curious about all of this. They want into that room. In. They've accepted Ace as a silent presence in a place they are denied, but now the little stranger is reaching out into their airspace. I see them standing in a half-circle behind Puzzle. Their heads bob every time Ace's skinny white paw shows itself. The dogs quibble at my feet as I approach the door; lots of knee bumps and chuffs. *We've been patient,* they seem to suggest, *but really, footsie is just a little too much.*

"Sit," I say, and they sit — their faces mutinous — to let me pass.

Ace is a different dog this morning. He stands on his back legs to greet me when I come into the room, twitching his naked pig-pink tail. He snorts and tosses his head, waving his paws: *Hi! Hi! Hi!*

"Well, look at you, little circus dog," I say to him. "I think it's time to join the family." Bright eyes, cold nose, cool ears, and dancing. "Welcome, kiddo, to the clown car."

Dog-dog introductions can be disastrous. It's never happened in my house, but I've heard stories: the sudden resource jealousies, the unexpected fights, the abject little rescue dog that emerges from quarantine with a mighty, unsuspected aggression, fangs going everywhere, even into the hands that saved him. It's called *trigger stacking* when a dog is exposed to too many new things at once and pushed past his stress limit. Double the reason to quarantine: our separation periods here have always been as much about easing a new dog into the house as they are about preventing the spread of illness.

I know my home dogs. The big ones are working dogs and very stable. The little ones are noisy and cantankerous but soft. I don't think courtly little Ace will come out snarling, but I need to be careful with all of this anyway. Two vets agree that he's been lost for a good while, on his own for months, and somewhere along the line he was attacked by a much bigger animal. I can't assume he's shaken all that off, that just the sight of one of the big dogs won't terrify him.

Puzzle is the first to finally see him. I slip her into the study when the other dogs are outside. She's the house matriarch; every dog here defers to her, and her advocacy beside him may smooth the way with the others. Ace knows Puzzle at once. They exchange sniffs. Ace hops up on his back feet to rest a forepaw on her shoulder. She gives his face a once-over with her tongue. It is the same kindly interaction I've seen Puzzle give the lost dogs we've met, gentle and slightly detached. She doesn't take too long about the greeting, either. When she turns for the door, Ace follows her into the corridor.

The little hospice dogs are next. I bring the two out to see him. Both are mostly blind and mostly deaf, oddly spry despite all that. Ace is small and frail still, but he's the bigger dog here. He stands quietly. From a distance, Mr. Sprits'l gives a single territorial yap before he approaches. Mizzen is more interested in the dribble of chicken juice down Ace's chest. The two old dogs greet him, sniff him, and creakily depart, sinking back into their beds with a groan.

Then come the much younger four-pound Poms, who respond to any change in the house with protest. The meeting is big! JiffyPop and MoonPie skitter up to Ace and back away and yap and sniff and circle and play bow and yap and skitter away again. If ever there were dogs who like to milk the drama, it's JiffyPop and MoonPie, Jiffy because it's her nature, and Pie because he dotes on Jiff and backs her up. Ace doesn't seem to know what to do with the smaller dogs, but he answers their circling with a butt-wiggle wag and a bow to play, only to find Jiff and Pie at the opposite end of the hall, muttering like angry bees. From his bed, Mr. Sprits'l watches the two little Poms approvingly. Conflict. Drama. This was his noise in younger days. Carry on.

"Sorry about that, kid," I say to Ace. He's stood his ground, swinging his ears and looking puzzled but not overwhelmed.

Now for the big dogs. SAR golden retriever Gambit and service dog pit-bull-mix Jake are kindly, well-trained dogs. But they are big in presence and personality. Together they fill a room. What will Ace, an attack survivor, make of them? Has he come far enough not to be frightened?

I open the back door, where Jake and Gambit have been waiting patiently. Through the mudroom, into the kitchen, the two trot. They see Ace by the refrigerator and stop so suddenly they skid a little on the hardwood floor. He doesn't look much like a dog, and he must smell very odd. Naked, gaunt, abraded little Ace has brightened at their arrival, fluffed up what little fur he has. Now he's standing alert, about six feet away from them, head tilted, ears drawn forward, and bald tail flicking. Big and little, the dogs creep together. They circle at a distance, then more closely, sniffing noses and tails. Soft eyes, wiggling backsides, curiosity, caution from all of them. It's a minuet of sorts, a precise, electric moment of introduction — and then, on Ace's part, joyful.

"Bah!" he rasps, his front paws down and his bottom up in a play bow. "Bah-ha-*ha!*" It's an odd, hoarse whisper rather than a bark.

Ace rears up on his back legs, throws a couple of forepaw boxes, and slips between Jake and Gambit out the back door. He's a fast little bugger, and slippery, too. The two big dogs look dumbfounded. Jake and Gambit collide trying to follow him. Across the deck, down the steps, Ace races into the fenced backyard. He's never been there before, but he takes the new space at a fearless gallop — a game of Can't Catch Me in the moonlight. The big dogs chase him with goodwill, stopping when he stops, freezing in place before tearing off after him again. Sometimes the big dogs reverse the chase. They round a corner to duck under bushes — a perfect hiding spot for ambush — but Ace tracks them easily, flushing them from the brush like birds. From the deck Puzzle and I watch. This isn't her game any longer, but she raised Jake and Gambit, and she has already connected with Ace. She follows the flash of three young dogs in the moonlight, her ears up and tail whipping lazily against my knees.

My mother, my father, and I in 1963.

6

THE HUMAN FACTOR

W HEN I WAS a kindergartner, I once had a bad fall. It was just before Easter, and that day my school had given each of us a long clear tube of candy eggs topped by a plastic bunny cork that could become a finger puppet. I had run down the street to a friend's house, intent on us making ourselves splendidly sick with a candy picnic, but when she wasn't there, I turned around to go home again. It wasn't far—seven or eight houses, maybe. I can still see our street clearly that afternoon—a flat residential lane that curved along the edge of a military base, edged with '50s ranch starter homes almost exactly alike. And so I was skipping home with my candy stash when a pair of military jets swooped overhead, and as I lifted my head to watch them, turning, too, somehow my forward momentum and change of direction tangled and I fell headfirst onto the sidewalk. I fell hard. In my imagination these days, it was a buzz-bomb dive into the asphalt, exploding candy.

The blow knocked me unconscious. How long I lay there, I'm not sure. But I remember waking up to a dark dog nuzzling my ear and the taste of cement and the coppery scent of my own blood, which was forming a pool around my head. I dimly recall seeing a scatter of colorful cellophane-wrapped eggs. Horribly nauseated, I was past caring about candy. My brain roared inside my ears. I lay facedown there for quite a while. I heard cars pass me on the street, and I remember wondering why no one stopped to help me.

I lay there long enough that the light, when I finally pushed up to my knees, had shifted from afternoon to early evening. The dog stayed beside me. A big guy, maybe a black Lab; I remember his warm, companionable shoulder against my arm. He rose when I did. Leaving eggs, toy bunny, and a generous smear of me across the sidewalk, I staggered home covered in blood. Dad was coming out to fetch me from my friend's house and met me at the door. He shouted at the sight of me, and the startled dog skittered wide and ran.

I remember Dad saying, "Did that dog do this to you? Did that dog do this?" and me wailing "No, I fell. *I fell*," and Dad swinging me up into his arms and calling for my mother. Mom almost fainted when she saw me but steeled herself to drive to the hospital, because Dad, propping me up, was afraid to let me go. They were young parents with a badly injured child, but in retrospect, they did all the right things. They knew enough to talk to me, to keep me awake, Dad holding a damp tea towel to my still-bleeding head and a bag to my mouth every time I got sick.

That fall put me in the hospital, badly concussed. Mom says I never got sleepy. Instead I got hyper. I kept asking why only the dog had stopped to help. Was I magical, invisible? Somehow, to my childish mind, that blow had made me so. I had some kind of kid superpower now, with a doggy sidekick when I needed him most.

When we went home days later, we passed the spot where I had fallen. Dad slowed the car and then pulled up alongside it. The candy mess had been cleared away, but the blood on the sidewalk, now dried to a rust-colored stain with homeward-bound shoe streaks and a few ruddy paw prints, remained. I remember my mother's hands shaking in her lap, her anger and guilt and wonder that I had lain there so long. I remember my father saying that anyone driving past should have been able to see me. I chimed in again about the passing cars, because I was firmly in the it's-not-fair stage and would not let the matter go.

Christ, my mother said, *her footprints are still there.* She was ready to storm across lawns, to bang on some doors. I think Dad could sense her fury and unreason, because he reached for her arm even as she twitched for the car door latch. She made my father promise that we wouldn't be those kinds of asshole neighbors. Right? Goddamnit, whatever it was, we'd stop. After a crisis, Mom's moods tended to swing and her language go south; her words had a hysteric edge even I had come to recognize. She had almost lost her daughter. Now she needed some fierce promise to change the world.

She was asking Dad, not me. *We'll stop,* I promised anyway. I leaned forward to the windshield, looking for the dark and blameless dog.

Honey, Dad said, *we'll stop.* He took his foot off the brake and reached across me, sitting between them, for her hand.

They did stop, too, in various ways during the years we were together. I remember a story of my father finding a toddler separated from his parents in an Austin thunderstorm; Dad sat with the boy, who could not give his name, in the window of the J. R. Reed Music Company on Congress Avenue, where Dad worked. Having called the police, Dad sang and amused the boy with silly songs on a Steinway baby grand until the boy's parents saw him from the window while running down the street in search of him.

Mom once heard a frail cry from a neighboring yard when she was taking out the trash and found an elderly woman trapped in a broken lattice she had fallen into. She had a broken wrist and was badly cut from her efforts to wiggle free of the old arbor. We didn't know her, but she had no family close by, that little lady, and I remember us driving her to the hospital and sitting there overnight while she was treated, my father making me a bed out of two chairs near a Coke machine. We were up all night. I had school the next day.

And of course there were the animals my folks stopped for, often with me in the back of their pale blue '64 Mercury Monterey, a car that my Dad worked three jobs to get and was extremely proud of. These were days when seatbelts were still something of a novelty, and I don't remember if this car even had them. I do remember riding precariously perched atop the Mercury's back seat, leaning against that car's strange rear "Breezeway" window half slid open. My folks would see a stray animal and stop, the force sometimes tumbling me from my perch, and then there would be a dog with mange or a one-eyed cat or a dazed, injured rabbit in the backseat with me. Those animals would scratch, bleed, or pee on the car's two-tone upholstery, and my parents never seemed to care. This was the drop-everything quality I grew up with. "Put Yourself on the Shelf" was a song Dad made up about being helpful, and he sang it to me often when there were dishes to be done.

We are no longer in the 1960s, and when Odie's owner spreads the word and local people ask me for help finding their dogs and cats more often, I learn quickly that what might have been simply curious neighborhood activity years ago looks suspicious now. I shouldn't be surprised. Even SAR call-outs, deploying K9 teams from a huddle of police cars and fire engines, can provoke misunderstanding, anger, or fear in some remote corners of an urban search sector. We search in uniform, carrying gear and following a K9 ablaze with reflective patches and what I call don't-shoot-me lights — flashing LEDs that light up the words *search* and *rescue* on our coats, packs, and the dog's vest. Still, Puz and I have been confronted a few times, verbally abused a few more, and we heard the anonymous *pop-pop-pop* of a warning shot once, on a late-night search for a special-needs man. *Get off my lawn*, writ large, though we were in a public alley.

No wonder, then, that lost-pet search, without the huddle of law enforcement vehicles, may need plenty of explaining. Suspicion has become a default. The work is easiest when you're posting signs, which explain the situation and invite help all at once. Blond, teddy-bear-faced Puzzle, as magnet dog, defuses questions sometimes. I keep one lost-pet flyer in hand to defuse others and to show to locals who might have seen the pet. But alongside bereft owners, neighborhood searches with a flashlight—typically sweeping for the glow of a lost cat's eyeshine—can pause passersby and police cars whether or not I have a golden retriever at my side. More than once I'm asked, *Who are you with? What is your contact number?* Already a uniform-wearing member of other search organizations, I have resisted being more than a trained neighbor helping neighbors find their missing pets, but I understand the wariness.

Many MAR workers gear up in the way of SAR personnel, with team shirts and reflective vests and glow sticks and LED hazard lights. I am reminded again of that necessary message. Missing-animal response is new to many people, and since it is no casual effort, it needs the kind of street presence that means business. And so, after a few people question me, I wear a reflective neon vest with LOST PET SEARCH heat-pressed across the back of it. And when demand becomes great enough, I add a phone line. Local police officers come to recognize the effort. In time, patrolling officers pause and point to the next street and call to me something like, *Loose dog running east two blocks over. That your guy?* And when some of the people whose pets have been reunited offer to help on the next search, the emerging group needs a name to go by. My mother unexpectedly gives us one. She's been watching an old video of Ace, shot just days after he recovered from pneumonia. The little dog popped up on his back feet and danced for me, his bald tail twitching. Mom messages: "Look—this is where Acey got his wag back." And WagBack becomes our name.

❧

They haven't spoken in decades, but my folks weigh in separately on this "whole lost-pet thing" I've been doing lately. They exchange volleys that never connect, parenting still. Dad worries that I'm overextended. Mom says they got the daughter they raised. Dad cautions that maybe I shouldn't be too much like my mother. *She could charm cats from the bushes and dogs off the streets, but she wore herself out (and wore us out sometimes, too).* That Dad remarried another animal lover and, with his second wife, went on to bring in stray cats so pregnant they were ready to pop, then found homes for the kittens, doesn't escape him. Sometimes he laughs and reminds me to do as he says, not as he does. Mom doesn't really know much about Dad's second life, but she speaks of the quiet resourcefulness she remembers (those jumper cables! that bacon!) with affection. But then sometimes she claims *any stick-to-it your father got, he got from me.* Old history, still bruised.

On his eightieth birthday, we wait for cake coming from the kitchen. My father is still recovering from recent surgeries. He is sitting in his favorite recliner with his new rescued kitten, a tabby named Pockets. Uncharacteristically, he's asked me to sit, to stay, not to help in the kitchen. He has something to say. Dad tosses crumpled paper for the kitten and asks, "How's my dog?" about Ace, whom he sometimes teasingly takes credit for saving. He asks about Puzzle and Odie and how the lost-pet work is going. Missing-animal response. So it has a name now, he muses. And theory, down in books. And formal training. That must be so different from search and rescue for people, he says to me, because how many lost animals even know that you're trying to help? They're smart, but not that smart. Or maybe we're just figuring out how to tell them. He is surprised that some people make a profession of this. He's not surprised there's this much to learn. It's tricky, he says, remembering the string of days we once put in on a school playground, dropping chunks of hamburger from Burger Chef, convincing a wary, grubby dog under a slide that it would all be okay. Dad dangles his fingers over his kitten's paws. When it came to lost animals, he muses, he and my mother had to wing it in an era when no one talked about this stuff. *You winged it, too,* he says. *You always had to be in the middle, winging it, too.*

We reminisce a little about stuck-in-a-shed Smokey and it-took-two-vets-to-save-her Rosie and Sonny the jumper-cable Lab and about a crazy terrier that lived behind us in Fort Worth that kept hopping into a neighbor's car and ending up in other cities. What was that dog's name? Jingo? Gringo? Tango? The dog had a tag, thank God, because Mango's hitchhiking was unreal. He would jump in through the back window, left partially open to let out the heat. And he would end up wherever that driver went. His owner had a heart condition. Dad says every time Fandango disappeared, the guy would pop another digitalis pill and cruise the streets for his little dog's carcass and hope for a collect call from Austin or Tulsa or Santa Fe. Dad finally helped the owner build a chicken-wire fence, because really, the old man's heart couldn't take much more.

Pocket rumbles as my father expertly scratches his throat. Dad speaks so rarely about my mother, about us in the past. For a long time it hurt to be so thoroughly dismissed. I understand better now. My parents were good at saving animals, kindred spirits when it came to loss, but they couldn't save us, too. Their grief, in its day, must have once run every bit as deep as my own. Dad and his second wife have worked hard for a better life. To preserve himself, and perhaps out of consideration for her, he had let our family history go. Even the good bits.

Now, he says quietly, there are things he'd go back and change if he could. Now he is telling me what he wanted to say. They are trippy and all over the place, those things Dad regrets: small things I don't remember, big things I do. He wishes he and my mother hadn't doubted my need for glasses, that they'd put braces on my teeth, that

I hadn't had to ask for a bra. *You were growing up, and we weren't watching.* He's sorry for those times when I had to live away from them and all the ways we hid the truth that I hadn't been home for months — long stays with my grandmother, or extended family, or friends. He says he hopes I never knew how bad things were sometimes. How hard my mother and he were trying, how dangerously they were out of sync. I did know how bad it was, but I don't tell my father so. We lived on the edge of catastrophe. When Dad speaks, I think of those desperate parents in buildings on fire who throw their children from high windows and hope for a miracle, and while I don't paint that image for him, I tell him it's okay. I landed okay. We all, in our separate places, landed okay. And we did a little good that remains.

Pockets smacks a ball of paper back to my father. We return to trading stories about the animals, the happiest moments we once shared. My father recalls one kitten we brought home from the shelter, a real high flyer, who was able to leap from curtain rod to cornice board to armoire across the house, never touching the ground. One time PittyPat went missing, and when my mother tapped her signature drum riff on the tuna can, the cat leaped out of a hole in the ceiling smack onto my mother's head, taking my mother's beehive wig with her. Flailing cat, wig-grabbing Mom. Tuna went everywhere. The other cats came running. They must have thought that spray of tuna was an act of God.

Dad laughs. The mood shifts. When I tell him about the high-tech humane traps and the night-vision goggles and the GPS mapping out there for lost pets these days, he chuckles and shakes his head, tapping his feet with excitement. He whistles when I tell him that I just bought a drone and will train with it for the purpose. Dad has never been a Luddite, never been one of those cranky I-had-to-walk-twelve-miles-to-school-in-the-snow kinds of guys. He's amazed by the technology, mostly pleased that it must mean that more people care. Still — he says that no matter what gadgets you've got, the human factor never changes. He doesn't use these words, but he's talking willingness, resourcefulness, and patience. Those strays brought out the best in us, he muses, going back to our time as a family. Someone, he says, has to let go of their own stuff and care enough to stop. And then they have to stick it out. Across the coming years, in love or on searches, his words will never be wrong.

Waiting for a cue I can only guess at, Ace
has a face always full of expectation.

7

GHOST IN THE HALL

ACE REMEMBERS WHAT HE LOST, and he wanders from room to room sometimes, looking for it. Though he's settled in and seems happy enough with us, there is a puzzled quality to his life here, as though he makes familiar moves that I don't answer in kind. Ace is loving and affectionate, but there is someone he looks for who I am not. From time to time he traces the life they once shared across the rooms of my house.

I've never brought home a dog so ingrained in ritual. Even the owner-surrendered rescues have adjusted here more readily. Wherever he came from, Ace was central to the lives of those who loved him. He shared short walks and long car trips, couch naps and long, long sessions at the television. He learned tricks for treats. Every day Ace reveals a little more, and I pay attention, before our habits here overwrite his old ones.

He got a lot of car rides in the old days. He wishes for them now. I knew he was a little traveler the moment we took him out of the shelter, but he was sick then, and it takes the well dog to show me how much he loves the car. Sometimes I think I could almost identify make and model from his specific reactions. The clunk of some car doors will wake him from a nap. A certain pitch of passing engine makes him keen. Not every car, not every door. When a pizza delivery guy in a '90s Ford Taurus uses my driveway to change direction, Ace wags and whimpers at the door like he is greeting a long-lost friend.

But while he readily climbs into a car at curbside, he is uncertain about the garage, which suggests to me that wherever he lived before, car trips began in a car parked out of doors. And those trips were made in the lap of a passenger. Ace has no interest in sitting with the driver. Once in the car, ears alive and eyes bright, he wants to sit with someone in the right seat, paws resting on a human's right arm, nose to the window but head not out of it, in maximum breeze position. I wrestle with my conscience about this. I'm not a fan of dogs in front seats, having seen the terrible, even fatal damage an airbag can do to a dog. But it's hard to ignore his yearning. How to manage both his happiness and his safety? A friend suggests I sit in the backseat with him, and we try a ride together like that, chauffeured by the woman who suggested it. We make weird little drives that go nowhere just to share his tongue-out joy.

In his former life Ace was allowed on furniture. He's allowed on furniture here, too. There's no hesitation about him that I've seen in other rescued dogs—the kind of furtive, side-eyed, I'm-going-to-try-this quality of a dog testing the rules in a new place. If there are homes where dogs don't get on furniture, Ace doesn't know them. He left quarantine in the study ready to jump on couches and sleep on beds, which is not a problem in my house if he can find six square inches of space not already covered by other dogs. Ace confidently assumes they'll welcome him and squeezes right in, but looks at me quizzically when tiny JiffyPop, Pomeranian guard of home territory, growl-grumbles at his pushiness from across the room. He has not yet earned her permission to be anywhere. (No one has.) He ignores her.

One early morning, a strange thump and a squeak at the back door wake everyone in the house. The cats scramble. Every dog rouses in full cry. I stumble out in my pajamas, sidestepping the goldens, the pit-mix, and the Pomeranians, sighted and blind, who got there first. Where is Ace? He's not among the pack. I find him sitting in the mudroom at the back door with one forepaw up, looking dazed. There is a step down from the kitchen to the mudroom, and I wonder if the sleepy little dog stumbled and had a fall. Scruffy and bemused, he shakes his head with a yabbityyabbity cartoon expression, like he's not sure what happened either. Puzzle noses him over, and after a long moment he stands, putting weight on the paw. But he gimps around a little, and I catch him looking uncertainly back to the spot where we found him.

It is another of Ace's little mysteries. I shake my head and write it off to a dog still learning the lay of the house, until one day, standing at the sink, I hear him dashing down the corridor with the other dogs behind and see Ace wheel around the corner from the kitchen to the mudroom. Ace loves playing chase, and he loves leading the big dogs, and at the height of today's game he doesn't hesitate, leaping off the kitchen step toward the back door. And then he face-plants right into it, full speed, headfirst into the bottom panel. It's a hard hit, the same thump from days earlier, and he bounces off the unyielding door with a yelp, shaking his head and huddling beside the dryer. The other dogs have skidded to a stop and peer down at him from the kitchen step.

What I saw makes no sense. Ace ran at top speed into the door. For a heartsick moment I wonder if he's going blind. But that can't be right, since he navigates so cleanly everywhere else in the house. None of the vets found a problem with his vision. When I pick him up, those dark button eyes are clear. I sit on the step to take a better look at him, and it's at that moment, from that level, that I see the back door as he sees it: a panel in three overlaid sections. The raised middle one is just the size and shape of a doggy door, which I don't have. But Ace must have known a dog door sometime in his past. He had flown into that panel as though he expected it to open, and he had been betrayed by it — I guess a second time. It is a lesson learned. I never see him try to run through the back door again.

I watch Ace make choices. If I am puttering around the house, he prefers to lie near Puzzle. If I'm working at my desk and Puzzle is near me, he lies next to Puzzle, near me. If I'm sitting on the couch — or any chair, really — with my feet on the floor, he has no interest in climbing up to sit on my lap. But if I stretch out to lie on the couch with the television on, he's immediately there, circling and scrunching up the throw blanket, flopping down to rest his head on my knees. The first time I lay on the couch like this, he looked overjoyed, relieved, as if he'd been waiting for it. He will sit for hours across my knees. He will give up Puzzle for this.

Ace has a curious etiquette with food. When I eat at the table, he doesn't mooch there, nor will he beg if I'm sitting in a chair. But someone taught him to dance for treats at the kitchen counter. He knows the difference between cooking and cleaning, and when food is out, it's a full routine on back feet, with twirls. If that doesn't work, he begs, sitting on his back haunches, forepaws lifted, poignant. He's every scruffy little dog in a silent movie with this. It works.

Give credit to the Maltipoo—he's adaptable. One early night after his quarantine, I stretch out on the couch with him. I've watched a little television and am reading now. For whatever reason, Ace walks up my body to stand on my chest. Peering over my book, he gives me a long hard stare. It's an uncomfortable message from a now-meaty little dog with steel paws boring into my chest.

"What?" I ask him, and still he stares.

My dogs have other signals that I can read even from the next room (MoonPie has a peculiar little need-to-pee tap dance in the hall), but this long look from Ace I first think is a request for petting. So I pet him. Ugh, no, that's not what he wants. Ugh, no, ugh. Normally eager for any kind of touch, he pointedly turns away enough times that I get the message.

I have a cat that gazes at me when her bowl is empty (I swear she does not blink), and I wonder if maybe that's what Ace is going for —maybe he's used to a late snack; maybe he wants more water in the bowl. But when I get up, though he bounces a little at the prospect of a dog cookie in the kitchen, he slips past me to the back door, where he waits, staring pointedly again, and sighs. No third time fool, he is not going to try for a doggie door that isn't there. When I let him out,

Ace dashes immediately to the grass, looking relieved. Poor little soul. I had no clue.

Hundreds of lost-dog pages on Facebook—a clutch of them from the area where he was picked up by animal control—but I find no hint of someone searching for lost Ace online. He lies at my feet in the study, curled next to Puzzle, who is stretched flat across the hardwood floor. She has her chin on my foot; he has his chin on her back. Together they have pinned me to my seat, and I give in to them, unwilling to disturb their perfect peace.

Lost dogs have a robust social media presence. Modern owners and lost-pet searchers often turn to NextDoor, Facebook, and—to a lesser extent—Instagram and Twitter, and it wasn't at all difficult to find a dedicated Facebook page for the area where Ace surfaced: *Lost and Found Pets in Conroe, Willis, and Cut-n-Shoot Area.* I scroll through the page's most recent posts to those going back six months, then a year. I type *Maltese* in the page's search field, then *Maltipoo*, then *poodle*, to see what posts return. People don't always know their dog breeds, and indeed, Ace is a right mix. A *poodle* search on one lost-pet page brings up a whole host of lost dogs, including a Chihuahua named Poodle, but I don't see a single notice for a missing dog that looks like Ace.

The current Houston-area Craigslist is also peppered with lost-dog ads, including plenty of Maltese and poodle variations, but when I reach out to the owners, the specifics don't match. Their lost dog has no teeth, and Ace has them. Their lost dog was neutered; Ace arrived intact. One lost dog's photo is so similar in appearance that my heart jumps, but missing Maltipoo Casey, it turns out, is female. "Are you sure?" I ask, but gently, because people do get mixed up, and Maltipoos can get pretty tangled back there, but the lady laughs and says, "Well, she had puppies, so pretty sure."

A month after he was picked up by animal control, there's no online sign at all that someone is missing Ace. I am bemused by that, until an airplane seatmate tells me a story about a lost dog in Oregon that opens my eyes.

The dog's name was Sailor, and the little mixed breed had lived with his eighty-year-old owner all his life. They were seniors together in an apartment complex with more stairs than was better for either of them, and that's what made the woman's daughter determined to move them to a first-floor unit. It was an upsetting transition for all concerned. The elderly woman had twenty years of life to get shifted — stacks of paperbacks and half-finished scrapbooks and cupboards full of birthday trinkets from every child and grandchild, clothes belonging to a late husband that she couldn't part with, and clothes of her own that no longer fit.

Sailor was a part of the move and very much in the way at the same time, and the trouble was, they couldn't really shut him anywhere, as the move involved every corner of the house. It was probably very frightening for Sailor, says Dana, my seatmate, because he'd lived so quietly. Dana lived down the breezeway and could hear Sailor barking in a way she had never heard from the mostly silent little dog. Those barks had a frantic, outraged quality and went on without pause for hours, piercing the apartment walls like a bullet through newspaper. Dana says it wasn't long before neighbors were complaining, even though it was obvious that a move was happening and that this wasn't going to go on forever. A few neighbors stormed to the manager. The apartment staff didn't do anything, but after a time, Dana tells me, Sailor's barks seemed to come from a different place and took on a peculiar ringing quality. Dana passed the daughter on the stairs and offered to babysit Sailor during the move, but the daughter refused. Sailor wasn't going to be any more settled with a stranger. In fact, he might bark even more. She already had her mother in the new apartment, and they'd put Sailor in the bathroom of the old place while they were going in and out. The barking continued. Dana wondered how a little dog would have lungs enough and voice enough for that staccato *yapyapyapyap* across hours. Others in that building grew more furious, confronting the laden daughter, slamming doors. Afternoon came, and evening, and Sailor was still at it.

And then the barking stopped. Dana said the silence, when it happened, was so complete it made her ears ring. The move must be over, she thought. Sailor must be moved and with his person and all is well. But within minutes she heard someone running on the staircase, and she opened the door and found the elderly woman's daughter doubled up on the landing, tearful and exhausted. She had finished the move and returned for the dog, only to find Sailor gone. He'd been shut in the bathroom, and the door to the apartment had been shut each time she and the movers left, too, but when it was finished, she came up and found both doors open and the little dog nowhere in sight. Dana said the daughter was so upset she had doubled over as though she were going to be sick.

Dana grabbed a flashlight and was the only neighbor to help the daughter walk around the complex looking for Sailor. She says she could tell the others were still pissed off about the day's worth of barking. She recalls fingers pulling apart miniblinds and faces peeking out from triangles of light, bursts of laughter, the blinds snapping back. She and the daughter met with more sympathy a few buildings away, but no, no one had seen the dog.

No sign of Sailor that night, or the next day, or the next. The daughter had to leave town to return to her own life, her own job. Dana put up a few hasty flyers in the neighborhood and one tacked onto the mailroom bulletin board at the complex, but no one came forward to say they had seen him. She says she went cold a few days later, when she found DOG IS DEAD scrawled across Sailor's face on the mailroom flyer—a violent confirmation of what she'd feared the day the dog went missing: that Sailor didn't escape from the vacant apartment but was taken from it and had been harmed.

Dana called the woman's daughter, halfway across the state.

Don't tell my mother, the daughter said. *I'm coming back on the weekend, and I'll do it in person, so I can be there if it doesn't go well.*

At home it wasn't going well at all. Dana said it was a terrible week, stepping outside to find her elderly neighbor standing wistfully in the new doorway in her housecoat and soft slippers, calling for Sailor, her constant companion for the past dozen years.

And then Dana's phone rang, six days after Sailor disappeared. It was the daughter, whose voice was so weirdly elated that at first Dana thought she might be drunk. The daughter needed a favor. Her fifteen-year-old son, who was on his damn smartphone all the damn time and who never looked the hell up from it, thought he'd found a post about Sailor on Craigslist. The description was unmistakable. Crooked leg and missing front teeth. Someone had found him the night he went missing; that someone had posted right away. The someone was also urgent: she had just a couple of days to find the owner or she'd have to give him away.

Now the daughter needed a favor. Could Dana possibly meet up with the finder and the dog and see if it was Sailor? Dana was thrilled, but she recalls hesitating, realizing that she might not recognize the dog on sight, that she risked taking someone else's lost dog, and that going to the elderly woman's home for a photograph might raise hope that would hurt her later. The daughter laughed. They had pictures of Sailor they could text her right now, from the same damn smartphone that her son never let out of his hand. Bless him.

Saved by Craigslist and a Web-savvy kid who lived more online than off. The dog was Sailor, who'd somehow ended up in a grocery store parking lot all the way across town. Dana felt sure he'd been taken from the unlocked apartment and dumped. She took the confused little dog from the relieved young woman who had found him. She dug in her purse and pulled out a twenty, which she gave over in thanks. Thank God for that grandson. Dana recalls how the dog, stiff and trembling with uncertainty, lit up when he saw his owner again. She remembers watching the frail woman's face go from gray to pink.

You could see the weight lift from her heart, Dana says. She went ten years younger, just like that.

And what if there is no Web-savvy grandson? Dana's story carries with me long after the telling. Something in it resonates with Ace's past, back to owners I've believed for a while now were elderly. I can't be sure, of course. It's all intuition, based on the old-fashioned tricks he knows and the modern ones he doesn't, the car rides in the lap of a passenger and the long, companionable sessions he seems to expect in front of the TV. Some quiet days I try out all the habits I have learned beside him, from the first morning face-to-face affection, to the shared scraps from the kitchen counter, to the kiss sounds that call him in from the yard. All bear witness to an ordered life very different from mine, and to an owner whose love remains where he or she does not.

The house where our lost cat Smokey resurrected
and where more than one missing dog was
reunited with a child who loved it.

A BOY AND HIS DOG

I HAVE A MEMORY of my mother's hard search for my classmate's lost dog. Mom had a tenderness for second-grade Billy, who seemed underfed and overbruised, and she had a tenderness for the dog, Checkers, an also skinny but sunny creature, effortlessly optimistic that every next moment would be good. In those days, where child-welfare calls to police led nowhere without some kind of witness, Checkers seemed to be Billy's only ally at home. Checkers lived for fetch and would bring back anything Billy chose to throw for him. Sticks, of course, but also rocks and newspapers and soda bottles and a doll that Billy had found somewhere and tossed flop-legged around the yard. I remember that doll's spinning limbs and tortured hair and Checkers returning it with a mouth softer than the throw had been. Billy was the kind of kid many parents worried about. He had a reputation for tantrums in the classroom, and sometimes he hit and threw sharp things and went to the principal. But Billy liked my mother, who made him sandwiches when he helped her in the yard and snuck extra PBJs for him to take to lunch.

When Checkers disappeared, Billy came to my mother first. I remember walking around the neighborhood with her and with Billy, shaking a half-bag of dog chow like maracas, the sound of Checkers's meals. Billy and I weren't friends at school. He could be mean. He pinched my arm purple once, and not long afterward I pulled a chair out from under him for bullying a smaller boy at recess, earning both of us the dreaded trip to the principal's office. Somehow, in the cause of lost Checkers, we forgot all that. I remember Mom walked one way down the street and told us to walk the other, holding hands for safety, all the way to the school. She told us to look left, look right, look twice for yourselves and once for Checkers. She gave us one of my father's skinny belts to use for a kind of leash. We walked all evening, and we were barked at by every other neighborhood dog, but we never saw Checkers. I remember walking Billy home, tearful myself over Billy's open tears.

My mother was determined to get that boy his dog back. I have the clearest memory of her later that evening, as she leaned over the kitchen table in the breakfast nook of our 1920s house. The wiring was suspect in that house, and the light from the single lamp above the table was fitful and poor. Making LOST DOG signs for Checkers, Mom wore a perpetual wreath of cigarette smoke from the Viceroy burning in the ashtray. Sometimes, in a moment of distraction, she had two going. My mother was concentrating hard, choosing words carefully, using thick sheets of paper from her sketchbook and a marker of the kind we had in the 1960s, the stinky kind that gave you a little buzz if you smelled enough of it. Mom seemed more frustrated than buzzed. She'd been at this awhile, making sign after sign, and every now and then she straightened up and rubbed the small of her back.

LOST DOG CHECKERS, she wrote, 1700 BEVERLY DRIVE. And then, on each sign, she drew a quick sketch of Checkers's face — a white dog with a white ear that stood up and a black ear that folded over and spots on his nose. She also wrote REWARD, which must mean she and my father were going to scrape something together, because Billy's family certainly was not.

My mother is an artist and, even more than that, a perfectionist, and as hard as she was working that night, she wasn't satisfied. The sketches were all right. They looked enough like Checkers to make the point, but even written in marker, those signs weren't going to be visible to people in moving cars. Mom was using a wide-tip versus a fine-point marker. That still didn't make the letters large enough to do much good, she told my father and me. And it wasn't like we were in a neighborhood where people strolled. The only people who regularly walked on the sidewalk were school-bound kids and the mailman. And she knew that one good rainstorm would puddle all this effort to nothing. Mom was frustrated and chain-smoking and worried about Billy, whose surly parents slammed the door in her face once, and worried about missing Checkers, who lived his life on a backyard tie-out when Billy wasn't home.

Mom wanted bigger letters for the lost dog's signs. "What I need is an even wider marker," she said, holding her thumb and forefinger a couple of inches apart. Otherwise she'd bleed the markers dry trying to make pages and pages of block print. There wasn't such a marker that we knew of. Besides, at this hour, all the stores were closed. She and Dad tried to think of alternatives. Mom had a box of pastels and a satchel of oil paints, but oil paints were too heavy for paper and the pastels would smudge and run really fast if they got wet. I helpfully offered my mother that last bit, because I'd read *Mary Poppins* and I knew how chalk could run. I remember her going to the kitchen cupboard and shaking her head over the four-pack of food coloring she and Dad had used to dye my Easter eggs. She had paintbrushes for width, but food coloring would be too pale and too runny.

"Finger paints?" Mom said to me, but then Dad said quietly, "Sus doesn't have finger paints anymore," and we all fell silent, remembering last year's unfortunate art on the wallpaper.

No finger paints. I brought everything I could think of from my room. A box of broken crayons, glue, some tubes of glitter, and a pack of shiny stick-on stars. That's where I was in those days: any art looked better with glitter and some stars. I remember encouraging my mother to use them — glitter would make Checkers special and the stars would make people stop and look. Mom never dismissed my contributions, but she had this "Oh, yes," with a lot of air in it, that told even second-grade me that the idea sort of stank.

It was my father who carried the day. He'd been rummaging in the bathroom. I remember him coming down the stairs with two bottles of Johnson's shoe polish in different colors. "The container is the applier!" the shoe-polish commercials said, and I remember him quoting that, popping the cap of one with a flourish, the bottle's dauber wider than any marker we had.

Mom and Dad made signs for Checkers deep into the night, long after I should have been in bed. They were so focused they forgot about me, daubing the lost dog's name on sketchbook sheets while I sat on the floor and played with my glue, stars, and glitter. Mom cut out the sketches she'd made of the dog on earlier efforts and glued them to the center of their new signs, the sketches puckering as the glue dried, giving Checkers a slightly frazzled look. Still, those shoe-polish letters made words that jumped right out at you. My father said so, reading to us as my mother held one from the great distance of the dining room to the kitchen.

"Lost Dog Checkers!" my father read, walking back and forth across the room. "1700 Beverly! Reward!"

My mother applauded.

"And a picture of Checkers!"

Mom curtsied, my father laughed, and I jumped up and down over ten LOST DOG signs at midnight, a star-spangled kid twinkling glitter across the kitchen floor.

Up and down the street, all the way to school, we thumbtacked those signs on phone poles the next morning. Our street and one street over. Four days later, Checkers was back. Did the signs return him? I don't know, but he was returned by someone a few streets over, handed off—with reluctance on both sides—to Billy's father. Mom always thought those signs somehow made Billy and his dog visible, proved that someone was paying attention. Five days later, Billy's grandparents came, loaded up the boy, the dog, and the balding doll, and took them all to Arkansas. *Somewhere safer*—that's what they told my mother, who found a reason to be in the yard and see all this and ask. Mom stayed in the yard when my father said we should leave and stop staring. She was the last one in my family to wave Billy and Checkers goodbye.

Houdini, an escape artist.

9

HOUDINI

THESE DAYS, OWNERS often resist making signs. Posting online is easier than making posters, and plenty of owners who reach out to me now when their pets go missing are reluctant when I tell them that one does not replace the other. Posts catch a specific online audience. Signs snag anyone local passing by. Flyers distributed by hand create a personal connection between searchers and neighbors. All of these are still vital ways to spread word about a lost pet.

Yes, online posts cast a quick, wide net, but they also leave a great deal to chance. There is a dangerous illusion that when we post to our own social network, somehow the whole world is seeing it. How many of your neighbors are on NextDoor or Facebook? How many of your neighbors are on NextDoor or Facebook *right now*? What about the stranger driving through town who finds your dog? She's probably not going to cruise local Web pages, but she might respond to a sign. Web-savvy residents might find a lost dog and think to check online for a post about him, but there's still every reason to spread the news to someone not so connected. I think of online posting as a wide, loose net, while signs near the place the dog went missing tighten the mesh close to wherever the dog was last seen.

Despite the speed of modern computers, flyers take some time to compose and to print, and some owners feel so pressed to be out searching that signs become a low priority. I completely understand that, knowing the urge to get out there. But if a dog isn't found or sighted quickly, it's time to get the word out at street level on a sign that will not scroll off a social media news feed twenty minutes from now.

Computer-generated signs on phone poles are a good move in areas with high foot traffic. Encased in plastic page protectors or laminated, they have a much better chance than unprotected paper of withstanding the rain. But what about passing vehicles on high-traffic roads where drivers rarely stop? Here, large block print and neon poster-board signs are a better solution. The now standard 5+5+55 rule suggests that drivers passing at 55 miles per hour can make sense of only five words in the five seconds it takes them to pass. Since freeway speeds are even greater, less becomes even more important. Make signs readable and brief.

Now, as more neighbors reach out to me for help with their lost pets and knowing how time-critical all of this can be, I decide to make a pack of reusable neon signs that only need to have flyers of the missing pet slid into waterproof pockets. The Fast Five, I'm calling that packet of signs. I let the neighborhood know I have them. Within a day of making the Fast Five, I'm putting them out on behalf of a Yorkie lost in a thunderstorm. The Yorkie comes home within the week. Five days later a King Charles spaniel goes missing, and it's a sign that brings him home three hours after he disappears. Found ten blocks away in a schoolyard, he is saved from his wandering by a family walking home from the grocery store. The family isn't on NextDoor or Facebook and the adults don't speak English, but they recognize the dog's face from the sign they just passed, and it's their ten-year-old who phones the weeping owner with the good news: *We found your dog.*

The young mother with three kids, a grieving husband, and a grueling job must have felt overwhelmed by the disappearance of her father-in-law's little black dog in the worst heat of summer. The pup — we'll call him Houdini — had lived with them for seven years. He was much older than that. Houdini had lived with them in the company of another Chihuahua, so it was not like he was a stranger to the house, the family, or the neighborhood. But Melinda tells me he had never really been their dog. Houdini had been deeply attached to her father-in-law, who had lived with them and who had died unexpectedly a month earlier. Until that time Houdini had never bolted from the house or yard — never a twitch of an attempt to escape. But now he was gone, and the family worried about the tiny dog's ability to navigate nearby busy roads and withstand the pressing heat.

Bound to jobs with long hours and little leeway, Melinda and her husband had not been able to really search the night he went missing. Her kids had walked the streets immediately after discovering him gone, but they found no sign of him, and none of the neighbors they asked seemed to have seen him either. The next day Melinda posted on neighborhood social media — a plea and a picture — and got an almost immediate response: a neighbor had seen him wandering a few streets over, just a brief glimpse of a little dark dog she didn't know.

I post back to Melinda, too, and send her my phone number. When we talk, I tell her that the neighborhood sighting is hopeful and a clue to direction of travel. We need to get signs out and work to get as many sightings as possible. Those signs need to be specific, too. In our small town there are plenty of little black Chihuahuas. At any given moment more than one is running loose. I have the Fast Five signs at home again, and I'd be glad to get them ready and put them out at nearby intersections where they might catch the eye of the most people driving by. She accepts, grateful for the help. The dog hasn't been himself since his person died. He's never done this before, and they've never had to search for him before, and they have no real idea what choices he'd make. But he's old and frail and arthritic, and we agree that he probably could not have gone far.

While I get the signs ready, I recommend that Melinda contact our local animal shelter. We are fortunate in having a compassionate, careful animal control officer and a good shelter with an excellent volunteer base. Melinda is at work and can't get there immediately, but she's going to call anyway and hope for good news. I make Houdini's flyers as fast as I can. Twenty minutes later I have the flyers made and the Fast Five neon signs ready to stake at intersections. I'm about to head out when the phone rings. I can hear Melinda's relief before she even says a word. The shelter has Houdini. Animal control picked him up the morning after he vanished. He was found about a mile away from home. It was a fair distance for a little dog to travel, across a state highway, too, but maybe Houdini's anxiety and enterprise had somehow bested his arthritic joints.

Turn around, stand down is a familiar routine in search and rescue. It's a strange sensation, too, loading up and heading out to search, thinking forward to everything that needs to be done and in what order, and then word comes that the subject has been found. Relief comes quickly, but it takes a little longer for the urgency to evaporate. I go home and strip the Fast Five signs of their Houdini flyers. I look at the funny, sugar-faced little senior with slightly twisted ears, dark eye patches, and an underbite. Something makes me keep those flyers — sentiment, maybe, or an abundance of caution. And three weeks later I am glad I did, when on a Sunday night Houdini disappears again. Another panicked post. The family isn't sure exactly how it happened. Theirs is a full household with kids and adults in constant motion. "Since my father-in-law passed," Melinda posts on our neighborhood social media, "any chance he gets, he runs."

This time Houdini truly vanishes. I get the neon signs up at nearby major intersections ahead of morning traffic outbound to work, but no sightings are reported by neighbors across the next few days. I make a hundred flyers and walk around the neighborhood, talking to everyone I meet and offering each a flyer with contact information they can keep. Most people are surprised by my approach; some are clearly wary of my motives. One woman flips her hand at me in a shoo motion and says "Do not want to buy" before I point to the picture of Houdini, then shade my eyes and turn my head in a little pantomime of looking. Her own little dog barks from the living room window then, and that poodle is persuasive where I am not. The woman smiles at me and takes the flyer. But she shakes her head. She has not seen him.

I walk the grid of streets at different times, often seeing Houdini's neon signs waving brightly from the corners where I staked them days ago. On one neighborhood canvass I come upon a local church that's having a food drive, staffed by a youth group from beneath a cluster of shade awnings. The effort is getting a lot of traffic, with donated food rapidly coming in and going out. I keep coming back to it, canvassing the young people as they turn over new shifts. These aren't local kids. They've seen the neon signs on the drive into the church parking lot, but not one of the young people has seen Houdini. They are a sweet group. One resourceful young woman offers to point out a flyer to every visitor to the donation table. Another suggests putting one in every bag of food going out. They invite me to stay and visit with people coming in. It's not a bad strategy; the drive is doing a brisk business, and for a while the little lost dog has extra help, with the food-drive volunteers pointing out his picture to donors while I pass out flyers to the visiting locals from this pocket neighborhood. Most of them have seen Houdini's neon signs. Some of them have seen the social media posts about him. But others don't know his story until we tell them. Most take a flyer and look thoughtfully down at the poignant close-up of his face. He's a fragile-looking creature, with those huge eyes and knobby joints.

"Bad for heat," says one gentleman, who doesn't speak much English. He taps the photograph. "Very small." He shakes his head sadly, folds the flyer carefully into sixths, and puts it in his wallet. I help him carry a pallet of boxed cereal to the food-drive table.

I log the steps taken and miles walked across a week of foot searching for some sign of Houdini. Three times I've walked the unlikely path he took last time, where he apparently crossed a busy state highway to get to the center of town and was picked up there by animal control. I can't quite make peace with that escapade. If lost dogs feel threatened in the daylight, some can become nocturnal (and some senior dogs are especially anxious and impulsive then). Maybe Houdini crossed that highway in the cooler dead of night, but I've walked that route now, and it tires me. It's hard for me to believe Houdini made it all that way in the course of one night missing, to be picked up there the next morning for his trip to the shelter. I show neighbors in the area his picture and tell them the story about his ending up here a few weeks before.

"Again?" the neighbors at the corner say, and there's a little judgment in the sound. They haven't seen the dog this time. They'll keep an eye out, they promise.

Having learned from the last time Houdini went missing, Melinda has checked the shelter daily. He is not there, and the staff tells her that no one has called to report a black Chihuahua found. We speak a few times by text or by phone. The young mother sounds tired and discouraged, pulled in too many directions by the demands of work, family, and her heart for a dog who is not hers — who seems to have lost his human center and is driven by an impulse she can't understand.

We've already made notifications with the online lost-pet services. I push Houdini on social media, posting updates on local Facebook lost-pet pages and cross-posting outward on pet pages across the Dallas–Fort Worth area. I stress the story behind the story — the grieving senior dog who has lost the person he loved most — hoping people will remember this lost Chihuahua amid a host of others lost in the area at the same time. Online and off-, we hope people will engage with Houdini and want to help find him.

Days two, three, and four pass without even the slim lead of a maybe sighting of a moving dog in the dark, which usually happens in the process. But now it is like every loose black dog has been taken by aliens. No word of any dog on the move that might be Houdini, anywhere.

How long will his family keep searching? How much are they

searching now? Our contact is limited during the summer days that follow. My once-a-day foot canvasses have shifted to early morning, before a foraging dog might retire from the heat. In the late evening I've been driving through the neighborhood, so often that a few people seem to recognize me. I round corners in the dark and see Houdini's sweet face framed on the neon signs still waving from intersections — a little miracle, really, by day seven, as those signs tend to disappear. Sometimes the city pulls them. Sometimes they get taken for other uses. I once saw a garage sale advertised with a sign stolen during a previous search, the sale information only haphazardly covering the original lost-dog information, the German shepherd puppy's eye still winking out from behind the words EVERYTHING MUST GO.

No matter how hard I nudge Houdini's social media posts, he goes unanswered. Neighbors who offered up early best wishes have fallen silent. They haven't seen him. The days are stretching on. Other pets have gone lost in the meanwhile. No reported Houdini sighting in seven days. I have walked the area so thoroughly and so often that, though I hope a kindly person has taken him in, I'm beginning to fear that the little dog was hit by a car on some back street or crawled off somewhere and died alone.

Eight days later I get a message from another town. An animal control officer in a neighboring city is responding to one of my posts on a lost-pet page. She works with someone who has seen the neon signs. At her shelter, she says, they have a dog that looks a lot like Houdini. She asks for my phone number and texts me a photo of the little dog, alive and well and in someone's arms — the same underbite, the same curiously up-twisted tip on the left ear. Melinda is overjoyed when I text the same photograph to her. It's him! But how did Houdini get to a shelter in a neighboring town?

How, indeed? After Houdini's family and I meet up at the shelter for their reunion and I watch the little dog light up when one of the teenagers cradles him, I take a moment to ask the animal control officer how Houdini had come in.

The story is a strange one. The Chihuahua was brought to the shelter the morning after he went missing. Someone pulling out of a parking lot at a hospital just off the freeway had seen the dog sitting at the edge of a field. His fragility and isolation—far away from any housing or protection at all—was enough of a concern that the finder had taken him to the closest shelter, two cities away from where he'd been lost.

Houdini had been in that shelter for seven days when the animal control officer saw my post. She looks on all the local lost-pet pages most days, she tells me, but it can be tough to keep up, because so many missing animals are posted daily, and it takes a lot of scrolling to review all the pets posted even on just one day. Luck had been with us; she had not seen Houdini's picture when it was originally posted, but one of the later updates had pushed it upward in the feed, and she saw Houdini for the first time. Then a colleague mentioned the sign for him that she'd seen more than ten miles away.

Some endings are happy and troubling at the same time, I realize, as I retrace the route lined with Houdini's neon signs. I'm reclaiming them to use for the next search. One of his neighbors, now familiar with me, taps his horn and stops as I pull up one of them.

"Dead?" he asks, his face expectant and a little sorrowful.

"Alive!" I answer. "And home."

The man shakes his head and smiles, as if he can't believe it. I can't quite believe it either. I pantomime a clap, and he taps his horn in a kind of tribute as he drives away.

At home I review the dog's travel on a satellite map. He'd been found a fair distance from home the first time he went missing—not an impossible journey, at a mile away, but a fraught one, across one of the busiest streets in the area. This time, roughly fourteen hours after he went missing, Houdini had been found 7.4 miles away, a trip that would have taken him through heavy traffic and overgrown wilderness and across an eight-lane interstate with a cement median and roadside construction debris so steep I couldn't have climbed it in SAR gear. I might stretch to believe that a skittish, motivated senior dog could make it a mile overnight the first time he disappeared, but clearly this was a different story. Had someone found him in his hometown and then transported him to the edge of that faraway field, or had he been picked up by someone kindly, then escaped from whoever had found him, only to be found by someone else? Or had someone purposely spirited this dog far from home? Had whoever taken him to the shelter been telling the truth? It was a strange and very specific story—a little dog at the edge of a field by a hospital two towns away—but I have no doubt that however Houdini traveled, he didn't get there on his own.

I slip his flyer from the signs. There is something uncertain enough that I keep them again, just in case. Sure enough, Houdini slips from his house another time a few weeks later, but this time it's a short trip. A neighbor reports almost immediately that she's got him and he's safe. Signs, posts, and flyers: Houdini has become locally famous. He's earned a romantic reputation in this neighborhood, as a slippery little escape artist whose talents developed late, sparked by a loss of his own.

The storm drain where Ace may have sheltered for months.

10

SURVIVAL MODE

T HE LOBBY OF THE Conroe shelter is much quieter the second time I enter it. The receptionist has a moment to give me on this weekday, but she seems a little surprised by my request. It's now a couple of months since Ace came with us to Dallas, and I've posted all I can about him on social media and have dug as far as I know how to online. I'm convinced that whoever lost him didn't post much on the Internet, if at all. My mother and I have chased hundreds of social media posts—so many lost little white dogs—and I'm back in Conroe again, hoping to learn more about his life before we got him. Perhaps if I return to the neighborhood where he was found, someone living there might remember him.

The receptionist taps in Ace's intake number. The shelter's records don't say much. An animal control officer picked up Ace as a stray on August 25 at roughly 6:30 in the evening on Bybee Drive, a residential street in east Conroe. That first, terrible photograph I have of him was taken shortly after he came in. Was animal control called by someone who reported him, or was he just found on a routine sweep? The notes don't say. Would the officer remember catching him, the dog's belly-crawl out of a ditch? The young woman gives me a dubious look and says there have been two months of strays since then, and Ace came from an area notorious for its troubles, among them its wandering dogs.

The receptionist asks if I'm going out there. I am. She pauses as if she has something she wants to say but isn't going to. She tells me to be careful.

Fifteen, maybe twenty minutes on this late Friday afternoon. An interstate and a state highway will take me there. The Bybee Drive neighborhood is not too far away. I pull into a motel parking lot and bring up a satellite view of where I'm headed — a roughly triangular area bounded by the state highway to the north, a farm road extending from the northeast to the southwest, and a corridor through woodland of high-tension power lines making the third leg of the triangle. Satellite images can make modern life look much tidier than the way we live it at ground level, but even from space this area seems transitional, uncertain — an uneasy petri dish of dense woodland, utility infrastructure, light industry, a jail, and pocket neighborhoods, new and old. Just south of the state highway I can see a naked development of newer, treeless tract housing that reminds me from space of an amoeba. South of that, a long road leads through what must be much older stretches of mixed zoning — small houses with generous yards and old trees in some places abutting white stretches of cement studded with metal buildings and tractor-trailers pressed together like Legos. Beyond the power lines, outside the triangle, is another mixed neighborhood of small houses and mobile homes.

Bybee Drive itself is one of three long east-west streets feeding off the farm road that takes me there. Those three streets are like the tines of an old-fashioned fork: Woodland Drive, Bybee Drive, and East Dallas Street make up the Woodland Estates subdivision, built in the 1980s and intersected by a single street called Lazy Lane. Stewart's Creek Park sits at the end of those tines — a few picnic tables, a pavilion for gatherings, some playground equipment, and a small sports ground. The park borders Stewart's Creek and has a paved, half-mile walking path that crosses the creek and braids north along power lines in the woods. That path is an area I don't want to enter alone, a local tells me. And maybe not even in daytime, and maybe not even with somebody else. That creek and swath of deep woods separate the

Bybee Drive neighborhood from the sheriff's office and detention facility to the northwest.

The shelter's notes don't say where on Bybee Drive Ace was found. I try to view the area as a small lost dog in summer would. The farm road end has less to offer in the way of food, shelter, and safety, especially in summer. That road sees some traffic, clips past the three streets of Woodland Estates, and leads almost immediately to a stretch of unyielding light industrial facilities. I get an impression of truck bays and metal doors and hot concrete.

The park end of Bybee, thick with trees, would be much better suited to a stray. There's plenty of dense wood to hide in, a creek for water, and a park with picnic tables for the occasional scrap. A dog could survive on the park end if he had to, particularly if visitors were kind. As I turn from the farm road onto Bybee, I wonder if any visitors were.

Certainly more than a few of the residents here wonder about me. I'm the stranger, arriving at the same time most are getting in from work, and more than a few people turn to stare as I drive past them. Maybe it's the slow speed or my turning head, looking left and right across the passing houses. Maybe it's my unfamiliar car. I wave at one man, who doesn't return it. Two houses down, a woman does wave back, then puts her hands to her hips and looks puzzled. I get the sense of an established neighborhood with recognizable traffic, and I'm an outsider, my intentions unknown.

Bybee Drive's wide lawns give way to scruffy, undeveloped ground just before the park. I drive all the way along it, from the farm road to Stewart's Creek, where Bybee abruptly takes a hard left. Pulling into the parking lot, I seem to disturb the drivers of two other cars there, a BMW and a Chevy of some kind. They are idling in the lot facing in opposite directions, their drivers talking back and forth from open windows. They watch me pull into the lot, and when I park, they immediately leave.

I sit for a long moment, getting a sense of the place before getting out of the car to walk around the small park, which is peaceful and clean. A dog could shelter fairly successfully from bad weather here—the pavilion and especially the central play structure, a sort of tower with tunnel slides and climbing walls, would provide plenty of places to duck away from rain and hide from worse threats. Though it's quiet now, perhaps enough people come here with picnics and fast food that a hungry dog could forage—or be pitied—enough to survive.

Back in the car, I follow Bybee Drive where it curves from the park to join East Dallas Street, then take a right on East Dallas, crossing a small bridge over Stewart's Creek. The transition is abrupt, shifting quickly from modest midcentury ranch houses to older structures and trailer parks rough with poverty and the passage of time. Here are older homes in disrepair and a small enclave of battered trailer houses, some with so rickety and patched-together a quality that my heart twists, thinking of the danger to anyone inside them during a fire. High fences of every kind separate many of the houses from the street, studded with PRIVATE PROPERTY or BEWARE OF DOG signs. I see a little girl of about eight in front of one house without a fence, pouring a pitcher of water over a laughing toddler sitting in an empty plastic play pool, while a young black-and-white bull terrier pup noses something out of a plastic trash bag with a hole in it. When I wave to the little girl, she waves back, and urges the toddler to also. The puppy ignores me, chewing something greasy he has pulled from the trash, while across the street two larger dogs leap at the fence, baying at him and his treasure, wanting it.

I have eight FOUND DOG signs in the backseat of my car and now wish I had more. In English on one side and Spanish on the other, I made them before I left home, hoping for good results from major intersections in an unfamiliar neighborhood. I felt like an interloper even before I made them, fussing unnecessarily over neon poster-board color (which color would be best seen but less obnoxious, more likely to be left alone)? In the end I settled for bright green neon wrapped around old campaign signs on stakes and stapled. The signs are two-sided, with four-inch letters that get right to the point: FOUND SMALL CURLY WHITISH DOG 8/25 with a laminated photo and a phone number. I didn't put a specific breed on the sign because years in rescue have taught me: breeds are often anyone's guess, and many people have no idea what their dogs are.

As I drive I consider the neighborhood and the roads that must be taken in and out of it. Where would the most residents see these signs? The park seems the most obvious place. I walk briefly along the creek and wind through the playground equipment, deciding finally to stake a sign near the pavilion, where it might catch the attention of passing cars, neighbors on walks, or those visiting the park with children. Two teenagers wearing headphones and practicing skateboard tricks ignore me, roaring and flipping across the cement. The ground is hard, and it takes some work to press the sign's metal stakes into the unyielding dirt. Mission accomplished, I turn and see a woman with a leashed shih tzu watching me, hands on her hips. She does not return my wave and gives me such a long stare, brow furrowed, that at first I'm uneasy; then I realize she may be reading the sign. I start to approach her — maybe she would remember Ace — but she turns away despite my call and walks rapidly down Woodland behind a silky mop of a dog moving at top speed.

Hoping to catch neighborhood drivers inbound and outbound, I put one sign at the end of Bybee and the third and fourth signs on East Dallas, one at the end intersecting the farm road and the other very near an elementary school and a small bridge leading to another neighborhood. Three women are walking in single file with a baby in a stroller near that bridge, and they stop, smiling uncertainly as they watch me wiggle the sign's stakes into the dirt. I hear one of them translate the English side of the sign to the others in Spanish.

I have photos of Ace on my smartphone, and the women willingly meet me, one shielding the baby from the slant of bright sun as I show them Ace's intake photograph and several others where he's in much better shape. The young mother, who speaks English, first

thinks I'm showing her two different dogs, and she puts her hand to
her heart at the sight of wounded Ace at the shelter. She turns to translate to her friends. No, says one, shaking her head, she doesn't know
this dog, but the other smiles shyly and then says something in a fluid
burst of Spanish, pointing into the woods toward the park.

The young mother turns back to me. Her friend recalls a dog like
this one that was sometimes in a storm drain near the park. At first
that dog looked okay and she had shared her baby's cookies with him,
but then he looked bad, and she kept her little ones away in case he
had a disease. But was it this dog? The problem, she tells me, is that
there are many dogs loose around here. She tells me I should come
back on trash day to see.

The two boys on skateboards agree. They are still at the park
when I return there, one grinding and skidding, the other sitting on
a picnic table, examining a wheel. They stared at me for a moment as
I came up the path to the pavilion, but they've seen the sign I staked
there, and when I tell them I'm looking for the owner of a lost dog,
they bend their heads to the pictures as I scroll.

One of the young men has lived in this area all his life; the other
comes here to skate with his friend. I ask them about pets in this area
—how they live and if people look for them when they're lost. The
visitor shrugs and defers to his friend, whose comments sync almost
exactly with those of the young woman I talked to earlier. There are
a lot of dogs here, and a lot of them get out and run loose, and most
people don't worry about it too much. They try to find them just by
driving around. Sometimes the loose dogs get into trouble, fighting
sometimes and killing cats . . . or even each other. I mention trash day,
and the young man who lives here laughs and nods and describes it
like an invasion sometimes, the way the dogs take over the area. He
makes a sweeping motion with his hands from the street into the
place where we sit. His words paint a picture of the hard, wandering
life Ace might have lived here as a desperate, resourceful, undersized
dog competing for scraps.

The young man doesn't know Ace. But there's a lady around here who breeds Chihuahuas and teacups and sells them. Teacups? His friend looks confused. The young man spaces his hands about a foot apart and tells him *small*. The ladies, he says, and the old ones like the small dogs. Here it is big dogs for outside, he tells me, and little dogs for inside on laps.

He says he could not tell me how many strays he's seen run through this park this summer, big and small. He's on foot. He doesn't have a car. He's on his skateboard to get here, and most dogs don't like the sound, so he rolls by to the fury of dogs behind fences and strays scrambling away from him in all directions.

When I mention that Ace came to my house knowing tricks, he looks surprised. Tricks are interesting. Different. He and his friend look at his photograph again.

"*Abuelo?*" the friend asks, and the young man looks startled.

He says there was this old man who used to come to this park with his wife and two dogs. Like a very old grandfather, an *abuelo*, and his lady. Not Hispanic. They walked here most days, but it was a while ago. A long time since he saw them, he thinks. Maybe as much as a year. He remembers only that the woman was thin like a bent stick and the man was not, and that he held her hand tightly, like you'd hold on to a kid. They would sit at a picnic table with their dogs. One dog was black and white, the young man remembers, and the other was light, and they were both small. But the old man, the *abuelo*, had them do tricks like beg and roll over. The *abuelo* and his wife were kind. Sometimes they brought a bag of powdered sugar doughnuts, and they'd give one to anyone who asked. His friend nods. He remembers those doughnuts.

The young man points beyond the pavilion, down Bybee, and says he never really paid attention, but he thinks that the couple walked in from the *nice* streets. He is sorry he can't tell me their names. He never really knew them. He remembers that for the longest time it was the two of them, holding hands, and then it was just the man and the two dogs sitting there with the doughnuts. And then they didn't come anymore. He says it's one of those things where you see someone every day and then you don't, and it's strange for a little, and then you get used to their being gone, and now it was like they were never even there.

A woman two streets over is briskly walking her own dogs when I call out to her. She kindly stops and squints at Ace's photograph. A quick, clipped, no-nonsense woman, she says *Shit* when she sees his shelter intake shot, then gets right to the point. Lost when? Found where? She asks good questions. She considers the picture a long time. She doesn't know this one specifically, she says, but there are a lot of dogs, a lot of dogs around here that look like that. Some of the dogs around here aren't lost, she says. They're just running loose. Sort of permanently loose. They go home when they want to. Or not. Things happen. It's scary when those loose dogs are big breeds that rush you in the street or stand there with eyes so hard you're afraid to move. It hasn't happened to her often, but it's happened around here.

She gestures south and says at one time animal control had a facility nearby, there were so many loose animals. But that was a while ago.

She points away from her neighborhood and says there's a local woman thataway who breeds dogs like Ace, backs a trailer onto her property and sells them out of it—not always, but you can tell when it's puppy season because at night you can hear the dogs barking in cages outside, and sometimes, when the wind is right, the smell nearby is foul. She says it's a puppy mill on wheels—not a nice situation at all. She's not quite sure why it happens, but every once in a while there will be this flood of little dogs through the neighborhood. Poodles and Maltipoos and Chihuahuas and Yorkies. Looks like a prison break, she says. Word is that for some reason this breeder lets her stock go now and then. People have different stories as to why. The trailer is moved, and it goes quiet, as if the operation has shut down. If they live long enough, some of those dogs find homes in the neighborhood. Some end up at the shelter. She taps Ace's photograph. Right kind. Right size. She asks if he still had his balls when I got him. Maybe this one was one of those breeder dogs.

Maybe. But someone who cared about Ace had him longer. I've had puppy-mill rescues, whose behaviors and fearfulness are in a totally different key. Mill dogs most commonly live kenneled and disconnected from those who own them. At some point Ace had lived with someone who cared.

The woman has lived in the area for years. She says these pocket neighborhoods are different worlds that share little. She shakes her head when I ask if she remembers LOST DOG signs for this dog and looks at me in wonder when I mention lost-dog posts online. I ask if it's possible Ace might have been lost from elderly owners around here.

Of course it's possible, she snaps, giving me a birdlike moment of scrutiny. There are plenty of us. Lost — or abandoned. Abandoned happens a lot. The lines blur a moment, and I'm not sure if she's talking about the elderly owners or their dogs. She says kids come in to move their parents out and then just leave the pets. She remembers one situation where the family left the parents' dog shut up in a mudroom, and the dog was there for days with no food or water before someone next door realized and decided to call animal control. The woman must see a flicker of hope in my expression. "Not your dog," she tells me, smiling. "That one." She points to the graying hound mix on the end of the lead, who hears affection in the woman's voice and thumps her tail.

When I mention the *abuelo* and his wife described by the two skateboarders, she listens to my secondhand description, looking down the street as though to imagine them. Man with a frail woman and two small dogs, one black and white and the other light-colored, walking to the park often with a bag of powdered doughnuts. All of them gone now for a year or a little more.

She turns back toward the park, thinking carefully. No, the woman says, she didn't know them. She doesn't remember passing them. But she doesn't have grandchildren and sees no reason to go to the park. Look at me, she says, pointing to her lilac QUILTING, COFFEE, AND DOGS sweatshirt. She has too much to do to sit in a park. She twitches the leashes, and her two dogs, called to attention, look back at her, panting grins. Odd as it might seem, she tells me she'd likely recognize the dogs before the people. People come. People go. She's lived here a long time and has a few good neighbors she's seen the years with, but she'd probably know the dogs in yards better than the people on the street. She's out with her two several times a day. She talks to all the dogs they pass. You shut down some when you're alone. You start talking to dogs. Yes, yes, she says to her wizened canines in a who's-a-good-boy? voice, clapping her hands and grinning at them. You'd shut down completely but for the dogs.

Hard rain wakes me in my hotel room — large drops out of a churning sky. A *frog-strangler*, my grandmother used to say. The woman in the lilac shirt from yesterday reminded me a bit of her, my father's mother — the same no-nonsense, frank look at the world. But my grandmother never had pets, an attachment she never understood in my parents, an emotional and financial indulgence she had no time for. There she and that lady would have parted ways.

I stand at the wide window and watch the rain pound cars in the parking lot, hoping for all of us there won't be hail. A barefoot man races out of the door of one room in a T-shirt and boxers, one hand punching a key fob and the other holding what looks to be a fast-food bag over his head. A crack of lightning makes the world so briefly bright I can see that his boxers are striped. He's left a car window open, I guess. Or maybe he really wants a smoke. The car lights up, and he throws himself into it, disappearing behind the wall of rain between us.

I think of the Stewart's Creek strays. Lost or loose-not-lost, they are out tonight, too. I try to imagine how and where Ace might have sheltered from this kind of weather. This would be no night to hide in a storm drain. I've searched for missing people on nights like this and have passed many animals outside in the weather. I've seen how neighborhood big dogs will huddle like cats beneath whatever cover they can find, heads ducked, tightening themselves into unhappy pyramids, the storm-phobic ones trembling in panic, waiting for the thunder and lightning to end.

Ace would take a storm with some advantages. He is not storm-phobic and not afraid to get wet. And he's resourceful. I can imagine lost Ace ducked under a car in a driveway or tucked beneath a picnic table in that pavilion. Either way, in this kind of rain he'd have been in for a soaking. Tonight's deluge pours faster than the ground can absorb it, making deep puddles and sudden streams in unexpected places. The strays out there tonight are likely getting soaked.

As quickly as the rain seemed to begin, it ends — a fifteen-minute burst of fury, and it's spent and gone. The flashes move north and the thunder resolves. The hard rain slows, then stops altogether. The man wearing boxers gets out of his car, pips the key fob over his shoulder, and the car blinks back at him twice. He retreats to his room. What do the lost dogs and the loose-not-lost dogs along Stewart's Creek do now? I wonder. Back to foraging, I guess. Back to finding a square foot of dry space to sleep.

The ground Ace once wandered sparkles a few hours later. The storm's low pressure hasn't yet given way, and signs, trees, houses here are in sharp relief, washed briefly clean by rain and caught by first sunlight out of a clear sky. I've headed back into the area early and found a sleepy neighborhood and an empty park, its ground sodden, play structures wet, and the creek rushing cheerfully south. Ace's three signs held up well against the storm. The ones staked streetside wave brightly from where I placed them. The one beside the park pavilion seems hardly weathered at all.

Feeling less like an outsider, more surefooted on this bright Saturday morning where I can see so clearly, I set out on a walk. I want to find the drainage ditch where a small white dog once hid, according to the young woman from yesterday, and to walk along the path behind the treeline that follows the creek. I've been cautioned about this path, but at this hour on a Saturday morning I walk it anyway. There's a crazy, almost sculptural quality to it that I'm glad to experience, winding my way along its curves, braided by power lines. This is an easy path to walk along, but I can see why people might be leery of it. Bordered by thick trees on each side and completely out of view from the street, I am both exposed and isolated here. I'm the only one out, the only one sidestepping a neat mound of coyote scat. Dogs like cleared paths, and dogs that have walked them with humans like them even better, but this one would be an easy ambush for a predator. I walk it with the same kind of caution an animal might: head up, eyes all around. The formal walkway curves early back through the trees to the park; a natural path worn by human feet leads farther northward to another neighborhood. I will give it a day, I think, and then I might move one of Ace's signs to a busy intersection there.

I walk the streets as Ace might have traveled them, stretching a bit to think like a dog. Ace is such a bright, perceptive little guy. I know him well enough now that it's easy to see him trotting paths of his own making—from this culvert to that trash bin to this hole in a fence where a dog might briefly escape pursuit. I can also see how he got into the condition he did. His curly coat kinks and tightens when it gets wet. Fleas and ticks in abundance would account for the wide sores where he scratched his skin into raw hot spots. And the consistent stories of loose dogs fighting could explain the worst of his wounds when he came to us.

Where did he come from? Why did no one take him in? I can't really know. But even human survival in some corners of this area seems hard-won. Certainly there would have been a point where the saving of him would look in every way expensive, even dangerous. I remember the words of the young woman from yesterday, describing a sweet, deteriorating dog they had known. At first they had shared the baby's cookies with it, and then it had looked bad and they had to keep very much away in case it had a sickness they could get. Their caution is understandable. It strikes me that for dogs like Ace, it's a short journey from lost pet to pariah. The burden of survival is very much their own.

The Boy Scout dog care merit badge.

11

AGAINST THE WALL

W HAT A DIFFERENCE a month makes," my mother says. "Ace looks so relieved to be found." Mom and I are talking on the phone. It's a rare conversation, and something in a photograph of Ace has prompted it. My solitary, fiercely independent mother has compromised lungs, and she's been housebound for a while now, her speech affected by her struggle to take in air. She refuses visits. She rarely answers the phone. When she does make a call, she jumps straight in without preamble, getting right to the point. Even then, sometimes there are long pauses while she gropes for speech. My mother prefers email and social media for this reason. And she thrives online, where, in the gray space of failing memory, she can retrace what she's said and what people have said to her. Mom is rich with banter and friends. *Still kicking!* she messages me most mornings, the proof-of-life agreement we made when she refused to move into the house I bought for her.

Mom's been following Ace's story on Facebook. Every day she looks at photos I've posted online. My mother has brought in enough strays to know how to read them, and she's right about the change in Ace's demeanor—in a series of photos across the first weeks we've had him, his fearful eyes and hunched posture have been replaced by something brighter and more confident. The damaged dog he had become is giving way to the dog he truly is. She is proud of his pluck and his stamina. She's proud that I'm healing him while honoring the love he knew before. She worried about me foot searching in Conroe for that maybe owner in a maybe place, but she gets it.

Mom's a little fretful as we talk. Sometimes she can't remember things, but she can sense the outline of them. Today she's called because those photos of Ace reminded her of a dog we once found at a gas station, but that's all she can bring up. Do I remember him, the gas-station dog? He was white, too, wasn't he? And small. Mom knows we didn't keep him. She thinks the story ended happily nonetheless. That memory has kept her up all night, this lost dog from fifty years ago, just out of reach.

I do remember that dog, a frizzy white terrier-something with blackish spots that we found soaked in a rainstorm, crouched against the wall of a gas station. I was six or seven years old. We were in the car with my grandmother, my father's mother, on our way to a café for breakfast. That was a thing we did on Saturdays when my grandmother visited. The café served free baskets of banana bread striped with royal icing, no matter what you ordered for breakfast. But that only lasted until 10:30, and if you missed it, then you had to wait a week for banana bread. We were running late on that Saturday, and I remember my dad driving with some urgency, making what he said were *California rolling stops* at stop signs, not wanting to disappoint us all.

Then my mother saw the dog and cried *Stop!*, and my father did so, full stop, without knowing why. He hit the brakes so quickly that we all lurched forward and back, hard, my grandmother's rain hat slipping askew. I remember Mom gesturing, frantic and wordless. She point-point-pointed to the left, stabbing the air, and Dad turned to squint at the gas station. Then he, too, saw the little dog, its head bowed against the rain.

Dad pulled into the gas station parking lot without a should-we?-yes-we-should word between them, and I remember him going for his door handle just a second behind my mother, who was already out of the car and splashing through puddles in her slim belted dress and high heels. She had left her coat on the seat.

"You're not *serious*," my grandmother said to the back of my father's head, and I can still hear her saying it while Dad, caught between wife and mother, looked staunchly ahead. My grandmother was a wonderful, generous woman in many ways, but she had concrete ideas, and once she had it in mind to do something—like this day's hats and high heels and breakfast with warm banana bread that stopped at 10:30—she didn't like a change of plans. And she was no fan of dogs. She'd never had one, did not ever want one, and tolerated those of family and friends by paying no attention to them at all.

And now here was my mother, back in the car in a dog-wet wool dress that would need expensive dry cleaning, carrying a quivering, muddy animal that gathered himself up on the tuck-n-roll upholstery, then leaped over the front seat of the car into my lap, where he shook as I tried to contain him. He shook-shook-shook dirty water all over my grandmother and me. I laughed, my parents shot each other wild glances, and my grandmother, muddy all over, briefly turned to stone.

"You can just get me some banana bread to go," she said very carefully, without looking at any of us, spotted gloves righting her matching spotted hat.

I called him Wiggles. But a name didn't mean I could keep him. My parents were firm on that point. They spent the day debating him. He was somebody's dog, my parents agreed. He was way too fat and too friendly to be homeless. He was somebody's dog that got lost and ended up at a gas station six blocks from our house. He had a collar on but no tag. What was the point of a collar with no tag? Maybe he'd lost it. Mom was making notes.

Did this dog live close to the gas station? Did he live close to us? Could he have slipped from someone's car when they stopped for gas?

That "What now?" that hangs over every found-pet situation, sometimes forcing finders to make quick choices, hung over us like a thundercloud. We were living in a rented house right next to the landlord, and the landlord had already stretched the point to allow Rosie the cat. He was in no way going to stretch further, even long enough for my folks to find the owner of this dog. And it was not like we could exactly hide Wiggles. He had a whole lot of energy and a whole lot of bark, and we'd already found furious Rosie on top of the medicine cabinet. The minute, *the minute* that dog had to go out to pee, we might as well send up golden fireworks, my mother said, and there goes the security deposit.

My dad hoped the rain would give us at least a little cover. I remember Mom peeking out the dining room window into the backyard, next to the landlord's driveway, so my father could take the dog out back to pee, which he did, ducking behind the nandina bushes that divided our properties, urging the dog to hurry.

"Housebroken!" he said when he came in, and Mom added it to her notes. They were already figuring out whether they had money for a classified ad in the paper, but it would be Monday before they could put one in and pay for it and Tuesday before the ad would show up. Three and a half days was a long time to hide this dog from a landlord.

Dad made grilled cheese sandwiches while my mother thought hard. I remember Dad leaning against the kitchen counter to eat his sandwich while I dismembered mine in long gooey strings at the table, Mom's untouched grilled cheese on the plate. Wiggles cruised the kitchen, nose up and chuffing, fascinated by the scent. We all felt the weight of *What now?*

"We can't just let him loose," Dad said out of nowhere.

I echoed, "We can't just let him loose."

Then Mom turned from the dining room window, away from the landlord's driveway and the nandinas and the fifteen-foot teepee that Cub Scouts had built in our backyard, and said to my father, *Merit badge.*

For part of my childhood my mother worked as a secretary for the Boy Scouts of America. I remember her in bigger offices and smaller ones as we moved from town to town. Sonless but always wanting a son to follow her daughter, she'd become a Cub Scout den mother somewhere along the way. I remember her first clutch of Cub Scouts when I was a kindergartner — they seemed like very big boys as they bent over a vacated wasps' nest — and another group when I was in first grade, who didn't seem to mind my perpetual shadow and my desire to help them build a teepee in our backyard out of bamboo and old sheets when they studied Indian lore.

Those boys came to the house a few times a month. I got to do a very few things beside them and didn't get to do a whole lot more. I remember mouthing the Cub Scout promise behind the door that separated me from their meetings. What I can't remember now is if they were due for a meeting anywhere near the time we found Wiggles. Even if it wasn't scheduled, somehow my mother organized a meeting, and quickly. Not just her Cub Scouts. There were older boys, too. They must have come in that Saturday or Sunday — I remember them dripping from the heavy rain — and they sat on the floor in half-circles in the living room, various parents behind them, while I sat on the stairs, chin on the heels of my hands, and watched.

Mom told the boys she had exciting news, a very special opportunity, and then Dad introduced Wiggles, and Mom told everyone about the dog care merit badge and how Wiggles could help them all earn it. And the Cub Scouts could help them. Some of the things they would do together, like right now, learning the parts of a dog, and then some they would do individually. Wiggles was available to any of the Scouts whose parents would allow it, in rotation, giving each boy a chance to train and care for him, logging the experience needed to earn the badge. It was a cool badge, she said, and she showed them.

An embroidered little dog snuggled up to a bigger one — it *was* a cool badge.

Resourceful she was, and, I must give my mother credit, reasonably honest, too. Though I don't think she went into our whole landlord situation with kids and parents, she did explain that Wiggles had wandered from home and that he was still lost, and that this was also a way the boys could serve the community. *Let's take care of Wiggles, but let's find out where he lives.*

My mother's desperation inspired great strategy. Though she was probably pushing the tolerance of the merit-badge process every which way, even the experienced Scout parents bought in. Who would take Wiggles first? I remember hands shooting up and parents laughing and looking uncomfortable and no one wanting to be that parent who said no to his son and the now-bathed, avowed house-broken, winsome dog. So Wiggles was out of the house before our landlord ever saw him. He left our house and never came back to it. My parents ran a classified ad for two weeks and pinned a notice at the gas station where we found him. Those Scouts, in the meantime, were logging care skills beside Wiggles even as they did what my mother told them to: they asked their neighbors to the left, to the right, two houses across the street, and two behind if anyone knew the owner of this dog.

We all wanted a happy ending, but I remember when Wiggles left my arms for the first Boy Scout who took him. Wiggles cried and licked my face in the going. It was the first time as a rescuer that I felt that taffy pull of my heart. It was the right thing to do, but it hurt.

Now, after telling my mom the story on the phone, I ask her if she remembers how many Scouts got to care for Wiggles. She does not. I have a vague sense it was a month or more and that not every boy who wanted to keep the dog got a chance to. But they all helped in some way, feeding, walking, and training him, asking neighbors and friends at school if they knew the owner of this dog.

What I do remember is the story of reunion. It was Halloween, and the family who were keeping Wiggles had kids coming in and kids going out, and the dog was barking nonstop. At some point the Scout in charge of Wiggles opened the door on a little black witch — a first-grade witch in an apple-green mask. The girl squealed at the sight of the dog, and the Scout dropped a bowl of candy when Wiggles went nuts to get to her, capering in circles, recognizing the child despite her disguise. She tore off that witch face and knelt to him and cried. Everyone cried, the story went: the witch, her father beside her, the Scout and his little brother, and their parents — really confusing a line of ghosts and cowboys on the sidewalk hoping for a Tootsie Roll.

My mother pauses at the end of our story. "Merit badge," she says, and laughs. She can no longer imagine thinking so nimbly. We reminisce a little more about those days in that house and about Wiggles, who landed with us at probably the worst time in our family history, just months before we parted for the first time. But that dog patched us together for a little while. His need made us braver. I remember my quiet, resolute father and my resourceful mother, crackling to save him. My mother says it's amazing what you will do for something helpless. It's amazing what you figure out when your back's against the wall.

*The house matriarch, Puzzle, nurtures
every animal that comes in.*

12

SAFE HARBOR

ANIMAL BEHAVIOR, terrain features and navigation, scent theory, decomposition, canine versus human perception, ethical concerns and legal issues, the psychology of loss: my education in missing-animal response seems limitless, and these are among the subject areas in play. It is rich, varied, grounded study. Many of these disciplines are familiar to me from SAR, their concepts adapted to a different kind of wanderer. Now, for the first time, I consider the options on a wilderness search for a lost soul who can smell me—and flee—when I am upwind. I rub my forehead over state laws and local ordinances governing animal ownership and care. I learn which medications can befuddle a lost dog's choices and what behaviors signal that a searching owner is near to giving up. And at almost every turn, from every source, I study canine communication—dog-dog and dog-human. No matter where the lost dogs go, if they are to come home, interaction with humans often makes the difference.

Kat Albrecht offers a MAR course for volunteer and paid pet searchers, and I take it, along the way reading everything I can from psychologist Stanley Coren, animal behaviorist Patricia McConnell, canine cognitive scientist Alexandra Horowitz, and veterinarian Sophia Yin, among others. I watch body-language videos and documentaries on the canine mind. I am hungry to learn not only how to search for lost pets but also the science driving that strategy. Like search and rescue for lost persons, missing-animal response is fascinating to study, and it shapes my dreams, with plot points that turn on scent curled in corners or a four-pawed night figure at the edge of dark woods.

What exactly do frightened dogs read in my golden retriever? Is it something vaguely maternal, some sense of protection or calm?

That mysterious quality first showed up in the search field when Puzzle was about two. We had just finished a woodland training search when a young border collie burst out of the brush, his head low and backside wiggling, dragging a dirty slip lead. Not much more than a pup, he was gaunt and ragged and peppered with burrs. A skittish creature, too—the dog would not approach me, but he was all over Puzzle, whimpering and circling. She was a good distraction. He hardly noticed when I picked up the grubby lead behind him. He was lucky it hadn't caught on something, pinning him to a place where he might have starved to death. As it was, the pup was hungry and dehydrated, but still far too nervous to take anything from me until Puzzle took what was offered first. His slender muzzle beside her soft nose, they jointly lapped water from her search cup. The little border collie couldn't keep his eyes off my golden retriever, nuzzling her until she gave a single lick to one of his ears, then set the pace for him to follow.

Locals knew the young dog's story. Recently taken into foster care and just thirty seconds through his new front door, he had bolted out of it again and run almost two miles into wilderness, where he had been lost for a little over a week. He was a scared, elusive, black-and-white blur that fled local hikers, who had repeatedly reached out to him. When he found Puzzle in the brush, whatever fright had made him run and keep running evaporated. Her canine assurance was enough to get him back to human care.

Since that time Puz has drawn other lost pets in from their wandering. *Girl's got a side hustle,* says a laughing friend about my search/ magnet dog. Puzzle has stopped dogs that were galloping loose across neighborhoods and puppies that have bolted from cars in parking lots. I will always remember two tiny black Chihuahuas, moving so fast their owners could keep up with them only in a car, who found her at the edge of a Dallas playground. It was the owners' misguided horn honking I heard before I even saw the little dogs streaking down the sidewalk. Gobbling freedom, they were all speed and joy and no street smarts at all. Down the sidewalk, across a street, through a maze of swings and slides, around a clubhouse, perilously close to a busy avenue they ran, almost into that terrible traffic, while their owners honked and a chorus of bystanders shouted "No!"—which seemed to make them run faster.

Then the two Chihuahuas saw Puzzle. They stopped short, and, after a split-second stare so keen it was like those cartoon dogs whose eyes bug out with hearts, they raced across the park, tumbling over each other to get to her. They were the smallest dogs I had ever seen— twin black asterisks with fawn eyebrows and red-tipped nails buzzing around my ankles—and they loved Puzzle, whip-wagging their tails and stretching up to paw at her face when she leaned down to them in gentle question. The distraction of her gave the owners time enough to catch up to their dogs. The little Chihuahuas were still leaning to- ward Puzzle as they were lifted up into arms to go home.

The golden reacts to these events with a whimsical expression, as if she's not sure what all the fuss is about. Stray dogs dashing up with breathless affection is an unexpected thing we have come to ex- pect. So now I carry treats and a slip lead with us on walks and keep another set in my car. While Puzzle gives the strays a sniff-over and a face wash, I can get a lead on even the wiggly ones.

Puz was not always so gracious. As a sunny, high-drive puppy can- didate for search and rescue, she came into my household ready to take charge of it, or try to, upsetting all the established manners of the animal family, which included small dogs and large ones, some of them very senior, and cats. I had been rescuing animals for a long time and was used to introducing new dogs to old ones. But when Puzzle came home in 2004, it had been a while since I'd had a large-breed puppy. And I'd never had one bred from a working line, as she was.

She was an instruction, that puppy. Puzzle was strong. She was fast. She was fearless and resourceful at ten weeks old. Anything was sport. Everything was opportunity for a game. Within a week of her arrival, she somehow jumped from point to point across furniture to the top of an armoire, defeathered a comforter, and nabbed a hunk of cheese off a kitchen counter three times her height. She dragged a potted ficus from one end of the house to the other, where I found the sad tree upright but stripped of its leaves, a skeleton. Puzzle in those early days entered the room like the bad guys in old westerns. Her little blond form would show up in the doorway, and dogs and cats alike would duck the coming damage. When redirected from something that she wanted but shouldn't have, Puzzle had a lot to say about the correction — long strings of puppy syllables as she looked me square in the eye. All that drive and energy would be good in the search field, I incanted, like a prayer, vacuuming feathers and sweeping up dirt. As hard as I tried to stay a step ahead of her, in those days I always felt two steps behind.

It was a good thing that Puzzle loved to search. As soon as the last of her puppy shots cleared her to put her paws on new ground, she started training to find missing persons. She took to the challenge right away, and our work together forged a powerful connection we would share for the rest of our lives. Puzzle was an easier dog in the field. What she wanted most was what I wanted, too. She worked hard and came home to sleep even harder, stretched across the floor on her back with her fat puppy belly exposed, legs akimbo. Sometimes the other dogs sniffed over her inert form, their ears swung back and expressions quizzical. I once found one of the cats standing over Puzzle's sleeping head, hard-eyed and paw poised, like *I could give you such a slap.* A second later that slap connected, and the cat vanished like a ghost while the stunned puppy spun awake.

But there were darker moments, too. Though golden retriever Puzzle was universally friendly to people, dogs, and cats of every stripe most of the time, she developed an early antipathy to one of my Pomeranians, Fo'c'sle Jack. I didn't understand it then and am not sure I do even now.

Jack was very dear to me. He was a fuzzy, merry little guy at four and a half years old—a therapy dog that visited sick children in hospitals, on the quiet and mellow end of the Pomeranian scale. With a full brown, black, and orange coat and large button eyes, Jack was the size of a toy and looked like one. He had never known trouble until he'd been attacked as a youngster by two border collies running off-lead, an attack that nearly killed him before I could wrestle them off. Ever after he'd been cautious around bigger dogs he didn't know well.

Young Puzzle came in at his weight but quickly outsized him. She was the bigger dog within a month. And she was all pounce and play. Though he seemed calm enough around her most of the time, I wonder now how many cues between them I missed. Did Puzzle sense Jack's wariness? Was there something about his always spiky, upstanding fur and his slightly protruding eyes, edged in white, that she misread as a raised-hackle, whale-eyed challenge? Perhaps she had an urge to resource guard food, toys—or me. All the dogs ate in the kitchen, their bowls widely separated, but sometimes Puzzle would take a sudden, side-eyed dislike to Fo'c'sle Jack five feet away and, with no more warning than a moment's side-eye and stiff stillness, would jump the little dog, whose terrified screams seemed to escalate her attack.

Though it happened only a couple of times, the situation was frightening, bewildering. We had other Pomeranians — why was Puzzle so focused on Jack? I scrambled to reconfigure meal routines and to avoid repeat events. I never wanted to see that side of her, never wanted to hear Jack scream again.

I wish I could say her excellent training at my side fixed the problem, but I can't claim credit for the change. I trained with her, certainly, in the search field and out of it, but the shift in Puzzle seemed more native to the evolving dog. As Puzzle matured, the pushiness gentled. She figured out her place in the pack of other animals, and her obedience skills took shape beside those of the older dogs. It was a peaceable kingdom most of the time. All the dogs stretched out across the floor, butt to butt or paw to paw. All the dogs gathered in the kitchen to sit politely for treats, no dog infringing on another. But every now and then there would be this electric glance between Puzzle and Jack that I came to recognize. Redirect, redirect, redirect — I learned to step in quickly and avert another terrible exchange.

Puzzle grew wiser. Fo'c'sle Jack relaxed. Though they never became good dog friends, the conflicts between them vanished. By the time Puzzle was a mission-ready search dog in the field, she was also the dog who'd found a job at home. She began to nurture the shattered senior rescues coming into the house. Chihuahua-Pomeranian mix Sophie, with congestive heart failure, had been taped in a box and thrown in a Florida dumpster before she was saved. Toothless Tupper had been smacked with a broom and spent days wandering hungry in heavy snow. Smokey and Misty had left their sheltered life beside a dying owner and were thrust into a what-comes-next they could barely understand. Blind and deaf Scuppy, twenty-one, had been found in the street after the children of his elderly owner dumped him.

Those dogs came to our house across years. In the quiet manner with which Puzzle attracted and calmed lost dogs, she formed different relationships with all the rescues we brought in. She lay beside creaky, arthritic Sophie, the Florida dog who could never quite get warm enough. She stretched out next to the bed Smokey hid under, engaging with the shy dog on his terms until Smokey's native playfulness returned. Very senior Scuppy fascinated her, and she became his second shadow, negotiating the house and yard the way he did, by scent. Tiny Pomeranian Tupper adored her on sight, and they snuggled extravagantly, Puzzle commandeering the length of the sofa and Tup tucked into the warmth of her belly or throat. In 2007, Puzzle was enchanted by a homeless kitten, a fuzzy, hungry calico glory that still had blue eyes, and Puz yearned so for the little creature that the kitten came home with us straightaway. Thistle was Puzzle's cat from that first moment—a love affair that just increased as they aged.

Puzzle never attacked Fo'c'sle Jack again.

I was grateful for the change in my golden partner. Puzzle evolved into the matriarch of the house, without any kind of insistence on her part. By the time she was four years old, she'd been searching for lost persons and nurturing animal rescues at home for half her life. By the time she was eleven years old, dozens of rescued animals had come under her care, some for just a few days on their way to new homes, others for the remainder of their lives.

That tradition continues. Sickly puppies, wobbly seniors, handicapped special-needs dogs: in her calm, casual way, Puzzle sees to them all. I do everything I can to meet those rescues where they are and to offer them a good life here, but Puzzle's gift is something beyond my human care. Having come from a terrible past life or a life that was good until they lost it, they all come in fragile. They find comfort in the golden retriever, and strength, and it seems to me some kind of understanding that they could trust only from another dog. *The nightmare is over*, her presence seems to suggest. *You're safe.*

The south wind is so strong it makes me tilt a little on this blustery day in November as Puzzle and I head out for a neighborhood walk. Must be twenty knots or better, I think. My eyes blink against it and my open jacket inflates. We usually have an audience when we leave, and this time it's Ace that watches us through a window. Though he does take walks with us, not this time. Devoted to Puzzle, he will stay at that window until we return.

Puzzle is delighted to be out on her own with me. A let-dog-be-dog walk, I call these meanderings where she walks at will on the end of her long lead, stopping when she wants to stop, sniffing what she wants to sniff. I follow behind and watch her ears blow north, the windswept sway of her plume tail, paying attention to what she pauses over and what she cheerfully ignores. Base of the phone pole: fascinating. Soggy newspaper: not interesting at all. She's really curious about a plastic green turtle toy at the edge of a sidewalk. It's got sticky pink goo all over its turtle head and turtle back, as if a toddler played with it after squishing fistfuls of cherry Jell-O. Food and human, the toy must be rich with scent. Puzzle sniffs it over and then leaves it. She turns back to look at me, her mouth open in a casual pant that looks so much like she's smiling that I can't help but smile back.

On these walks I give Puzzle the *wander* cue and let her choose the direction. We head first to a neighbor's yard covered in Asian jasmine, where Puzzle likes to roll. Then, after she's covered herself in leaf fall and prickly bits, she shakes herself happily, ready to be off again. We turn at a corner and walk face-first into the wind. Puzzle's pretty face streamlines and my long hair flies. We have plunged forward about a block when we hear the terrified shriek of a small dog coming from a direction I can't place.

By scent, sound, or sight, I don't know, but Puzzle has him before I do, a small white dog running toward us, so much like Ace that at first I'm confused. How did Ace get out the door? But as he gets closer, I can see that this is a different dog. Smaller. Less stocky. He wails as he runs like a dog that's been beaten or is terribly afraid. We have stopped where we stand, wild in the wind, and the poodle mix runs straight for Puzzle as though she's safe harbor.

He's maybe twenty yards away when we see what he's running from: a pair of loose larger dogs, muscular mixes that briefly pause at the corner, as though they aren't sure which way the little dog went. They catch sight of him, and they are off in perfect tandem, bounding down the sidewalk, each stride eating the distance between them. But their pause has given the shaggy creature time enough to reach us. He runs to Puzzle and is oblivious to me. What sense does she make of this moment, with a small dog at her chest and two large ones running toward us at top speed? I can't know. But none of this looks good, and I pick up the poodle reflexively, swinging him up so quickly into arms that he gives a startled yelp, and I drop him over the low fence that bounds the front yard where we stand. I hear the soft thud of him, briefly see him scrabble in the grass.

"Run!" I shout to the dog pointlessly, and hope he does, but now the big dogs are upon us. A shepherd of some kind. A Lab mix. They are barking and growling, animated, jumping against us, hackles stiff and tails raised. I push Puzzle toward the fence and block them from her there, turning my back to the dogs and ducking my head and holding very still, looking down at my own dog. Male dogs won't attack females is the truism you hear, but I have taken a bad bite for Puzzle that disproves that. All I can think of now is her sweet, exposed throat. Below me, my golden knows the dog-dog nonverbal cues better than I do. Even she is very still, her posture soft as both dogs nose what they can of her. She wants no conflict. She has ducked her face to the fence, looking staunchly away. The two big dogs have lost all interest in the small dog they were chasing. Puzzle is more intriguing. How long do we stand there, curiosities for these dogs in the way that turtle was for Puzzle? It feels like a robbery with the threat of violence. I feel them huff at my shoes, knees, and elbows, reading across me every dog I have in the house. The growling shepherd noses my pocket. I have dog treats there. The nuzzle doesn't feel friendly. The dog's gaze is hard.

Take the treats, I think. I am not ready to expose my hands.

As the one dog works at my pocket, I feel both dogs deescalate. Their breathing slows and their tails lower. Their stiff hackles smooth. It's then that I catch sight of the white dog I dropped over the fence. He is back now, right here with us, nose to nose with the Lab and straining through the fence toward this notion of treats, his curly butt wiggling. What the hell? A moment later the poodle mix is running the fence line, from the Lab to the corner, where a man in jogging clothes has rounded toward us.

The man laughs as he sees me standing motionless in place, calling that it's okay, it's okay, they're really friendly. And they are now —or at least they're distracted. Torn between the treats in my pocket and the approach of their owner, the two take a moment before cantering to the man. Beside him, behind the fence, the poodle capers in tandem with his step.

Thank you, says the man, as though I've done something heroic, standing woodenly there on the sidewalk, blocking my petite golden against his eighty-pound bounders. He hooks his fingers beneath the collars of both dogs. *Thank you so much.* He had no idea they went out the gate behind him. He had no clue which way they went. Behind him, the little poodle squeaks for equal attention.

My throat and mouth are dry. I croak something tangled about the chase and the hard run and the hackles, about the little white dog ducking under Puzzle and his frightened cries.

The man shakes his head ruefully. *Oh. Yeah. All for show.* The dogs are all his, and it's a chase game they have in the backyard, too, the little dog egging the big ones on. He and his wife have been trying to work on it, because sometimes the neighbors call. The squeals sound that bad.

Well, it felt very dangerous, I tell him.

It looks real, doesn't it? But you were never in danger at any time, he says. He whistles to the poodle, who follows him along the fence. Turns out the yard I tossed the little dog into is his own.

A thank-you note from a neighbor.

13

THY NEIGHBOR'S DOG

A CE IS A NIGHT CREATURE. In the dark of a new season, he chooses to sit outside alone, head up, ears drawn forward. I watch him through the back door. The porch light is off. His pale figure sits poised like a sheepdog or a gate guardian on the deck, from which he can see the entire backyard and a long stretch of neighborhood beyond. Sweet-natured, playful, obedient — Ace is one of the family now, yet somehow remains in a world of his own, especially at night. His head turns, and his puffs of breath cloud the chill.

Winter is coming, and we're all glad. This was a summer that never seemed to end. The dogs have spent months stretching as flat as they can across the hardwood floors, melting into it. But today they raced around the backyard when the cold front passed. They turned their noses to the north, sensing the wind shift and smelling the new scents in it, electric when the temperature dropped. They ran and they wrestled. The big dogs made their own agility course back and forth over the garden fence, Ace hassling at their heels. The Pomeranians chased each other in tight circles, buzzing across the grass like bees. Even the hospice dogs managed a stiff-legged frisk on the back deck. Crisp air and sunshine: it was a glorious day. But now, as the sun sets and the temperature drops, one by one all the other dogs have come inside. A night creature herself, even Puzzle, whose right shoulder gets stiff, has withdrawn for the pleasure of a blanket in front of the electric fire.

I tap on the back door in question. It's the family code: *Want to come in?* Ace glances at me and turns away. He wants to stay outside. He cuts a poignant figure out there. If I weren't convinced that dogs recognize their shadows but never dwell on them, I might project all kinds of human poetry on Ace's thoughts in the half-light. But watching him, I'm pretty sure he is all dog out there in the dark. Eyes large and black beneath curly eyebrows, Ace prickles with awareness. His nose bobs and his ears weave forward and back. Every so often he cocks his head sideways toward the crawlspace beneath the house. When a dog barks from a few backyards down, Ace rises, rasping back in his peculiar way—no anger or fear in the sound, an easy, doggish response to something another dog has voiced. Their fellowship lasts a minute or two, and the other dog goes on barking, but Ace settles, no longer interested in the exchange. He stretches out on the deck with his head between his paws, ready to doze.

And then he is up, fiercely up and off the deck, a levitation so quick I can't follow it. Ace springs down the steps and across the slate and along the fence and back toward the house in a furious, nose-low gallop that ends in a slam against the lattice that I can't see from where I stand. By the time I'm out the door and across the deck, Ace comes up with a mouthful of rat he has flushed from beneath the bird feeder. It's an ambitious catch, a large Norwegian roof rat, still struggling, and Ace must hold his head so far back to carry it that he missteps right into me, dropping the dark creature, which springs away with a squeak.

Ace leaps and I yelp "Sit!" simultaneously. After a skittering moment, Ace freezes, looks up at me for a dubious half-beat, and sits. The rat escapes. Good dog with that sit, and a grudgeless dog, too, because even having given up his rat, Ace beams up at me in the moonlight, tongue out sideways, trembling with excitement. It was a good play day for a family pet, but this—now *this* is what a little dog can do.

If what we knew about the Maltese came from old portraits, we might think these dogs had no strength to stand at all. Maltese pups famously sit with figures of antiquity in oil paintings, curled on laps, cuddled in arms, occasionally nesting in swaths of satin train from a seated lady's skirts. They are cosseted and portable, wearing ribbons and jeweled collars dripping little bells. That is one history of the Maltese dog, but not the only story.

As with many ancient dog breeds, the origins of the Maltese are controversial. The first known representations of the breed are found on Egyptian artifacts dating from 600 to 300 B.C. Those images suggest that the Maltese was one of the breeds worshipped by the ancient Egyptians. The breed is depicted in Greek art and literature dating from about 500 B.C., including works by Aristotle, Martial, and Pliny the Elder, among others. The Roman emperor Claudius is said to have owned a Maltese. Both the Greeks and the Romans believed the dogs came from the island of Malta, calling the breed the Melitaie dog.

Clever, companionable, resourceful, engaging—the Maltese remained a popular pet companion through the Middle Ages, Renaissance, and later eras. They were valuable dogs, tradeable as commodities, particularly popular with the upper class, statesmen, and royalty. Elizabeth I and Mary Queen of Scots both owned Maltese dogs. Bred for centuries to be genteel companions, they were particularly happy lap-sitters and bedfellows, and some believed the dogs also had healing properties. Maltese dogs were placed on pillows beside the heads of the ill and the sorrowful, or across their stomachs or chests. The dogs' warm willingness to stay beside the infirm earned the breed the nickname "the Comforter." It is said that Mary Queen of Scots was allowed to have her dogs in the days of her final imprisonment and that she was so desperately afraid on the day of her execution that she hid one of them—a Maltese—beneath her skirts on her way to the scaffold, where he was found and rescued after her death.

Great debate surrounded the breed in the late nineteenth and early twentieth centuries as dog shows came into vogue. Was the Maltese a spaniel or a terrier? Body shape and coat type suggested spaniel to many, but the English, particularly, were adamant that the Maltese was a terrier, a ground-scenting hunter. The dogs were known to be excellent ratters, with some citing historical evidence that Maltese dogs had worked ships in earlier eras. The debate was resolved only by the declaration in the early 1900s that the dog was neither spaniel nor terrier, rather a breed that should be classified as a type of its own —the Maltese dog.

I've had a part in the rescue of more than one Maltese or Maltese mix, but I've never had one in the family. Now I see the divide in the dog on my back deck and understand better why Ace and I have so far failed to connect. I give him abundant attention and affection, and he responds to it gently, but for months I've felt like we had little in common. Perhaps we just aren't a good temperamental fit. Before doing deeper breed research, I had assumed that Ace was a particularly clever example of an ornamental dog long bred to sit in the lap of its owner—a perfect dog for an elderly person or a more sedentary one. As much as I love him, I'm not much of a sitter, and there have been times I wondered if he might be happier in a more sedate home. It takes a midnight scramble and a roof rat to reveal that there is more to this dog than I know. Ace hasn't settled here because he has been adrift; neither lapdog for a quiet companion nor resourceful survivor on his own, he needs something else in this life beside me.

Does he want a job? I put my hands on my hips and ask him aloud there on the back deck. He doesn't understand, of course, but he tilts his head at the sound of my question. He is so ready for *something* that he throws sparks.

Clearly Ace could be a first-class ratter of rodents running along my fence line. But I have something else in mind.

We start with fur. I'm going to try training Ace to search for lost pets, and I need fur samples from animals outside our family to test his interest. Fascinated neighbors offer bags and bags of carefully labeled cat and dog fur. I ask for only small samples in zip-sealed baggies, but some donors give me extra-large bags crammed tight with enough fur to knit another dog. I request that each bag be labeled with the name of the dog, the age, the breed, and the date collected, so that I can record Ace's searches precisely in his training log. Some add to that description with little doodles or stories. There's a tenderness there; those labels express the love, pride, and worry these owners feel for their pets. PROUD MUTT GOOBER says one label, the name bordered with hearts and stars, or WEE'UN, YORKIE, 16, TINY OLD DIABETIC!! A child has put a note with the fur sample from her black-and-white spaniel mix, a puppy I returned home once. *Thank you for finding Pepper,* she has written. Another bag tells a story: *Found cat named Picnic because he walked up and asked for our fried chicken.* One owner has surely given his border collie a Marine cut. Though I asked for only a clipping, the young man provides two large bags of fur and a note: *Accidents happen & Dutch is fast. Plz keep some for his smell if he gets lost.*

These days Ace is so eager to work that he hovers at the edge of rooms, waiting for a sign. This is a glorious game to him, as it is to the SAR dogs. He's learned the rustle of gear and samples that preface Puzzle's training searches, and when he can, he watches her through low windows while she works. I can't know what he makes of her mad spring away from me and the dedicated sweeps across the search areas he can see from where he stands on his back feet, but he has heard the rev-up language and the *find* cues often enough that he has absorbed some of the excitement, yearning alongside Gambit, the other SAR dog in training, whose turn is always next.

Ace's awareness and his focus do him credit. While the other little dogs peer over windowsills only when the reward treats come out (and they yap bitterly, sensing injustice), Ace leans to the glass. He seems to follow the procedure when Puzzle works, the way the golden herself did as a puppy trainee following the searches of the mission-ready dogs.

The little dog is a quick learner. He has nose and plenty of drive. Ace is curious when his own training begins; he's a little nonplussed when, this time, the big dogs are put in the bedroom and he's the one guided to the mudroom for the *ready, set* language that starts the training process. I've already placed a sample of fur in an open tin on the back deck, just steps away from the door. We begin with the *find* cue, and when his curious nose leads him to the unfamiliar scent in an environment he knows well, I praise and reward him. He seems startled by the familiar words given to others. He's heard those words through walls. Now they're applied to a choice that he's made. For that first fifteen-minute session of four mini-searches, I use the same fur, the same tin, and move it farther away each time. He is quick to associate the *find* cue to the task, finding the fur each time a little more readily, even on the fourth and final search of the session, when the tin is sitting on a chair cushion and he must snag the scent from above his head rather than skimming low across the ground.

Ace's first day of school. Search training starts this simply and this small. Over days and weeks the work will get more complicated. We'll rotate fur samples; we'll raise them high and tuck them low; we'll teach him to find one scent and ignore others in a space. We'll start using "target pets" and trace the paths volunteered dogs and cats have been led across distances. Does Ace work well nose-up, catching scent in the air (called *air scent* or *area search*), or does he more naturally *trail*, nose low/nose high to the scattered scent of an animal's path across the ground? Both disciplines can be useful in the search for lost animals.

Together we'll figure out how Ace works scent and what his aptitude truly is for this challenging job, a job with demands far beyond following scent to its source. Search dogs need stamina. They need stability. They must be committed, resourceful, and confident.

In this nosy little survivor, I see potential. I would like for him to be successful — for us to be successful as a team — but there are many ways to be brilliant at this or to falter. Right now it is enough to see this little dog shake off some of his sadness. He meets every new challenge with ready joy.

Helping my mother study, I was intrigued by what mortal creatures are made of, what supports us and drives our actions.

First fear, then fascination — my mother's nursing school studies taught me something, too.

14

A LITTLE AMBITION

W E WERE RUNNING AGAIN. Though I was still a child, I had long since learned the signs of family flight and its particular chronology: late-night conversations between my parents that escalated to shouts, a few empty boxes and the emergence of many that had never been unpacked at all, hasty goodbyes, a car trip of indeterminate length, and a day-old doughnut in my hand as I stepped for the first time onto the grass or asphalt of a new backyard. This time I'd come home as we were leaving it. I arrived after a long visit with my grandmother, landing a week before expected, in the middle of their—our—hasty move somewhere else. My folks were startled to see me. They were furiously bright. I would later learn that they—we—were fleeing missed back rent and the threat of eviction, but at the time all I knew was that something terrible had happened, that they were full of big words lofted over my head. I heard those words, repeated them, and asked. *Propositioned, coerced*: these were big words for a little girl, my father said. My mother had lost her job because of these mysteries. My father still had his, but we were stretched thin, he said. They both had also gone back to school, which was a thing I didn't know parents could do. Dad was going to learn how to run computers. My mother had decided to become a nurse.

"This is it!" cried my dad as we pulled up to the curb of a house he'd rented while Mom was in class, our fifth house in three years. He didn't say it with the emphasis of finality, as in "This . . . is it!"—the last house we'd move to, ever—but rather "*This* is it," the prize in the box of Cracker Jacks, as though of all the houses we could have picked, this was the one we had chosen. For the moment. In those days my parents read Ram Dass. Their favorite book was *Be Here Now*, so all their "this is its" were understood to be temporary.

Dad was no actor, but his desperate cheerfulness always got an effort grade in my book. When he smiled, the early lines on his face crinkled all the way up to his eyes, as though he were genuinely happy, but I saw how he looked at my mother there in the car. It was an anxious look, the way a frightened passenger stares out the window of a 757 and hopes the wing stays on. Glory or disaster—which one? He looked at her, looked at the new house, looked at her.

The new house was long and narrow, extending lengthwise from the street like a box of matches, painted peach and swimming-pool aqua. I liked it. But Mom stared out the window, lost in her own thoughts. For a moment all I could hear was the *tonk-tonk-tonk* of the car's turn signal, still going from when Dad had pulled over. Then my mother roused and tapped the passenger glass, pointing at a fat white cat in the window of one neighbor and a pair of perk-eared mutts wagging behind chain link on the other side. So small a thing could shift my mother's mood, and the animals made this strange place seem less hostile, must have made her feel at home. Her irritation at my father's anxiety faded, and she smiled, clutching her *Anatomy and Physiology* textbook and her *Merck Manual* as she got out of the car. *Don't lose the cats,* she said to me. She was still smiling as I brought in shelter kittens Archy and Mehitabel slung over each shoulder. They gripped my bare skin, wild-eyed and purring. They leaped from me with double *plunks* onto the buckling parquet floor. No matter that our new home had a dead bat in the hallway and rusty water coming out of the tap—this was going to be one of the good days.

There were many good days in that crazy little '60s tract house on an old air force base. My parents had shaken off the shadows of their recent disasters, and we seemed more sure-footed as a family. Mom sewed lime-green gingham curtains for me, and for my new bed my father painted a century-old four-poster white. It felt like I was staying and like they didn't already have one foot out the door for somewhere else. Archy and Mehitabel seemed right at home, too. The kittens liked to dash through the long house and then slide into my room at the end of it like they were stealing home plate.

My father told me that Mom had suffered what was called a nervous breakdown. She had briefly lost the ability to read and write. She launched herself into nursing school anyway, picking her way through texts deep into the night until every word got a little clearer. I can still see her beneath the crook-neck pole lamp, haloed in the smoke from her Viceroy, scooting claw-prickly kittens off the pages as she read. Mom made flash cards in a shaky hand that steadily improved. I watched her bite her lip and manage block print on the little lined cards, stiff uprights for the *D*'s and *T*'s and *K*'s and precise curls for the *B*'s and *P*'s, as I had done in first grade.

I sat on the couch cross-legged and pored through her *Anatomy and Physiology* text while she worked. That book fascinated me with its bizarre words and curious descriptions and especially with its illustrations of the human body overlaid with transparent colored plates. I liked the feel of those transparent pages in my fingers, the rich colors in the art of human innards. Each human body started with a paper page and a simple outline. That body would get bones with one transparent plate overlay, and then organs, and ligaments, tendons, muscles, and skin with another and another and another. Mom was quick to fury if I disturbed any of her bookmarks, but I was careful, and I flipped through those *A&P* transparency plates again and again, making men and women whole, riding the thin edge of my private fears, because I had a secret: I was terrified of skeletons.

It was a fear that began when I was a toddler, and I distinctly remember its origins in two old movies that they were already airing on TV when I was very small. One of them was *Teenagers from Outer Space*

(1959), a black-and-white film about an alien teenager who abandons his crew's mission to eradicate life on Earth when he falls for a human girl. Originally titled *The Ray Gun Terror*, that film's alien weapons could vaporize humans down to skeletal remains, and the aliens blasted plenty of people in their quest to clear the planet and breed water-tower-sized lobsters. The plot's inherent goofiness went right over my head when I was three or four, and images from *Teenagers from Outer Space* sent me screaming down the hall—a skeleton in a swimming pool, a skeleton dropping from a gun battle, a skeleton slumped over a desk. (Curiously, nothing else around those ray-gun blasts was ever torched, though I think I remember that the water in the pool boiled a little.) In tears because I was so scared, I inevitably crept back into the living room, where my father, a science fiction fan, was glued to the set. I ducked my face under the couch, wanting to be near him but not wanting to see the bones.

I think the other movie was probably 1954's *The Naked Jungle*, about a column of army ants attacking a cocoa plantation in South America. Charlton Heston and fewer skeletons in that one, but the image of a skeletonized body in a little boat stayed with me, and I somehow believed that the army ants would come up and get me from Panama (where I was born on a military base), like they marched in the movie. I imagined all of us picked clean by ants in our Texas beds—the cats, too—and sometimes at night I cried.

Why these movies didn't leave me scared of ants and lobsters, I have no idea, but the fear of skeletons remained throughout my childhood, that terror lessening to a thrilling kind of scared when I peeked through my fingers and felt my stomach turn, shifting in time to an understanding that would be useful in the search field thirty years ahead. I would sit with my mother for hours as she studied to be a nurse, flipping those *Anatomy and Physiology* transparencies forward and back. Here is a man, entire. Sans skin, here's the man down to his heart and his lungs and his guts. Here: these red lines are arteries and these blue lines are veins, and here is the central nervous system, a spidery yellow scribble across him, all the way to his brain. And here at last is the man down to his bones. He's grinning, as skeletons do, and he has no secrets at all.

Weeks later we were walking the streets, my mother and I, nicknaming the neighborhood pets after body parts. It was another way to push critical terms into her head, and my creative mother had a genius for remembering through association. Mom had her A&P midterm on Monday. She was hobbling a little. Her back had seized up after six weeks spent reading on the couch. She needed to move, she said, she needed to breathe, but she needed to take her studying with her. That meant she needed to take me, too. Thrilled to be included, I held her flash cards in my hand, and sometimes I quizzed her with terms she had to define, or I flipped the cards over and gave the definition that required her to give the term.

I pressed the card to my forehead (glabella) when she was thinking of an answer. *Right*, I would cheer when she gave the correct one, and I waved the card from the tips of my distal phalanxes. It was autumn, and the wind was shifting, uneasy. The dead leaves of pecan trees skittered around us and crunched underfoot. The world seemed nervous, Mom said. She was nervous about everything: nervous about school, nervous about the future, nervous about her hamster-wheel thoughts, nervous that she'd been an honor student in high school and might be a failure this time around. She moved quickly even with her hobble. I trotted to keep up with her, lifted a little on the balls of my feet, smiling as I remembered the names of bones contacting ground through my Keds.

But between flash-card bashes, as we called them, Mom and I greeted the animals that had come to know us, and we laughed over the secret names and accents we'd given them. The big bulldog that snorted was Trapezius. The flashy black poodle with the white chest was Sartorius. Tibia was the long-legged cat that slept half dangling from a windowsill, like a leopard. The two dogs across the street, one big and one smaller, were Vastus Lateralis and Vastus Medialis. Latissimus Dorsi was the shy Chihuahua mix that peeked out at us from under patio bushes. Mom let me nickname her bolder brother, who could climb his chain-link fence and sometimes rushed us, baring his teeth and nipping. Gluteus Maximus, I called him, because he was a dog that would leap to bite your backside. Gluteus Maximus, because also he was kind of a butt. When I was ten, I thought that name was the best joke in the world.

Mom aced that A&P midterm. In that single semester we were closer than perhaps we would ever be again. Her manic-depressive swings had stabilized through medication and, I think, the new confidence going back to school—and being successful there—had given her. The strain on my father's face lifted, which made my own heart light.

I think my mother was surprised by how good she was at this. I wasn't. I was just a kid, but I knew she was smart. And intuitive. And brave. I remembered her calling out the big mean neighbor who had overbred his German shepherd years before. I had seen her step ahead to block me from the rushing Gluteus Maximus (his real name was Buddy). That dog came over the fence once after us, and my mother, instead of running, stepped up and shouted, *"Buddy, go home, goddamnit!,"* and he skidded into a reversal and galloped back the way he had come.

I sensed that my mother was strong in hidden, fearsome ways. Though she never spoke about it, I had heard stories of her nursing her dying father through a swift-moving pancreatic cancer when I was not yet two. At twenty-seven, she had done it all for both of us, the attending and the comforting and the cleaning of pee, vomit, and poop for her father and her baby, while her diminishing father turned his face to the window and wept and her heedless baby threw her bottle at the wall. Mom's mental health had spiraled downward after the loss of her father, her manic-depression in perfect sync with my father's anxiety attacks, and when it was bad in our house, it was very, very bad, and often I had to go away and stay with family, it was so bad — but there was something my mother found again in nursing school. I watched her learn to read and write again. I witnessed her rise. Even as a kid, I saw something mythic in the strength my mother had for others and, paradoxically, rarely for herself.

Of all the pets we named for muscles and bones, of course it was the butt-dog, Gluteus Maximus, that got lost. We had heard his family calling for him, up and down the streets of our small, airstrip-bordered neighborhood, for a couple of days. *Buddy, Buddy, Buddy,* they cried at the north end, their kids echoing *Buddy, Buddy, Buddy* from the south. Sometimes the family walked his timid sister, Betsy, to try to attract him, but Betsy had luxating patellas. Her knees were bad, and Buddy never came out for her at all.

We weren't quick to help. My father had taken a second job to stave off bankruptcy and was gone most nights, and my mother was now in lab classes that left her exhausted and half blind at the end of the day. Dissection after dissection. The work began with animals and would conclude, the next semester, with human cadavers. Slice, pin, identify, examine. Practice opening and closing. Clamp, snip, suture. All those body parts we'd studied in A&P were now made flesh. My mother's eyes reacted to the formaldehyde as she bent over frogs, pigs, and cats on the dissection table, and she came home sad for those little farmed bodies and blurry-eyed from the white goop her eyes had made in defense against the fumes. Buddy was lost? No way did she want me out there by myself on behalf of the missing butt-dog. She didn't trust him not to rush me and bite.

So Buddy was gone for a good few days before we got involved. Neighbors had seen what they thought might have been him in the twilight, slinking through underbrush or rounding corners fast. He left plenty of evidence behind. They weren't happy. Buddy was digging under fences and mounting their own dogs in heat. Their kids had to come in earlier, scared of this tiny monster with sharp teeth and a gift for silence and surprise. The butt-dog just wasn't popular. You never knew where you were with him. He climbed the fence to charge at random; he dug his way to anything he wanted, and he was suspected of savaging a few cats my mother and I had helped other neighbors bury. Loved by his family but completely untrained, even with his people Buddy was a bug-eyed, relentless leg-humper. And he was a swift-moving nuisance to the rest of us, bad news out of no-where that would bite. I heard one woman say sarcastically to another that it would be a darn shame if Buddy ended up on the airstrip. They shot dogs out there. *Bang,* she said, and she mimed a rifle's recoil.

On the weekend after he went missing, my mother and father and I finally joined the search. Mom had seen the sad family kids asking drivers at the intersection leading in and out of the neighbor-hood, and her heart twisted. She had a grim notion that if Buddy wasn't found and contained, some local would kill him. So she and Dad walked the streets on the kids' behalf as much as Buddy's, hand in hand with me alongside, trying for a sighting. With so many unfenced yards and plenty of dog and cat food out on patios, my mother didn't think the dog had gone very far. She also wasn't surprised he hadn't come home. Why would he want to give up this unfettered freedom after years of two hundred square feet of parched grass? My mother said she could kind of feel for Buddy, even though he was a pain in the ass. She imagined the dog carousing around our eight-street neigh-borhood like a sailor on shore leave. I remember her saying that, *a sailor on shore leave,* a reference I did not understand.

Something must have clicked with her when she said that, be-cause the next week my mother and Buddy's owner found the little dog a mile or so from our neighborhood. He'd traveled east toward another town, not west toward the airstrip. He'd shimmied under barbed wire and padded through hayfields to get there. A dark dot moving against the autumn-dead pasture, Buddy was easy to spot, in orbit around the home of a Labrador retriever breeder with several bitches in season. (They were five times the size of him. The mechanics were impossible, Mom said, and this I understood.) Buddy was skinny and thirsty and frustrated and half glad to see his owner come for him and half full of regret that he had to go.

Buddy's owner asked Mom if she'd drive them home. Though it had been awhile since she'd driven with a stick, Mom agreed if he would hold the little dog, still wired and nippy with lust. She somehow managed to get them all home again in the man's old truck, working the stick shift with her right hand and steering with her left. She said our big round neighbor cuddled Buddy with surprising tenderness. *Just a little ambition*, he said, laughing about the dog and his would-be harem. He said he guessed he needed to build a better fence. My mother observed that Buddy might be happier castrated, too. They drove the rest of the way home in silence.

Castration really would be the best thing, she said to me later. *Cremaster muscle, pampiniform plexus,* and *vas deferens*. A simple procedure. No bones involved.

Ace loves the game of it. On an early training search, he proudly woofs beside a tin of dog fur he has found.

15

FINDING HIS VOICE

A N EARLY WINTER AFTERNOON; the air is unseasonably warm. Ace and I have been working the challenge of covered scent, his search samples tucked deep beneath objects or under a trowel full of dirt. It is new and difficult work for the scrappy little white dog, and he has thrown himself into the game. Sometimes successful, sometimes not, he is learning how to indicate where he's found the hottest point of scent and show me his frustration when he cannot get to its source. Ace has not been much of a talker — a few dry rasps and squeaks is all I've heard from him — and I'm trying to nail down the other ways he shows me his first scent interest, stronger indication, and alert. "Every search dog is a new conversation," a SAR trainer told me, and Ace has a body language as frenetic as Morse code.

It's mucky work after this morning's rainstorm. I come in dirty and Ace comes in even filthier, muddied from damp soil and worm castings, every twig and spent leaf clinging to his curly coat. We are sniffed over, somewhat enviously, by the other dogs. It's a toss-up deciding which of us to bathe first. Ace is a proper mud pig. If I take a shower, bathing him is going to get me dirty all over again. If I give him the first bath, the worst I might do is streak him a little.

Acey wins, and he doesn't care. More evidence of his former life, he takes to grooming sessions like a pro, standing still for the bath, the clip, and the comb-out, even tilting back his head and closing his eyes when it's time to rinse the sides of his face. Ace has always seemed to enjoy the warm water, and I still use the shampoo the vet recommended when he first came here, an oatmeal shampoo gentle on irritated skin. In those early days I also tied a cup of dried oatmeal in a bandanna and used it to sponge the rinse water over him. That oatmeal must have felt soothing after walking wounded for so long, most of his skin raw with sores. Those first weeks after pneumonia, Ace would close his eyes as I rinsed him again and again; sometimes he seemed near to falling asleep where he stood.

Today there is nothing sleepy about him, but he watches me prepare his oatmeal shampoo and rinse poultice calmly. Shampoo, oatmeal, clipper, scissors, tweezers, towel. This cleanup is going to take some time. While the dirt will come right off, the twigs and leaf shatter will have to be unwound, combed, or cut free, and Ace has the kind of coat that kinks tighter when it's wet. I spend a long time working on him dry, just getting the vegetation free. (That same early SAR trainer, who ran a splendid collie, said that for every hour you search, expect two of grooming the search detritus off the dog. She was not wrong.) Ace is patient with all of it, turning only once in question when I try to pull free a twig bound too close to his skin.

He quivers with excitement, though, when he hears his bathwater running, and when I lower him into the elbow-deep water, he shudders and groans a little, the way a dog will when you scratch just the right place. His curly coat waves softly in the water, and beneath it I can see the pink and cream of healthy skin. Five months after rescue, Acey's wounds are gone, even the granulating shadows of wounds are gone, and only the dark hash marks of the bite across his hip remain. He wiggles a little with pleasure as I sponge the oatmeal rinse water over him, and it's an uncharacteristic restlessness that escalates when I begin to rub him dry with a towel. Oh, the pleasure of terrycloth! Every nerve seems to come alive then, and when I turn to put the towel aside, Ace suddenly crouches at the edge of the counter and springs for the floor. It's a long way down for a stubby little dog. He makes the jump as I'm turning back to him, and I catch him sideways like a football not meant for me, thrown hard.

"RrrrrrrRRRRRRR!" Ace croons as I lower him to the floor. Every dog's head comes up, and mine does, too. It's a sound Ace has never made here, half howl, half roar. And then the damp dog is off and running hard through the house, harder than I've ever seen him run. *Zoomies,* dog folk call this mad canine dash. Ace has the zoomies now. Down the corridor, around the corner to the living room, he ping-pongs across one couch, then leaps onto another and slides his damp self sideways, nose first, along it, shimmying like a porpoise. "Rrrrrrrooooooooarrrrrrrrrrr," he croons as he makes a second run across the upholstery and again when he nose-scoots his way across the living room rug. Perhaps it's leftover adrenaline from the searching. Perhaps the bath afterward was wonderful, too. Ace at this moment feels good, very good, and he dashes from room to room, on a mission only he knows, cheerfully taking on every dog and cat he passes.

"*Hey!*" he barks at one of the cats, who swings back her ears and narrows her eyes. Ace has found another new sound, a bark we've not heard. "*Hey!*" he barks again, at Gambit. Ace gives the big golden a play bow, and before Gambit can get to his feet to reply, Ace is away again, into another room. "Hey! *Hey!*" he shouts and leaps over Puzzle, who rolls over to paw at the dog no longer there. She stays in that position, upside down, and shoots me a bemused look. But Ace's next bark seems to inspire her, and she scrambles up to gambol out of my bedroom and after Ace like a puppy. The cats leap onto chair arms to swat them on the fly-by. The littlest senior dogs hug the corners, wide-eyed, as Ace provokes everyone to rabble. This is madness and they want no part of it, but they do want to watch.

And so Ace breaks his months of silence. *Uh-oh*, my mother messages me when I tell her Ace found his bark after a bath. *The first olive out of the bottle.* She's heard that Maltese are barky. She's pretty sure that Ace will become a talker now. Maybe more than is comfortable. And he does. The Maltipoo seems thrilled to have found his voice, in all its variations, and he has a wealth of things to say. He squeals at rats, groans over belly rubs, barks roughly at the sound of strangers at the gate, squeaks a staccato *pip-pip* when he's excited, and croons a *rooor-rooor-roooooon* in protest when things don't go his way. Ace has a lot to communicate, all the time. But it's his "Hey!" that has sparked something in Puzzle. He learns that if he yaps it enough into her ear, she'll chase him, then turn to be chased herself. It becomes their cue for scrambling, tumbling play.

I would really like at least one of these sounds to become part of Ace's search habit. Many K9 handlers hope for and train for a bark alert to signal when a search dog makes a find. Puzzle barks an alert for human remains detection, but she vocalizes much more softly on approach to a living subject, along with a puppylike belly-crawl and wagging. Because Puzzle and I have been working with elderly and special-needs missing persons in recent years, we need that gentler alert. An Alzheimer's patient stuck in a ravine could be terrified by a search dog roaring in his face. On a search for missing pets, it would be great if dancing little Ace could give me a vocal alert, but I don't need him barking furiously at the animal he's found. My mother bets me five dollars he'll voice some sound on his searches, as he now seems to do for everything else.

It is a time of exploration and experimentation for all of us. Little Ace has shown that he's motivated, trainable, and eager to play search games even when they get harder. And he's shown that he has a nose for it. But will he have a voice? For weeks it seems unlikely. And then one day, challenged by a pierced tin of fur behind a grating, fur he can smell but cannot get to, Ace paws frantically at the grating and mutters "Roorrr." It's his frustration sound, a good signal of hot scent, and

I praise him as I open the grating to give him access to his find. But when he gets there, Ace puts his nose to the tin, sits, and gusts a snort very like a *hmmph*. It could mean anything, of course, but Ace sounds disappointed and disgusted, like he would rather have made this find all by himself.

*Sometimes your lost dog is
closer than you think.*

16

THE BASTARD SEARCH

BEFORE SHE EVEN says her name, the woman on the phone tells me what she calls her dog. She says she almost didn't reach out to me when Teddy went missing, because she thought maybe she'd found him; she was sure she'd found him; she might have found him, and would I look at what she found, because she needed to know and didn't want to know at the same time. Lora had heard from a friend of a friend that I might help her. She'd been told that I, too, have Pomeranians, and that if anyone would understand how crazy she was about this dog, it might be me. Her Teddy is a four-pound sable Pom, a rescued dog that was debarked—a rather barbaric surgical procedure done to reduce his vocalizing to a raw whisper—before he came to her. He is brown and orange with a little black, like a small teddy bear. I can imagine him quite clearly. I, too, once had a sable Pomeranian I adored. My Fo'c'sle Jack died five years ago. Her Teddy has been missing for four days.

Lora tells me how Teddy went missing—slipped by her while she was talking to the UPS guy at the door, she thinks, because really, there was no other way. She tells me Teddy doesn't have a collar on because she'd been about to give him a bath. That's a common excuse for a collarless dog gone missing, the lost-pet fib equivalent of "the check's in the mail," but maybe this time it's true. She says by the time she realized Teddy was gone, she couldn't open her front door because her hands were already slick with oatmeal dog soap. Teddy is friendly to some but shy with men, and when he first disappeared, she hoped some neighbor would find him fast or that other barking dogs or something would tell her which way to run.

She had run most of that afternoon, seeing nothing like Teddy. Nothing that evening, nothing the next day. She spent almost that whole first night out on the streets, she says, calling him. She talked to neighbors she saw. She posted a few flyers on phone poles and in the community center of an apartment complex and at the information desk of a nearby retirement home. She posted online where she could. She made a Bring Teddy Home page, which had six followers, all family who lived in another state. Mostly, she says, she walked and cried. A little dog like Teddy had no defense against predators, animal or human. He does have a microchip, and its information is current.

He was my best friend, she says. Past tense. She repeats that she might have found him. She describes the spot, and it is not unlikely, in a treeline along a creek at the edge of a park a few streets over, a spot very like the place where Ace wandered. Teddy would not have been the first dog to shelter in a green belt near population. For a spooked, disoriented pet, it's a place to hide, to watch, and to forage when the dog feels safe. In the years I've been working and following case histories of lost dogs, many have been sighted along a greenbelt, where they were making their temporary home. Those skittish greenbelt dogs have been either casually lured out with a magnet dog or recovered with a food lure and a humane trap.

But Teddy's owner found fur in those bordering woods, and blood, and what looked to be part of a tail, and she is pretty sure Teddy met a terrible fate. This was yesterday. The friend of her friend mentioned that I had recovered the body of her own dog. Lora hates to ask, but would I go in there and find him and bring Teddy home?

When I pull up to the place in my car, I marvel at the woman's impeccable directions. She'd worked dispatch for a police department before she retired and moved, and it shows now in her precise sequences of streets and corners and the curve of a parking lot that ends with a trashcan and a light pole and a sign that warns that dogs must be leashed. She told me to park my car there, right under the street-light, and from the trashcan walk about forty feet to the edge of the woods. She said I'd hear the water where the low creek splashes over some rocks. The fur she found is at the base of a cedar tree. I should see a tuft of tail fur waving against the low green.

It's been a day since she walked that greenbelt, and we have plenty of carrion scavengers in the woods. If it was Teddy she found, there might be less of him now. I glove up and walk grimly forward, carrying a plastic bag, a little blanket, and a trowel. Recovering bodies is some of the darkest work in human search and rescue and no less in the search for missing pets. That's life lost right there, and so often someone's heart broken. And in my experience death has never been pretty, never a shaft of god-light falling on a serene, untouched face. I think of my father and his little brown bag when we trudged down the hill to bring home Smokey the cat all those years ago, and I pace forty feet to the band of woods with my jaw set just like his.

The going is tougher at the edge of the greenbelt, because this is typical Texas scrub in the early spring. The place has a rough beauty on this Monday morning. I stand still and listen for the sound of water. I hear it, the faintest gurgle and splash. But I look around and cannot see what she described. Cedars to the left of me, to the right of me, and straight ahead. I am allergic to them, and I stand sniffling like a child lost in the forest, wondering if the carrion eaters have already finished Teddy off.

And then I see the swath of death Lora had described. It is to the right of me, maybe six feet. Old blood, a vague clump of something, a tuft of fur. I step toward it, smelling the faint, cheesy odor of decom-position and seeing clearly what she also must have found. And less. It is an ugly sight, but even three feet away, I know this isn't Teddy. That little skull isn't canine. That's a tuft of squirrel tail waving in the wind.

Lora's voice is brittle when she answers the phone. She must have put me in her phone's contact list, because her hello is the kind of hello people give when they know who's calling and that the news on the other end of the line isn't going to be good. She hates me and she needs me at the same time.

Not Teddy, I tell her first thing, and there's a long moment of silence before relief and confusion tangle and she says something that sounds like *ButitlookedsomuchlikeohmygodwhatthehelldoIdonow?*

She needs to keep doing what she's doing, I tell her, and harder. She needs more signs, wider online outreach, more contact with neighbors, a physical check of every shelter within fifty miles, beginning with those closest. Though I don't live nearby, I'm glad to help as much as I can. I hear Lora sigh. Mourning, she had closed a door that now was open again. And I hear her waver. She is poised in the place many lost-pet owners stand, where love and grief and urgency make them falter at the task list and wonder if it will all be pointless and whether they should just seek closure and accept that Teddy or Duke or Muppet is gone. It is a choice I can't make for her. I can nudge her a little, encourage her. I can help, I say again. I can take on most of the online work and visit the shelters closer to me than to her. Lost pets have been found after much longer periods than Teddy has been gone.

We prioritize a to-do list together. She was so sure about that dead squirrel in the treeline that she had torn down her earlier Teddy signs, but she will make new ones. She will hand-carry flyers to the closest vets and pet supply stores, because some online services that promise to send flyers to these businesses don't always get it done. Don't forget to put a sign in your own yard, I tell her before we ring off. A big sign. With a picture. LOST DOG LIVES HERE. You want to make it as easy as possible for the finder to find you, because many will make the quick wrong choice, needing to get a lost dog off their hands.

We talk a few times in the following week. Once more she asks me out to view remains that are not her dog, again not a dog at all.

Lora is a tidy, procedural woman. She has done the things she's promised, and more. Together we discuss next steps. We widen the ring of shelter visits and website checks. I reinforce the online posts. We will contact local rescues with an APB on Teddy. That cute little dog could easily end up in the rescue system straight from a shelter or a citizen. There are laws in most states requiring stray hold periods for all lost dogs and cats (because of low reclaim numbers, some states do not require this for cats), but much depends on when Teddy might have been found, when and where he was surrendered, and whether his microchip was scanned appropriately at intake. Microchips bring many, many animals home, but occasionally the ID procedure falls short.

Lora walks for her health. She sat for thirty years at her job, she says, and so she's a walker now. She walks twice a day most days, sometimes three times. She remembers where her signs are. Where flyers have been taken or damaged by the weather, she puts up more. But she says foot searching for Teddy is getting harder. Every trip out and every trip back reinforces her gut instinct that Teddy is gone for good.

Lora sees the shape of her lost dog in many things, living or dead. This is not a new sensation. Years ago, a car crash took her husband and son. She does not apologize for grieving for Teddy in the same way she mourned her husband and her boy. It is a different love, she says to me, but it *matters*. Now, as then, she thinks she sees the one she lost sometimes, and her heart jumps, and then it's a different dog or even not a dog at all. She nearly ran across the street at a teenager on the sidewalk the other day, accusing, and then it turned out the teenager was holding a baby with some kind of fuzzy toy. Lora laughs with an edge to it and says she has made herself stop at every Teddy-colored roadkill. Not wanting to shame herself or bother me to come out on another false ID, she's been bending down to sad rabbits and opossums and squirrels. And cats. And dogs. Lora has never been squeamish—she was a police dispatcher, for God's sake—but this has all made her terribly sad. She says she's having awful dreams. *I know you are right, I should keep looking,* she tells me. She is trying to get to the place where the search becomes a habit that hurts less.

When is it time to give up? Owners always wonder, and no one answer is correct. I remember reading a Facebook post by a young woman on the East Coast. Her dog had vanished in a hillside neighborhood at the end of their morning hike. Those two hiked every morning, and then one day she raised up from tying her shoe and he was gone. I remember the picture she posted of herself in hiking gear beside the shining, athletic black dog, looking eager and earnestly into the camera. *I will search for you forever,* the young woman posted, and forever in her case was four years before she found him, alive and well in a sanctuary for homeless old dogs. He was now a gray-muzzled senior with a limp she didn't know, but he was home.

I recently worked with an owner who thought the cause was futile when his dog was two days missing; at three days he gave up, and at four adopted another dog from a shelter — the same shelter his lost dog ended up at on day five. There he was on the couch with the little newbie, and then the phone rang and someone said, "We have your dog." It was a happy ending for both his old dog and his new one and for him, he later told me. *Deus ex machina,* he said, laughing, but he wondered about the deadline he had set on a dog lost for so short a time.

Kat Albrecht has written about the human-animal bond and its influence on the search for a missing pet. Often, in her experience, those who have a stronger attachment to their animals search longer and harder. Owners with less connection search less long, if at all. I have seen that often myself, but I've also seen a sad reverse: owners so gutted with loss that they can't bear the not knowing. It hurts too much to wonder. Needing closure quickly, they subscribe to any narrative: thieves, freeways, passing strangers, owls. I have no idea how long Lora will search for Teddy. No stranger to loss and its aftermath, perhaps that's why she so quickly assumed — still believes, I think — he is dead.

She is much on my mind when I get a garbled voicemail. The number is Lora's, and the voice is, too, but brighter and faster, like a younger Lora who pulled an all-nighter on coffee. She has called me from the alley behind her house, where she stood up from mourning yet another dead animal and saw Teddy in the high window of a garage apartment behind her, looking down. He was grinning, as Pomeranians do, barking soundlessly through the glass.

A *bastard search* is the term used for lost people and animals when the missing soul is at home or very close by, sometimes witnessing the search on his behalf. It happens on missing-persons searches; it happens in lost-pet response. Plenty of lost-cat searches are bastard searches. Teddy the Pomeranian's was, too. Lora had been in that alley often. No doubt Teddy had seen her out there before. I will eventually learn the sweet story of the night cleaning lady who found and sheltered the little dog, who missed the posted signs because she slept days and drove to and from work in the dark. But for now, in the babble and garble that is overjoyed Lora, *alive* is the word I hear most clearly through the phone, and she says it over and over, the introduction to her message, and the middle, and the end.

The last photo of my parents together,
taken in 1976.

17

TOGETHER AND APART

O N A MOONLESS spring evening, my father was waiting in a parking lot to drive me home from dance class. He was alone, as usual, but he had the radio off, which was odd. If Dad could have scored his entire life to big-band music, he would have. I remember him silent against my chatter, his window open and his arm extended as he drove, his bandaged left hand grabbing fistfuls of air. The bandage was new. He had cut his hand doing dishes when a glass broke, he said.

We came back to an unlit house. As our cat met us across the night grass and I bent down to scratch his fine, arched back, my father said from the porch, "You and I are going to have to work out a schedule for doing the dishes."

"What about Mom?" I asked.

That's how I learned that my mother was gone. I wonder now if Dad had planned the darkness so he wouldn't have to see my face when he told me. There had been some problems, big problems—old ones they had never been able to resolve, he said, fumbling with keys. He couldn't seem to find the right one for the door. Tonight my mother had packed a bag and some boxes and left for an apartment she'd rented two days before. While I was in dance class, he had helped her move. He'd sliced up his hand in her new sink. She'd send someone back for the couch.

I remember the sensation in my middle when Dad told me, as

if I had swallowed an unripe apple whole. They had rarely been wonderful together, their love characterized by tension rather than tenderness, but they were my parents. So much made sense now. People
go before they go. Lately Mom had been as absent in the house as
she could possibly make herself. She had retreated to a guest room
and rarely come out of it except to go to work. Dad watched *Star Trek*
reruns and puttered late at night repairing antique pump organs in
the garage. We were down to the one cat, Bertie, and neither parent had mentioned bringing in another. But I was gone four nights
a week at dance class and hadn't been home to hear the short, bitter
exchanges between them that must have led to real fury. My father,
who recoiled from anything like the arguments he'd grown up with,
was an easy target. After her childhood lived in the forced gloom of a
paranoid schizophrenic, my mother found her voice and her throw-
ing arm.

In recent months I'd come home to objects mysteriously broken
in the house: a shattered living room mirror, an electric skillet with
two legs snapped off, twin holes that showed that something had
completely pierced the hollow bathroom door. My parents' explana-
tions didn't always match up. The few times we were all together, there
was a desperate cheer between them—short sentences, false laughter; they flailed like people in deep water who drown each other trying
not to drown.

And so my mother left. She sent a half-drunk redheaded
stranger for the couch. It was weeks before Mom spoke to me—she
called several times, said "Susie?" and, in panic, I guess, hung up. It
would be months before her mail with a forwarding sticker was deliv-
ered by accident to our house. That's how I learned where my mother
had moved. I was driving by then. I found her apartment one morning and waited against the door for her to come home after work. If
she was surprised at the sight of me, she didn't show it. She was coast-
ing on lithium.

Her apartment was an alien space — a one-bedroom with yellowed pinch-pleat curtains, the acrid smell of many tenant smokers clinging to the black flocked wallpaper, green shag carpet, and matching fridge. My parents had never had alcohol in the house. There were unfamiliar bottles in the kitchen cabinet here — Bacardi, Wild Turkey, sour mix. There was the green Mediterranean couch from our house. Above it Mom, who had always hated violence against animals, had hung framed bullfight posters on the wall. It was a deadly quiet space, already cluttered with half-open boxes she would never unpack. Mom said she wasn't exactly happy here, but it was the life she needed. Ever an insomniac, she had purposely chosen night shifts as a nurse, a way of life that had never worked when she was home with us, because we couldn't be quiet enough. Not our fault. Not her fault. Just the way of it.

What Mom really missed was an animal in the house. I had never known us — her — without at least one cat, and I could feel that absence, too. Animals connected my mother to the world outside her struggle. Mom said the management allowed pets grudgingly in this apartment complex, but the deposit was sky-high, and there was a monthly add-on to the rent. She couldn't afford it yet, but as soon as she could, she hoped to go to the pound and bring home a cat.

"Maybe you could go with me," she said, lighting a cigarette, and for a moment we had a history and were something more than strangers again.

Our phone rang on the back side of an evening thunderstorm. Dad had thrown open the windows to catch the coolness of it, and Bertie the cat had raced through the house charged with static. The phone rang, and my father assumed it was for me, and then his face changed, and I knew immediately it was my mother. They were at that fragile stage of parting when they were trying to be friends. Dad's voice was guarded now: shield up, prepared for anger, tears, mania, or any other of her shades of war. But no, this time Mom was calm. Upbeat. Charming, even. She needed a favor. A friend in her apartment complex had just lost a dog during the storm, and he was physically unable to search for it. Would my dad send me out there as soon as possible to help her hunt for the dog?

"It won't take ten minutes," Mom said. She'd seen the frightened terrier running through traffic and crashing through tall grass in the field across the road. Dad agreed to send me, and, after he hung up, told me that he would also come.

"Your mother sounds . . . pretty good," Dad said. I don't know what he hoped for or didn't by then. But he combed his hair and slapped on some Old Spice, and we both loaded into the car with a pack of lunch meat and a grubby slip lead we'd used before for this kind of thing. We didn't say much as we drove across the puddled, steaming streets to my mother's place on the other side of town.

My mother's apartment faced the parking lot, and she met us there, dressed as though she were going out. She was a little flustered. She had not expected my father. I think we were both taken aback by her beauty. Mom was wearing a silk jersey wrap dress familiar to both of us — a favorite of my father's and a dress I would have borrowed had it not been so mature — deep gold with a pattern of shields and knights and pennants bearing lions rampant in red, green, purple, and blue. She had a lipstick that matched the red of the dress exactly, and she was wearing it now, along with perfume I didn't recognize and the gold hoop earrings Dad had bought her for her birthday long ago. Her thick auburn hair blew free.

"You're dressed up for a lost dog," Dad said.

Mom laughed. Tonight's dog had not been part of the plan. But the storm blew through and out he ran, and she'd been keeping an eye on him from her window and hadn't had time to change. "His name is Herc — for Hercules," she said, conjuring an enormous dog in my mind, but this was a white terrier the size of a shoe. She pointed to the field across from the parking lot. If we watched long enough, she said, he'd peek out of it. He'd been scared by the storm at first, but now, spooked by everything, he seemed to have lost his head entirely.

Mom knew this dog. Herc was scared of loud noises and shy with strangers, but he loved car rides, too, and she thought he might come to her if she said, "Let's go for a ride," and she was the best option going. She was going to move the car to the edge of the field, where she would be standing next to the open back door with the lunch meat she'd asked Dad to bring. She asked my father and me just to go sit quietly on the other side of the field, to keep an eye out in case he decided to run the other way. We weren't going to pressure him, but if he wanted to seek us out, we'd be there. Everything was built on the hope that Hercules would be less scared of us than he was of anything else.

Dad handed her the lunch meat.

"Olive loaf?" she said, rolling her eyes.

"All we had," Dad snapped. *"Tonight's dog wasn't part of the plan."* In the half-light of the parking lot, I saw his words connect. My petite, beautiful mother drew herself up like a cobra—an almost-divorced-obviously-just-came-in-from-a-date-in-red-lipstick-worn-for-somebody-else cobra—and Dad folded his arms and faced her, ready to answer. They were poised for a spectacular fight right there, but at that moment Hercules slipped from the tall grass of the field and stood at the edge of it, paws on the curb of the busy street. Head down, tail down. He looked small and scared and unhappy, and was soaking wet.

I said, "There he is," not caring if my parents heard me or not. They were too much for me. Already walking away, I was here for the dog, some part of me aware for the first time how easily pets become a backdrop to human theater. Whatever good intentions had brought us out for this one had evaporated over lunch meat. I wasn't immune to the drama, either. A scared, hurt, furious, and self-righteous teenager, as I walked away I might have had in mind to make some heroic save to show them, to just show them how ridiculous they were being.

But there was a waver in Hercules's posture at the curb. Something about him telegraphed change, and I stopped at the edge of the street, fearful that my approach would make him disappear deeper into the field. But no—instead of running away, he sprang from the curb in front of coming cars toward me, as if I were someone he recognized, someone he'd been waiting for. Cars veered. Brakes screeched. Flashing across the headlights, the terrier was missed by one car but clipped by another, and with a sickening thump spun yelping onto a slim grass median between six lanes. I remember the dog's shriek and the silence that followed it, a void that made my legs shake. Dead, I thought. Or dying.

But Hercules rose. He hobbled up to a signpost and crouched there, one forepaw drawn.

"Oh my God," shouted my mother as it began to rain again, hard.

I stepped off the curb toward him.

My father called to me, "Susie, don't move. He's still able to run."

A little rain, a lot of rain, was not going to stop Saturday night traffic. Rain wasn't going to slow that traffic down, either. Now there was no way to step into the road safely. Soaked through, my parents and I stood in the parking lot with our eyes on the dog, hoping for some letup on this road that led to the lake—high school and college kids mostly, driving slowly past fast-food joints and roaring away from stoplights when they went green. Some of those bastards saw the dog on the median and honked at him. Some honked at us. My pretty mother's wet silk dress was skin-tight against her now, and sometimes the same cars came back to honk again.

The physics of the situation were terrible, almost every outcome poor.

We stood there in the intermittent rain, mostly silent, waiting out the situation, until some mysterious cue took the traffic somewhere else. There were pauses now and then. We could think about crossing the road. The rain, too, moved away.

With a nod to my mother, Dad tugged my sleeve to cross the street with him — not toward the dog on the median but at a distance from Hercules toward the field — leaving Mom in the parking lot with a handful of olive loaf and our car door open wide. Dad and I split the rest of the lunch meat as we walked.

Hercules had been watching us intently. At our movement, the dog stood up as though making *friend or foe* sense of us, his injured paw still raised.

Containment. Attraction. That's how I'd now describe what we were doing then. *We won't pressure him,* Dad kept saying. The dog could make choices. If he thought of Dad and me as a threat, seated twenty yards apart at the edge of his familiar field, he could choose to leave the median to cross toward my mother. If for some reason he was uneasy about crossing toward her, he could choose to come back to the field nearer us. (He could also choose to bolt headlong down the street in either direction. We could only hope he wouldn't.)

Ours was a hazy plan built on patience and the belief that this confused dog wanted human help, if his brain could settle. Hercules's need had moved center stage again. We were too far apart to say so, but I think we were all prepared to sit this out with the dog the whole night, figuring out what we were to each other. Every now and then Dad would scoot a little closer to me, gesturing that I should do the same, tightening the human boundary he believed the dog would not cross. Across the street, Mom sat in the driver's seat of Dad's car, twitchy for a cigarette and without one.

The streets were almost silent when Hercules stood up again and, after a moment's hesitation, crept off the curb. Dad whistled my head up from where I'd bowed my forehead against my knees, half asleep. We watched the little dog limp his uneasy way down a center lane before he curved to the opposite side of the street, toward my mother and the car in the parking lot. None of us rose or called to each other, but my mother, with elaborate casualness, tore a piece of olive loaf into shreds. The dog approached and stopped and backed and half circled and stopped, bobbing his nose a little at the scent of lunch meat, sitting once for the longest moment and gazing at the open door of the car. It was a half hour's uncertain dance while the three of us willed him to make the right choice.

What changes a dog's mind? What changed my mother's? Without looking at him, she stood up out of the car, absently tossed more olive loaf toward the terrier, then, with the sound of a kiss, called, "Herc — want to go for a ride?" and patted the backseat.

It was like two spies sharing a code word. Fear replaced with recognition, the dog cantered awkwardly toward her on three legs, ignored the olive loaf, and jumped into the backseat of the car. *Clunk, clunk:* my mother shut both doors. She'd done it. We'd done it. Hercules was safe. She turned to give us a thumbs-up, a flash of old, shared joy.

We didn't linger afterward. Mom spent a moment in the backseat with the dog, assessing his bruised shoulder and leg. As she palpated his muddy little body, he licked her fingertips. Then she gathered up the willing terrier to take him home. Thank you, she said, and no, she didn't need any help.

Dad and I got in the car. We shivered as the air conditioner defogged the windshield, not leaving, waiting to make sure my mother made it safely up the rain-soaked stairs. Did she know we were still there? I had thought we'd lose sight of her when she took the dog back to whatever apartment he'd come from, but instead Mom carried Hercules to her own. The door swung open as she got there, and a man — the redheaded couch-moving friend — met her unsteadily in the doorway. He wore boxer shorts and an open robe. He took his dog from her arms and tilted his mouth toward hers. I saw her shake her head and duck his kiss, and in the same smooth movement she shut the door.

"That's Bob," my father said. He switched on the radio. A block later he said, "Your mother always does better when she's saving something." There was resignation in his voice, and tenderness, the sound a story makes when it ends.

Puzzle and Thistle.

Silent Mary Pickford.

18

CATS IN TIGHT PLACES

TWO CATS WIND through our lives here at home. Self-possessed and confident, long-haired calico Thistle and plushy, slightly goofy black-and-white Mary Pickford have picked up no canine habits in this houseful of dogs, which I hear happens sometimes. Completely devoted to their own comfort, they are all cat and then some, batting Venetian blind cords, curling up on fresh laundry seconds out of the dryer, claiming the laps of humans who badly need to get up and pee. We're all clunky beside Thistle, who glides across the spaces the rest of us seem to tread. And we are nonplussed by Mary Pickford, who seems to see ghosts that must still have ankles, because she rubs along them, looking up into faces only she can see. Almond-eyed and silvery-whiskered, both cats are committed to hard stares from high places. They sometimes glare at each other; often they swing their ears back at dogs whose existence annoys.

The cats make a few exceptions. Calico Thistle was part of the family first, that tiny stray kitten Puzzle encountered and immediately adored. It was a moment of sweet connection, the fuzzy kitten trundling forward, Puzzle working over the orange, black, and white belly with her dog tongue, and the little cat reaching up with soft paws to grip the golden's muzzle. She was Puzzle's cat immediately and named Thistle, for her prickly claws and her beauty, shortly after. Thistle came home with us and rarely left Puzzle's side. Dog and kitten played occasionally, but mostly they cuddled, the golden's body curled around the kitten as she grew. Later, the adult Thistle learned to settle beside an exhausted Puzzle after we came in from searches, the cat's paws curled over the weary golden's own. Theirs is a love that has not faded. Puzzle and Thistle have been a bonded pair for eight years now.

Tuxedo cat Mary Pickford was adopted from an animal shelter a few cities away. Then a young cat in a cage beside smaller, cuter kittens, she was bypassed by adopters over and over because her looks were common and her ways a little strange. Pickford purrs constantly but inaudibly, a rumble that can only be felt. She shapes meows that cannot be heard. Named for a silent film star because she is black and white and soundless, Mary Pickford grew into a round, big-boned cat very quickly with us. She is an oversized cat with dainty eating habits and a thyroid problem, queenly and a little oblivious.

Most of the dogs are beneath her, but Pickford finds Ace fascinating, for mysterious cat reasons I don't understand. They have staring matches across the sofa — her unblinking scrutiny versus his solemn, button-eyed gaze. They spar now and then, Ace chattering and spinning before the bearlike, silent Pickford with fat white paws. Sometimes Ace instigates. Sometimes she does. Ace belly-creeps up to the musing cat to nibble at her tail, and she rises from her sunning place to right-hook his play bows and ear tosses. Sometimes Pickford is equally stealthy. She lurks over Ace from chair seats, pouncing on him when he's looking the other way. There is something cartoonish about it, the chubby, voiceless cat on the groaning chair, the ungraceful leap of a sumo wrestler in a fur coat onto the startled dog. Their shared spark is one of those happy accidents we find sometimes in rescue. Scruffy upstart Ace rouses sleepy Pickford and gives her back some kittenhood. And Ace, a dog still starved for connection he was too long without, is a little less alone.

Ace has been with us just four months when Mary Pickford goes missing in winter. I have come home from days of travel and she's just not there. An inside-only cat, and a very large one, I can't

imagine she could have slipped out of the house without my seeing her before I left or after I returned. But—take no cat for granted
—plenty of lost-cat case studies have taught me that it's possible. In
haste I start to search the house for Pickford like I'm ransacking it,
then check myself. That's not the smartest move. A ransack is only
likely to make a cat commit more to her hiding place. I quietly put
up the dogs, then work my way across the house and the fenced
backyard with a flashlight, peering in corners and beneath decks and
furniture, hoping to light up the glow of her eyes. I've learned that
inside-only cats who escape outside usually tuck themselves up and
hide close by, overwhelmed by a choice that now seems like a mis-
take. Sometimes such cats will stay hidden for days before hunger
and desperation force them to cry out or show themselves. If Pickford is outside, I can only hope she isn't stuck somewhere. There
would be no hearing her if she chose to meow.

The hasty search over, I shift mattresses, disembowel closets,
peer again under every large piece of furniture I have. How many
hours before I let the dogs out of my room and at large again? Rowdy
and overinterested in my search for the cat, they were a noisy distraction; I'd put them away to keep the situation calmer. And it wasn't like
they could help. Both of the search dogs are human-specific, and the
rest have other jobs. They aren't trained to find anything at all. Pickford had been all over the house for years now. The presence of her
scent would not be remarkable anywhere here.

Once the joy of release from my bedroom is over, most of the
dogs settle. But not Ace. I am mentally retracing my steps when he
begins worrying at a space beneath the couch. It is low-slung, heavy
thing and the clearance beneath it very low, but he is nosing back and
forth and around the sides, his head bobbing with interest—in search
terms, this is called a *head pop*—at one corner. I have looked under
that couch more than once. Tipped it back, even. Nothing. But Ace is
on to something. Interest, I would call it in a search dog, interest escalating to indication. He is persistent and increasingly excited. Before

my eyes, Ace flattens himself like a mouse and scoots under the couch, hips and legs splayed wide. From beneath it he chatters, and it's there I find Pickford, who has slipped herself up through a hole in the couch lining and is stuck fast beneath the seat. She is invisible up there, no white of her showing — a black cat in a black hole in black lining. It is quite a feat to get in to where she is, and it will take couch surgery to get her out, but with a long snake of my arm I reach in and find her, fingertips grazing the pads of her fat little foot.

I rock back on my heels and look at scrappy Ace with new eyes.

A long-haired cat the color of light on autumn leaves, Thistle is graceful where Pickford lumbers, keen where Pickford is vacant. Thistle carries herself like the stylish cats in those Parisian prints by Steinlen. She is art unto herself, curling around objects, winking at us, green-eyed. Thistle would likely have made some beautiful kittens had she not been spayed. That spay has never really convinced her; despite it, her maternal impulses remain strong. For all her sweet, nurturing ways beside Puzzle, Thistle has less endearing habits. About twice a year she has imaginary litters that she moves from room to room, and she goes to great lengths to catch and take food to them. Or at least that's what she thinks she does.

Since we have no mice or birds in the house, every winter and again every spring Thistle takes paper she has dragged off counters and prized out of file folders to her invisible kittens. Strong and determined, she seems to have a particular fondness for fat envelopes and stapled sheaves. I once found a sixty-eight-page contract beneath my claw-foot bathtub. A small sketch pad between the washer and dryer. More than once she has pried open the flap of my purse and carried off my checkbook. Thistle pulls open drawers, steals the electric bill or a notebook with all my encrypted passwords, and drags away her prizes in the middle of the night. She gives herself away at this, waking me with the particular croon a mama cat makes to her little ones, and

I've learned to leap out of bed and intercept her before the dogs do. The dogs respect neither her fantasy nor the importance of this year's W-2 and will shred anything they find, dismembering her kill as if it were their own.

It's easier when Thistle's imaginary litters nest in corners or under the bed. If some vital document goes missing when I'm not there to hear her thieving, I can at least get down on all fours and try to find the bank statement in plain sight — again, ideally, ahead of the dogs. But with winter litters especially she prefers warmer, more private places. The linen cupboard. The armoire for winter coats. I once found her in a box of Christmas decorations, where she'd scruffed the tree skirt to ribbons. Thistle would have kittened up in Pickford's couch hole if I hadn't sealed it. Mostly she chooses closets, and there I am undone.

I find clutter exhausting and keep a straight house, but tidy closets I've never been able to manage for very long. Fibber McGee, my parents used to call me, after the radio character whose junked-up closet avalanched on him every time he opened the door. My closet is the stuff of impatience, inheritance, and excess. *I have nightmares like this,* my least judgmental friend says. *Your closet is a portal to the damned.* I've shopped at the Container Store and studied those marvelous Japanese storage strategies and still just don't get it. In my bedroom closet, a boot and a chain-link belt sit on a pink Voodoo Doughnut box full of dried eucalyptus and stray socks. That's my slid stack of gummy photo albums from high school, and those are my grandmother's and great-grandmother's older scrapbooks, their glue tabs loosened, bulging with photos of very old houses, cars, and puppies that were new when the shutter clicked, and proud strangers beside them who died before I was born. Silk dance dresses and 5K Fun Run T-shirts hug the BDU pants I wear on searches. My grandmother's sequined flapper cloche rests on the tip of a small ironing board that leans on an open box containing Puzzle's baby collar, a pair of silk long johns, an etched pink 1930s mirror, and two bound galley copies of my first book. It's bad. It's humbling. It's the dark secret I get to about once a decade, the closet pristine for a few days before the rot creeps back in.

For Thistle it's heaven. In or out of nesting fever, that cat loves my closet. She has learned when the shifting old house loosens the catch of the door, and she stands up on her back feet to bump the crystal doorknob or hooks a paw under the bottom of the door to swing it ajar. Maybe it's a grand, mysterious experience for an indoor cat, this constantly changing terrain to conquer in the dark. Lithe and light-footed, she can do it, too. I find traces of Thistle's adventures. I can track her journey through the closet by what's squashed, what's tumbled, by the band of shed fur across the sleeves of every hanging sweater and the smudge of paw prints across the deco mirror's pink glass. Sometimes this frustrates me. Most often I sigh and get out the lint roller. Lately I've rationalized that if nothing else, Thistle's habits in my closet can teach me a little about the hows and wheres of a cat who chooses to hide.

She is certainly nesting in the closet as late winter turns to spring. Thistle has been at it again with her invisible kittens, and there have been some fitful nights for the dogs and me as she attends them. We are thick with sleep at 2 a.m. when she starts thieving, but it's a race, always, to get to the stuff before the dogs do. When I catch her, she scrambles. This season Thistle has added pads of sticky notes to the mail, pocket calendars, and checkbooks she's pilfered, and she's given away her nesting place by dropping the stolen items in a trail leading to the closet door. I'd shut it; I always shut it, but she's managed to pull it open, even with a hand towel wedged underneath. We're on about night five of Thistle's caterwauling when I wonder if I'm going to have to baby-proof every door, drawer, and cabinet in the house with those little lock straps used for crawlers and toddlers. And if I do, will even I be able to get back in them? I sit on the edge of my bed, head in my hands, and think *Really, cat, it has come to this.*

I read a Baby-Proofing 101 article online, then visit a home improvement store and come home with packets of plastic wedges and
bumpers and latches. All of this assumes I can install them correctly,
and all of this, I realize, assumes that my enterprising dogs won't chew
them off in five minutes of sport. It's an afternoon's work. You don't
realize how many doors and drawers are in a house until you have to
secure every one of them. The dogs find it all entertaining — I am their
peer on all fours, kneeling, crawling, a-fixing, cursing. Big and little,
they follow me from room to room and watch, sniffing my handiwork
afterward.

Drowsy Mary Pickford, too, studies me from a kitchen chair,
her paws tucked and tail wrapped, like an oversized loaf of black-
and-white bread. But Thistle, usually the nosier of the two cats, hasn't
shown herself at all. After a fleeting question about whether I've just
locked the cat up in one cupboard or another, I remember that I
haven't yet made it to my bedroom. Certainly she's in there. She could
be anywhere in there, even having a perfectly innocent sit on the windowsill. I head in to secure drawers and bathroom cabinets, leaving
the closet of horrors, where Thistle nests her latest imaginary litter,
to do last.

But I can't find her in it. She's not there. The door was ajar when
I got to it, but there is no cat to be found. I make noises and rustle
clothes, scoot clutter enough to stomp a few times on six square
inches of bare floor, but nothing seems to stir her from any hiding
place. Now I'm a little worried. I look over my shoulder at the kitchen
— ten cabinets, ten drawers, one pantry door — and the office, twelve
drawers and a closet, and down the hall to other rooms also battened
down.

The dogs eye me. It's been a strange afternoon, and all our normal
rituals are off. After nosing my face and peeking into the cupboards
I've reopened, they leave me. They drift away with some uncertainty
and backward glances, waiting me out until suppertime. Puzzle flops

down in her favorite spot in the corridor, smile wide in a casual pant, and Ace leans companionably against her, twisting around to scratch an ear with his back foot.

Ace. The dog who loves cats, and the dog who keeps tabs on all of us. I beckon him into my room. Puzzle follows. The golden is only mildly interested when I open the closet door, but Ace, who has never been inside it, is immediately curious.

"Where's Thistle?" I ask Ace. "Find the kitty," I say. We've been working on this lately with clumps of cat fur. He pops on his forepaws, ready. I flip on the closet light and leave the little dog to it. Five minutes later a few soft thumps are followed by a clatter, and a furious Thistle zips past me into the hallway. Ace must have flushed her. Ears back, tail out long, she leaps onto a chair and shoots me a look of loathing. I expect to see Ace right behind her, but minutes later I realize I haven't seen him. He hasn't come out of the closet.

Puzzle seems to know he's in there. She's not too worried about it, still stretched out where she was when I opened the closet door. She raises her head, looking on with interest as I head in there myself. I can see the evidence of search and find. There is a new disorder to the rubble. A few clothes have fallen from hangers. A plastic bin of scarves has tumbled onto the floor. I can see at once where the dog stepped on and overturned things, and I can see where he must have uprooted Thistle, from a very back corner behind a yellow sign that reads CAST AND CREW ONLY, where two old quilts and a duvet with a hole in it are tucked.

No sign of Ace. I am pushing boxes and tossing shoes and thinking I might need a search dog for the search dog when I hear a sound so like a whisper that I stop. Closing my eyes, I hear it a second time —a shy, *pssst-beg-pardon-hate-to-bother-you* kind of sound from beneath a pile of tumbled clothes. It takes a bit of digging, but that's where I find Ace, who has somehow slid himself into the arm of one of my father's huge Aran cardigans. A whitish dog sausaged into the sleeve of a whitish sweater, he's stuck fast and not easy to see. Only his nose and mouth peek out.

"Good job getting the cat out, Acey," I say as I find him. "Before you got stuck yourself, dude." I scratch his back through the cable-knit. The sleeve writhes. Ace's pink tongue pants from his tight little mouth. "Hey," he whispers. "Hey, hey, hey."

Mija.

19

ON OUR STREET ALONE

T HE TINY DUST-COLORED black-and-brown dog in the middle of our neighborhood's busiest street is a scuttling, wary creature, so confused by horn blasts and the rush of passing traffic that she unwisely chooses to run headlong down the center of the road. She can't recognize safe harbor. She is fast on the end of the loose leash she drags, and it's frightening her, too—a retractable lead that can expand and retract with the dog's movement on a big plastic handle. Designed for owner convenience, that lead is now an adversary, the handle bobbing and skidding behind her across the asphalt, sometimes closer, sometimes farther away. Every so often she casts a startled glance behind her as she runs. She thinks she's being chased.

Her name is Mija. I have seen this Chihuahua-Yorkie cross before, bright-eyed in the arms of her elderly owner, who is temporarily living here after heart surgery and who walks Mija twice a day with the assistance of her daughter. Some routes, some days, take them past my house. Mija is obviously treasured. On the lead she's a merry, prancy little thing. The owner picks her up when her health walk must continue but her dog is tired. Mija wears bows that tie up the long hair that would hide her eyes, and she's always on a matching retractable lead, whatever the color of the bow.

Those extension leads must have seemed a godsend in the early days of the woman's recovery from surgery. They are a great idea in theory, allowing a dog to walk as close to the owner or as far ahead as it desires, at greater distances than a typical leash allows. But there are serious issues with extension leads. They've caused rope burns and other injuries to humans and other animals, inadvertent garroting accidents—even amputations—in meetings with other dogs. It's not difficult for a strong dog to yank the lead's handle out of an owner's hand. Now, loose Mija's lead presents another problem—it can dangerously entangle a dog.

Mija runs right in front of my car as I'm stopped at an intersecting street. She is so quick a blur that at first I think I'm seeing a squirrel, until the clatter of the pink lead handle defines her. I'm not the only one she passes. I see a contractor dash into the middle of the street and try to step on it, but the little dog is faster than he is. His well-meaning rush only escalates her fear. And here is the situation: chasing a dog in this kind of panic can lead her to all the wrong choices (she's making plenty of them now on her own). It's important that she slow down and critical to keep her in sight without adding to her sense of being pursued. I turn in the direction she is running but drive well back, passing the construction worker, who shrugs and shakes his head helplessly.

Mija is not easy to follow. She blazes down the street where I have to pause at stop signs. Block after block the little dog runs, never once slowing, committed to this wide road. Pedestrians' heads swivel. A few stop and point. One lady puts her hands to her knees and appears to whistle. Mija disregards them all; if anything, their scrutiny makes her run faster. Approaching drivers must not know what to make of her. She's almost the color of the asphalt. It's an awful thing to witness, those close calls punctuated by furious honking, the dreadful certainty that at any moment I'm going to see this Mija killed. *Turn,* I will her, wishing for psychic powers, for telekinesis, for dog-speak. *Turn. Left or right, I don't care.* But not in front of traffic.

A half-block ahead of me now, I see her slow and pause so improbably at a stop sign that I bark a jerky laugh. She has heard the approach of something on the cross street I can't see, and she veers away from it, turning to the left, into a corner yard, and then reversing course to run away from the sound. She passes me at top speed as I stop for the thing that's spooked her: a street-sweeping truck, roaring and brushing past. The moment it takes to negotiate past the truck makes me lose her. By the time I turn around to head north, she is gone.

At least she's heading in the right direction, I think. Mija lives north of me, I'm pretty sure — at least five or six blocks from where I last saw her. I drive slowly. No sign of the dog in the yards of the houses I pass. No sign of the dog in the middle of the busy street. I hang on to that small positive and continue to roll slowly forward, flashers on. Cars pass me. One angry man leans on his horn and flips me off out of the sunroof of his car.

Mija seems to have teleported, she is so completely gone. I roll down the window to ask a jogging woman on the sidewalk if the little dog passed her. The woman is also skittish, stepping to the inner edge of the sidewalk and giving the car a wide berth until she can make sense of me through the window. She pulls out her earphones, furrows her brow. Dog? No. No loose dog. She points to the road she's just run along and gestures the course she has taken. She looks northward and squints. No. She has not seen a dog.

I glance at the clock in my car. Mija's been out of sight for six minutes. I know her only by acquaintance and wonder now if she has tired enough or calmed enough to seek her own way home. She's traveling closer to streets she should know very well. My own dogs lead me home on cue easily. Has Mija walked local routes enough that she can make her way back?

At least she hasn't returned to the center of the busy street. I can see a block or so ahead of me, and she's not there. I pause briefly at the corner where my house sits, torn between making a full stop and posting online to our neighborhood group about her or continuing to cruise the neighborhood in the hope of catching sight of her again. Surely, I think, our dog-friendly neighborhood will recognize all that's wrong about a loose dog dragging a retractable lead. Maybe someone else will post a sighting.

I decide to turn down the route I've seen Mija walk with her owner, and then I spot the pink flash of the lead handle she's dragging. She's not on the road and not on the route she walks with her owner. She's turned down an alley directly across the street from my house, an L-shaped gravel path that leads behind two streets of houses. By the time I get to the alley she has made the turn down the long leg of the L. She is tired. She has slowed.

Containment, I think, wishing hard for someone to block this end of the alley while I head to the other end. But there's no one nearby to ask. I can't follow her. The noise of my car on the gravel will frighten her more. I drive to the other end, park my car on the street, open the windows, and sit. She does not appear. One minute. Two. No sight of her. She must have reversed course again, gone back out the alley the way she came in.

Moments later I hear the roar of backyard dogs at the alley fence line. They have heard something or seen something or both. And whatever it is, it's not going away. A dog like Mija would run from that kind of sound, I think, and usually territorial barking will taper off. But this continues. I grab the leash I now keep in the car and head gingerly down the alley, the crunch of my steps giving the dogs something new to bark about.

The alley is green and somewhat overgrown, lined with limbs, weeds, old wood, and downed sections of fencing. There are gaps between a few fences that she could have slipped through to get out of the alley and onto the next street. I hope she hasn't. Even if she hasn't, if little Mija is hiding in any of this, she could be difficult to find.

Those backyard dogs are a waypoint of sorts. Their excitement leads me to where she must have just been—and again it's the bulky pink handle of the lead that I first see. Mija had rounded the curve of the alley and for some reason chosen to run along the brushy fence line rather than the alley's center. Though I can't see her at all, the handle of the retractable lead is now stuck fast between the branches of a large tree limb that appears to have been on the ground awhile.

Maybe eight or nine feet long, the limb is braided with brush. It's the kind of limb I am wary of on searches. More than once I've stepped near this kind of wood only to find a copperhead beneath. No sign of Mija. I wonder if she caught the lead handle as she ran and pulled hard enough that the line snapped free. It happens sometimes, but usually with larger, stronger dogs than she is. Mija's a wily little thing, though, and determined. Maybe she managed it.

She did not. I hear the dry, faint rattle of her growl before I see her. I find her still attached to the lead, tangled in brush and line, wedged beneath that fallen branch and the privacy fence beside it. She is pinned fast like a bug in a web. She is terrified when I pull back the brush and reveal her. Completely unbalanced by all that has happened, Mija is not happy to be found. She's a completely different dog from the one I've met in passing, wiggly and friendly and ready to kiss a stranger. Now she bares her teeth, showing more pink gum than I have ever seen from any angry dog, and lays back her long, frizzled ears. Her eyes bug with defensive fury, their whites showing. She's a burr on batteries. Her growl seems to go on forever, without much pause for breath. When I pull free a weed that pricks right across her eyes, Mija lunges the half inch her binding allows, tags jingling, white teeth clicking close enough that I feel her hot breath on my hand.

Those are some pink gums, I think. Those are some very pointy white teeth. Would cornered Mija bite me while I try to help? Almost certainly she would. I can't blame her. She's trapped, cornered, scared witless. But she would bite.

The backyard dogs near us roar with excitement. They are pressed as close as the fence allows them, climbing on each other to get as close to the action as possible. One dog can get his nose through the patched fence, and he sticks his muzzle out to us as far as he can. It's a tight fit. His constrained barks squeak oddly and his eyes tug into a squint.

I have to ignore them. I've got a few things to figure out. First, and most important, I want to make sure Mija doesn't have that leash line wrapped dangerously around her throat, abdomen, legs, or tail. It would take no time at all for a scared dog to snare herself in a tourniquet that could kill her. Even my examination could make trouble if her fear makes her writhe enough to tighten the cord that has pinned her into place. She is not going to make this easy. I remember the heavy search gloves in my car. They would pad any bite from Mija, but their thick, cumbersome fingers wouldn't make working with this cord easy. It's no use. If she's dangerously bound, I'm just going to have to risk a bite.

I drop to my knees in the brush, settle in, and force myself to breathe slowly. I remember stories from childhood about animals who seemed to recognize human help when they were in trouble. Androcles and the lion come to mind. Some Little Golden Books. Boy, those were good stories. Quivering Mija is calm enough when I'm looking away from her, but any direct eye contact or any too-close movement of my hands starts up that low growl again. She's even less happy when I talk to her, low and soft. I have soothed some injured people in the search field. Mija has not opted in.

But after I pull a prickly clump of weed free of her chest, we make a sort of peace. Maybe she's figured out that I'm helping her. Maybe she's conserving her energy to fight. I don't know. We operate in denial. Using both hands and my peripheral vision, I don't look directly at her, and she too looks away, quivering, stoic. I get a few tangles unwrapped like this, side-eyed. We do okay. Mija has boundaries, though. When I lean forward a little too much or look too directly at her while attempting to untangle the line, her nose wrinkles and her teeth bare. That ready growl clicks intermittently at the back of her throat, like a tiny rollercoaster on a long rise. She's like the occasional embarrassed person you find stuck on a search: *Just shut up and free me and don't tell me too much.*

Weeds pulled away, now I can see Mija clearly. She is caught firmly in an intricate cat's cradle, but at least she hasn't bound body parts blue. I rock back on my heels, look sideways at her, and consider.

We have three choices here. First, I could attempt to untangle the line completely, which would leave her on this lead, and then I'd have her. Difficult, time-consuming, maybe impossible. Second, I could cut the line free with my SAR knife after fetching it from the car. But then Mija would be loose, and I'm not sure I could cut the line and hang on to so frantic a freed creature, even in thick gloves. If I dropped her, she'd run. I have no doubt about that at all. Third, I could put her on the regular leather leash I have with me, then cut the line of the other. That, of course, would require getting my hands on her collar, very close to those teeth.

Maybe I get too still, look at her too long, because Mija turns to give me her full face as well. Her growl rises. She pulls back her lips even farther—a beautiful dog baring the toothy smile you'd expect from dogs guarding the gates of Hell. I can see the tags on her collar —a rabies tag and another, pink and heart-shaped, with rhinestones. There is faint, worn writing on it that I can't read from the distance the little dog demands: Mija's name, probably. Maybe an address or a phone number. The illegible tag is tantalizing. *Nice lady who owns this dog, I could really use you right now.* I feel a wave of concern about that elderly woman. How had it happened that a fully leashed Mija got free?

Search work demands resourcefulness. I think of my mother making signs with shoe polish and my father fashioning a leash from jumper cables. Sometimes my own light breaks late. What I can't see, my phone's camera might catch, and then I can blow the image up. I reach for my phone and make the most of Mija's furious stare, snapping a picture of the tag. Success! When I turn away and enlarge the image with a spread of my fingers, the owner's phone number can faintly be seen.

The phone rings and rings and rings again, six rings before an impersonal, automated male voice tells me to leave a message. Damnit, I know that voice. It's cloned on my own home answering machine. And then I recognize that the area code I dialed isn't a nearby one. Mija's tag carries the number of her owner's faraway phone at home.

My sigh of frustration must mean something to Mija. I look up and find her gazing at me, ears drawn forward, her expression soft. She is almost the dog I've met a few times on walks. Maybe our fifteen minutes together has taken her adrenaline down a notch. I put down my phone, wrap my arms around my knees, and just sit with her, looking away. The backyard dogs' interest resolves, then gives way completely when they are called to their supper. We are alone.

We can't stay here. This alley gets used by people coming home after five, and Mija and I sit right around the blind bend of it, in a spot that a driver might not see before it was too late. Without looking too much at the little dog, I pull out the leash I have in my pocket. I have no idea if I can clip a leash on her with just my peripheral vision, but I'm going for it. In movies, someone would pick up a stone and throw it and the distracted little dog's head would turn, and they'd get the leash clipped on in that nanosecond. But hyperaware Mija wouldn't buy it. I'm going to avoid big moves. So I hold on to the leash clip and pull free inconsequential weeds around her, singing "Can't Take My Eyes Off You," which she doesn't seem to mind.

I'm stalling and I know it. I'm running out of weeds to pull. And so I reach for her with both hands, ready to be bloodied, fumbling briefly with her collar as she struggles and managing to clip my leash around the collar itself, while the black clip of the retractable lead is still attached to the collar's metal D-ring. A five-second process, maybe, and a clean one. Writhing Mija didn't bite me. She didn't even try.

I am about to leave her for a quick jog to my car and SAR knife when Mija shivers where she's caught, then shrieks a double yap. Now she is distracted, and I briefly hear what the dog must have—a woman's voice calling her name. Other neighborhood dogs take up the opportunity and bark, too.

"Here!" I call. I wobble when I stand up—both feet are half asleep. When I look around the alley bend, I see the woman, the owner's daughter, passing on the street. Calling Mija's name, she hasn't heard either of us, not even Mija's high-pitched bark. "Mija is here!" I call to her, and she turns and looks dumbly at me, as if she can't quite believe it. It takes her a few moments to be able to cross to the alley.

She kneels to Mija where she is bound. Here is the help most needed. Mija wiggles and squeaks to the woman, completely ignoring me while I unwind what I can, snap free what I can, and finally get the retractable lead free. The daughter tells me that she's the one who lost Mija, that her mother is back in the hospital, and she's the one who put the leash on the dog and opened the door before ever really having hold of it. And Mija ran, God knows why. She ran through the gaps in the front-yard fence like it wasn't even there.

She lifts Mija onto her shoulder and takes the worn cloth leash I have clipped onto the dog. No more retractable leads, I urge her, because this is what can happen, and worse. She understands. Her impaired mother likes those leads, thinking they give Mija more exercise than she herself could give, but the daughter says that she can probably be persuaded to change. When she tells her mother the story—a much shorter version of the story, she says, that will not stop her heart—her mother will probably change.

Though I offer to drive them both home in my car, the daughter shakes her head. I have done enough, she tells me, and I get the sense she needs to compose herself with the dog. We part in the alley, and as the woman turns, I see Mija's fusty black-and-nut-brown face over her shoulder. Relaxed now in arms, ears perked, she wrinkles her nose at the sight of me nonetheless, baring those teeth from a distance, flashing me her fierce and gummy little grin.

*Ace trying a
short trail.*

*Ace snagging
airborne scent from
under a deck.*

AIR AND GROUND

E VERY RUN BEHIND a working dog teaches me something that I will bring to the next search partner—about old scent and new scent and the way scent sticks or travels, about what a dog who loves the job brings to the effort, and about what it takes to partner that dog well. Puzzle is always an instruction. The terrain I am working with her now is a rough one, and this senior dog takes it much more gracefully on four paws than I do, behind her, with my thick boots and pack. She is swift, and she is strong. Behind her, I galumph.

Today's training replicates an actual search for an aphasic young woman who wandered from a lakeside camping area years ago. Puz and I are trailing a volunteer playing the part of that young woman. It is a scent-specific search: out of all the human scents in this area, Puzzle should isolate and follow only the young woman's. Our search includes a steep hill wrapped in meandering, untended limestone trails, and—though we don't yet know it—will end where the hill spills down into a valley that edges the lake. From the PLS—the point last seen—Puzzle took scent from the volunteer's sock (*smell that*) and was cued to find more of the same scent (*find that*). The golden loves this work. She made a few circles across the chunky gravel of the parking area, and from there she immediately headed out, ignoring distractors planted along our route, including the volunteer's young son.

It is a good morning for search: warm but not hot, a light breeze blowing. This scent trail, three hours old, must still have good integrity. Puzzle is keen. Head up, head down, head up, head down, nose to rock and vegetation, she follows the trail's meander all the way up to a flat rock near the hill's crest, where she sniffs and circles the rock several times before moving on. Perhaps this is where the young woman sat for a time to rest or enjoy the view, before hiking to the curve around the top of the hill.

K9 trailing is most often seen on a long line, a stretch of lead twenty to thirty feet in length, the dog ahead and the handler behind. A long line enables the handler to keep connected to the swiftly moving dog, whose eagerness could outpace his partner's. But there are exceptions. Puzzle and I learned to trail on a long line. We still trail on long lines at night and in urban situations, where the line may keep her safer, serving as an important tether between us near traffic and passersby. But in wilderness the long line can make the search a lot harder, especially on hills like this one, where even the crude walking trails are edged with overgrown brush and thorny mesquite. Long lines behind a fast dog can get tangled and tangled and tangled again, and handlers must learn how to negotiate the brush and the pauses, untangling quickly. Some dogs do all their trailing on long lines. Frustrated by such delays, Puzzle early showed me that she could trail offline, working her way ahead at a steady pace and from time to time pausing to turn her head and check in with me, making eye contact before moving on.

Puzzle is offline today. Now she crests the hill and makes that check-in, waiting a beat for me to get a little closer before she is over the crest to make her way down.

"How did you teach her to do that?" a trainee running with us asks. "How did you teach her to stop and look back for you?"

I didn't teach her to do that. It was something Puzzle just gave me when she was about six years old. No longer the headstrong puppy, she seemed to understand that we had to collaborate at this. Even without that thirty-foot line, she keeps us connected. This search is no exception.

She must be close to the volunteer victim. I can see Puzzle's signa-

ture tail swoosh and the quickening that suggests she's getting closer to the hottest point of scent. The golden skips past a final distraction, a volunteer whistling his way down the trail with a fishing pole. Then she drops her nose low, snakes into the tall grass, and backs out of it again to rise up on her back legs and make eye contact with me, the first stage of her alert. Point made, Puzzle belly-crawls her way back to the woman. It is the gentlest approach, the happy dog's tail wagging so hard it makes the valley grass whisper, *shush-shush-shush-shush*.

Ace, dashing across the grass, is also showing me something, but I'm not yet sure how to read him. I wonder what Puzzle makes of his early efforts at search. Dog-to-dog, perhaps she reads him better than I do at this early stage. She is wagging at the window as she follows Ace's progress across the yard. Every so often Puzzle puts her paws up to the windowsill, and I can see the tail fluff waving behind her head.

As with SAR, lost-pet K9s can serve in different search disciplines. As with SAR, there is a long journey from a puppy who enjoys nose work to the mature, reliable dog who can meet the challenge of search again and again. Ace is not a puppy, and he brings a more mature, grounded quality to the search games I've introduced. He seems to enjoy any activity that challenges his brain and his nose. Today Ace isn't trailing the path of a traveling animal. Instead he is nose-up to snag scent that is airborne, working a small area search.

Ace is questing a fat tuft of tabby-cat fur that is somewhere in this small square of land. He has made some investigative sweeps across the space and has shown some excitement at the garden, but he has not yet narrowed to the spot where the fur is tucked deep in Turk's cap, which has just begun to leaf out. In this environment, rich with the scent of dogs he knows well, I want to see if he can ignore all of it and focus on the kitty stranger's scent instead. SAR dogs are trained to find humans and proofed against finding animals. I hope to train Ace to search specifically for cat or dog, on cue.

Puzzle watches Ace intently, in a way she
just ambling in the backyard. Her sunny face bea
dow down at us. Content with her own search
other dogs cued to *find* and watch those dogs sear
up in frustrated anticipation. This morning's tra
searching for all the dogs. Puzzle has made her
she's watched Gambit's hard runs and now Ace's b

Though area search and trailing press for the
to find what the dog is trained to find—they have
and answer different needs. Area search is used in
where search subjects may or may not be—the ki
might be used, for example, in disaster-torn place
many victims or none. These searches are generally
The dog is charged to find any source of the target s
in an area, all dogs in an area, all of a given endange
area—whatever the target scent is. Area searches m
ing or the dead. The area search discipline can be an
for MAR. Perhaps a pregnant indoor-outdoor cat has
house and birthed her kittens somewhere outside. A s
ing an area could quickly clear the spaces the cat did
alert to the space where the huddle of kittens lies.

I remember reading about an area search for a
few years ago. The senior horse was not a jumper and
gates surrounding his pasture were all intact, but the
to have vanished from the place he had known and w
life. Friends and family had walked the area. A small pla
ter had been deployed, without luck. A search dog and
better success with an area search. Somehow a section
had formed a small sinkhole that had given way beneath
the horse, who fell into the hole, maybe fifteen feet or
earth had tumbled down after him, and brushy scrub h
the hole and the horse even from the low-flying airplar
only slightly injured, was trapped there for days before t

ture tail swoosh and the quickening that suggests she's getting closer to the hottest point of scent. The golden skips past a final distraction, a volunteer whistling his way down the trail with a fishing pole. Then she drops her nose low, snakes into the tall grass, and backs out of it again to rise up on her back legs and make eye contact with me, the first stage of her alert. Point made, Puzzle belly-crawls her way back to the woman. It is the gentlest approach, the happy dog's tail wagging so hard it makes the valley grass whisper, *shush-shush-shush-shush*.

Ace, dashing across the grass, is also showing me something, but I'm not yet sure how to read him. I wonder what Puzzle makes of his early efforts at search. Dog-to-dog, perhaps she reads him better than I do at this early stage. She is wagging at the window as she follows Ace's progress across the yard. Every so often Puzzle puts her paws up to the windowsill, and I can see the tail fluff waving behind her head.

As with SAR, lost-pet K9s can serve in different search disciplines. As with SAR, there is a long journey from a puppy who enjoys nose work to the mature, reliable dog who can meet the challenge of search again and again. Ace is not a puppy, and he brings a more mature, grounded quality to the search games I've introduced. He seems to enjoy any activity that challenges his brain and his nose. Today Ace isn't trailing the path of a traveling animal. Instead he is nose-up to snag scent that is airborne, working a small area search.

Ace is questing a fat tuft of tabby-cat fur that is somewhere in this small square of land. He has made some investigative sweeps across the space and has shown some excitement at the garden, but he has not yet narrowed to the spot where the fur is tucked deep in Turk's cap, which has just begun to leaf out. In this environment, rich with the scent of dogs he knows well, I want to see if he can ignore all of it and focus on the kitty stranger's scent instead. SAR dogs are trained to find humans and proofed against finding animals. I hope to train Ace to search specifically for cat or dog, on cue.

Puzzle watches Ace intently, in a way she never
just ambling in the backyard. Her sunny face beams th
dow down at us. Content with her own search games
other dogs cued to *find* and watch those dogs search wit
up in frustrated anticipation. This morning's training
searching for all the dogs. Puzzle has made her own
she's watched Gambit's hard runs and now Ace's busy i

Though area search and trailing press for the san
to find what the dog is trained to find—they have diffe
and answer different needs. Area search is used in a ge
where search subjects may or may not be—the kind
might be used, for example, in disaster-torn places th
many victims or none. These searches are generally not
The dog is charged to find any source of the target scen
in an area, all dogs in an area, all of a given endangered
area—whatever the target scent is. Area searches may
ing or the dead. The area search discipline can be an i
for MAR. Perhaps a pregnant indoor-outdoor cat has slip
house and birthed her kittens somewhere outside. A sea
ing an area could quickly clear the spaces the cat did n
alert to the space where the huddle of kittens lies.

I remember reading about an area search for a m
few years ago. The senior horse was not a jumper and t
gates surrounding his pasture were all intact, but the a
to have vanished from the place he had known and wa
life. Friends and family had walked the area. A small pla
ter had been deployed, without luck. A search dog and i
better success with an area search. Somehow a section
had formed a small sinkhole that had given way beneath
the horse, who fell into the hole, maybe fifteen feet or
earth had tumbled down after him, and brushy scrub l
the hole and the horse even from the low-flying airpla
only slightly injured, was trapped there for days before t

AIR AND GROUND

E VERY RUN BEHIND a working dog teaches me something that I will bring to the next search partner—about old scent and new scent and the way scent sticks or travels, about what a dog who loves the job brings to the effort, and about what it takes to partner that dog well. Puzzle is always an instruction. The terrain I am working with her now is a rough one, and this senior dog takes it much more gracefully on four paws than I do, behind her, with my thick boots and pack. She is swift, and she is strong. Behind her, I galumph.

Today's training replicates an actual search for an aphasic young woman who wandered from a lakeside camping area years ago. Puz and I are trailing a volunteer playing the part of that young woman. It is a scent-specific search: out of all the human scents in this area, Puzzle should isolate and follow only the young woman's. Our search includes a steep hill wrapped in meandering, untended limestone trails, and—though we don't yet know it—will end where the hill spills down into a valley that edges the lake. From the PLS—the point last seen—Puzzle took scent from the volunteer's sock (*smell that*) and was cued to find more of the same scent (*find that*). The golden loves this work. She made a few circles across the chunky gravel of the parking area, and from there she immediately headed out, ignoring distractors planted along our route, including the volunteer's young son.

It is a good morning for search: warm but not hot, a light breeze blowing. This scent trail, three hours old, must still have good integrity. Puzzle is keen. Head up, head down, head up, head down, nose to rock and vegetation, she follows the trail's meander all the way up to a flat rock near the hill's crest, where she sniffs and circles the rock several times before moving on. Perhaps this is where the young woman sat for a time to rest or enjoy the view, before hiking to the curve around the top of the hill.

K9 trailing is most often seen on a long line, a stretch of lead twenty to thirty feet in length, the dog ahead and the handler behind. A long line enables the handler to keep connected to the swiftly moving dog, whose eagerness could outpace his partner's. But there are exceptions. Puzzle and I learned to trail on a long line. We still trail on long lines at night and in urban situations, where the line may keep her safer, serving as an important tether between us near traffic and passersby. But in wilderness the long line can make the search a lot harder, especially on hills like this one, where even the crude walking trails are edged with overgrown brush and thorny mesquite. Long lines behind a fast dog can get tangled and tangled and tangled again, and handlers must learn how to negotiate the brush and the pauses, untangling quickly. Some dogs do all their trailing on long lines. Frustrated by such delays, Puzzle early showed me that she could trail offline, working her way ahead at a steady pace and from time to time pausing to turn her head and check in with me, making eye contact before moving on.

Puzzle is offline today. Now she crests the hill and makes that check-in, waiting a beat for me to get a little closer before she is over the crest to make her way down.

"How did you teach her to do that?" a trainee running with us asks. "How did you teach her to stop and look back for you?"

I didn't teach her to do that. It was something Puzzle just gave me when she was about six years old. No longer the headstrong puppy, she seemed to understand that we had to collaborate at this. Even without that thirty-foot line, she keeps us connected. This search is no exception.

She must be close to the volunteer victim. I can see Puzzle's signa-

ture tail swoosh and the quickening that suggests she's getting closer to the hottest point of scent. The golden skips past a final distraction, a volunteer whistling his way down the trail with a fishing pole. Then she drops her nose low, snakes into the tall grass, and backs out of it again to rise up on her back legs and make eye contact with me, the first stage of her alert. Point made, Puzzle belly-crawls her way back to the woman. It is the gentlest approach, the happy dog's tail wagging so hard it makes the valley grass whisper, *shush-shush-shush-shush*.

Ace, dashing across the grass, is also showing me something, but I'm not yet sure how to read him. I wonder what Puzzle makes of his early efforts at search. Dog-to-dog, perhaps she reads him better than I do at this early stage. She is wagging at the window as she follows Ace's progress across the yard. Every so often Puzzle puts her paws up to the windowsill, and I can see the tail fluff waving behind her head.

As with SAR, lost-pet K9s can serve in different search disciplines. As with SAR, there is a long journey from a puppy who enjoys nose work to the mature, reliable dog who can meet the challenge of search again and again. Ace is not a puppy, and he brings a more mature, grounded quality to the search games I've introduced. He seems to enjoy any activity that challenges his brain and his nose. Today Ace isn't trailing the path of a traveling animal. Instead he is nose-up to snag scent that is airborne, working a small area search.

Ace is questing a fat tuft of tabby-cat fur that is somewhere in this small square of land. He has made some investigative sweeps across the space and has shown some excitement at the garden, but he has not yet narrowed to the spot where the fur is tucked deep in Turk's cap, which has just begun to leaf out. In this environment, rich with the scent of dogs he knows well, I want to see if he can ignore all of it and focus on the kitty stranger's scent instead. SAR dogs are trained to find humans and proofed against finding animals. I hope to train Ace to search specifically for cat or dog, on cue.

Puzzle watches Ace intently, in a way she never watches a dog just ambling in the backyard. Her sunny face beams through the window down at us. Content with her own search games, she can hear other dogs cued to *find* and watch those dogs search without ramping up in frustrated anticipation. This morning's training has been area searching for all the dogs. Puzzle has made her own searches, and she's watched Gambit's hard runs and now Ace's busy intensity.

Though area search and trailing press for the same outcome—to find what the dog is trained to find—they have different functions and answer different needs. Area search is used in a geographic area where search subjects may or may not be—the kind of search that might be used, for example, in disaster-torn places that could have many victims or none. These searches are generally not scent-specific. The dog is charged to find any source of the target scent. All humans in an area, all dogs in an area, all of a given endangered species in an area—whatever the target scent is. Area searches may be for the living or the dead. The area search discipline can be an important one for MAR. Perhaps a pregnant indoor-outdoor cat has slipped from the house and birthed her kittens somewhere outside. A search K9 working an area could quickly clear the spaces the cat did not choose and alert to the space where the huddle of kittens lies.

I remember reading about an area search for a missing horse a few years ago. The senior horse was not a jumper and the fences and gates surrounding his pasture were all intact, but the animal seemed to have vanished from the place he had known and wandered all his life. Friends and family had walked the area. A small plane with a spotter had been deployed, without luck. A search dog and its partner had better success with an area search. Somehow a section of the pasture had formed a small sinkhole that had given way beneath the weight of the horse, who fell into the hole, maybe fifteen feet or so down. Soft earth had tumbled down after him, and brushy scrub had concealed the hole and the horse even from the low-flying airplane. The horse, only slightly injured, was trapped there for days before the search dog scented the animal's living presence and alerted to the spot where scent rose. The search ended in a remarkable save. Area searches like these can be particularly useful for missing cats (and some dogs), which are inclined to hide. Remains detection—that is, searching for the scent of the deceased—is also done by area search and is, sadly, important to lost-pet search as well.

While trailing is an easy concept to visualize—the search dog on a long line, pulling the handler along a scent trail someone has made—area search can be more difficult to imagine. Picture an acre from a satellite view. The top side of the acre is the north side of it. The left side of the acre is the western border; the right side of the acre is the eastern edge. The wind is coming from the south, blowing across the southern border into that acre. That south wind will carry scent northward, and the search dog and handler begin their search along the northernmost side of the acre, opposite the direction the wind blows from. If the desired scent is in this acre, that south wind will blow across the scent's source, carry the scent northward, fan it out, and make it possible for a dog to snag that scent from a distance. So dog and handler must sweep east and west back and forth across the land, gradually moving from the north border southward across that acre, determining whether the desired scent is or is not there. The team's goal is to make the find or clear the area.

When a search dog picks up the desired scent on any sweep, his body will make a change, a stage of the search called *interest*. Puzzle makes a signature head pop when she first snags scent. I know another search dog whose hackles fluff, making a stripe of sticky-uppy fur all the way down his back. Each dog is different. After a dog has indicated interest, it will turn its nose toward the scent and begin to work what is called the *scent cone*—attempting to move from an area of faint scent to scent that's strong, stronger, strongest. The cone is wider and fainter the farther away it is from the subject, tighter and stronger the closer the dog moves toward the scent. In this example, the dog will likely be working north to south. He continues to sweep, but now he is moving in increasingly smaller sweeps as the cone narrows. His body changes, too, at this stage, called *indication*. There is often a gait change, perhaps a postural change, a different expression or tail carriage. At the end of the cone is the scent source—the missing person, the stranded pet, the dropped weapon, the wounded wildlife, whatever the dog has been trained to find. The dog alerts the find with a bark, a sit, or some other consistent signal. The area-search premise seems simple, but every search condition is unique, and every dog is an individual that works the scent and communicates what it's finding in a different way.

Golden retriever Gambit, my young SAR dog in training, I jokingly call the love child of a racehorse and a cannonball. High-energy, muscular Gambit is Puzzle's close relative, but he's not a trailing dog at this point. He may never be. Gambit loves area search over all other things. He would take this hypothetical acre search at a gallop, making wide sweeps back and forth across it, perpendicular to the wind. We've been working on a more measured pace, because Gambit might blow through a scent cone at this top speed and be forced to wheel around and come back from a fair distance to pick it up again. Not a problem once, but on a long search night with multiple sectors, he could wear himself out. Puzzle is less voracious and more immediately precise. When working an area search like this one, she leaps from the *find* cue into a canter that slows to a trot. She sweeps at a steady pace that is slower than Gambit's. But Puzzle rarely blows through the scent cone and has to turn back. She has always worked smaller, more narrow sweeps—fine embroidery to Gambit's saddle stitches.

He does not share her breed or her background, but Ace, a dog of short legs and low clearance, searches nevertheless, more like Puzzle than Gambit.

Even a half acre is a fair-sized search area for a little dog. For Ace today I have carved the space up into smaller squares, like a sheet cake. We clear one square and then move on to the next and the next. No cat fur here, no cat fur there, no cat fur here either. Ace has trotted steadily through the first three small areas, but now the fourth, which includes the garden, has snagged his interest. He begins worrying at the space in circles and tight sweeps, making an erratic passage, because when Ace gets excited, he travels sideways, his butt yawing forward as though it's in a race with his head. Following that movement, interpreting his meaning through Ace's crazy every-which-way fur, is a little like partnering a crab in a fright wig. Maybe in time we can forge a common language. Right now all I know is he's snagged the scent, which, rising from the vegetation, seems to be more scent cloud than scent cone.

I know where the scent sample is, but he does not—yet. This is where I can see how long Ace will stay interested and how quickly he tires of what is, to him, a game. Scrabbling through the spring growth, he clambers awkwardly over the stumps of plants still dormant. Then he puts his nose to the Turk's cap and frisks when he finds the cat fur, a straight-up bounce on his front feet. It is a happy alert and an electric one, as though he's snorted a nose full of bees.

As Puzzle nears her twelfth birthday and retirement, a few friends ask if I'll retrain her to search for lost pets, too. Most of them know Puz has a gift as a magnet dog, and for her to actually search for them, in their minds, is a natural sidestep. Why wouldn't I train her, at least for a time, to find lost pets? Friendly to dogs and cats and a proven trailing dog for humans, Puzzle could have a lot to offer. I'm grateful for their faith in my sunny partner. And of course I could be tempted for selfish and unselfish reasons. I know the good this dog is capable of, the light I see in her when she works. And I dread the day when Puzzle and I no longer deploy as a team.

But this is also true: K9 lost-pet search is no easier than the search for missing persons. The terrain is as difficult, the weather as temperamental; the missing souls are usually smaller, and here we're even more likely to have a frightened, resistant subject or one on the move. MAR dogs have to have just as much hustle as SAR dogs. To my mind, done ethically, MAR K9 work demands a dog just as physically capable as a SAR dog.

And I must think of my golden, who has almost twelve years of being proofed against finding animals. Why frustrate and confuse her this late in her career? No, when her bum shoulder and achy hips draw her time as a search dog to a close, Puz can be a sweet magnet dog for other dogs when the occasion arises, and we will contribute to some scent-work research that does not demand hours across concrete and vertical leaps that land hard.

And so it is the little found dog out of Conroe who might carry this torch. While search dogs aren't needed for every lost-pet search (as they aren't needed for every missing-person search), a trained, tested dog could be a real help on some of those early mornings at seven when a beagle puppy has learned she can squeeze beneath a fence at six. A trailing K9 can tell searchers which way a dog has traveled. An area-search K9 is better suited for situations in which multiple animals are missing or when an animal may be trapped in one place. Logging Ace's scent work across the neighborhood, I hope that he is a candidate for either service, but we will be months in trial training before we know.

Ace is a finder, and in some ways a gatherer, too. I'd almost think he had some sheepdog in him, the way he monitors us all. Watchful and acute, he reminds me of the collies and shepherds I've known. I remember one SAR K9, a wonderful collie, who would position himself in central, strategic places in hotel rooms that groups of us shared at the end of a search day. Any time one of us moved, that collie's head raised and he would roll up onto his chest, assessing. He would move if we did, positioning himself to see all of us and the door, as if we were his to protect. Ace lacks that collie's magnificent profile, but he shares the same vigilance. He is quick to wake, aware of every movement in the house, and he seems to keep tabs on all the animals—this cat in that room, these two dogs curled up together over there. He walks into a room and with a sniff or a glance takes inventory. When an animal or a human leaves the room for another space, he raises his head and notes it.

Ace is devoted to Puzzle. The golden retriever and the Maltese are an odd couple in many ways, and it's amusing to watch them together, the silky, self-possessed senior golden with a fusty-faced, always slightly unkempt mop of a dog spinning in her trail. I'm glad to see the bond between them, not only for Ace's sake but for Puzzle, too. Puz has recently seemed remote from time to time, a little withdrawn in ways I can't reach. I've been concerned, even though her senior wellness exams have shown her to be healthy. The search-team vet is glad to see her trim figure and happy bounce across the grass. Unpredictable and intermittent, perhaps this subdued thoughtfulness is part of the aging golden in her off hours. Whatever is going on, Ace rouses her with his teasing and his chatter. Puzzle is deeply patient. Sometimes she seems amused. She will flatten his play bows with a good-natured paw and hold him down for a motherly scrub across his face, the price of her attention.

Ace has taken his place in the pack of big dogs with a cheerful confidence that they want him there. It is not the life he once had, but it's the new life he's claimed, and I am glad to see him brighten. Puzzle is too fond of him, and Jake and Gambit too bemused by his certainty, to protest that he's taken some of their nap space. He has weaseled in among them, sleeping where they sleep, barking at the same passersby, and because they now all have jobs they train for daily, Ace is a part of that action, too.

A memento from the dog
that saved my mother.

21

THE DOG IN QUESTION

I T WAS THE WORST TIME to find a lost dog, my mother said when
she called me. She hated to bother. She knew I had to go to work.
But she wasn't sure of my schedule, and she thought I might have
some coming days off. There was this dog she kept seeing near the
hospital where she worked, and he was skittish as hell, but he kept
coming back. She was worried because he was looking skinnier and
now, at the end of a midwinter ice storm, awfully cold, too. She'd been
trying to get food to him. She'd been tossing him extra hamburgers
while she sat in the parking lot and ate her own. He recognized her
now, and she could win the dog's trust, but his condition was deteriorating faster than his acceptance improved.

"Can you help?" Mom asked. "It won't take ten minutes."

It never did. We both knew a skittish stray could take hours or
days. I lived fifty miles away from where she worked by that time, but
I think Mom was sure of me, and she was right. Of course I would
come. My mother was not yet retired but no longer young. I hated the
thought of her lingering in dark parking lots at the end of her three-to-
eleven shifts and worried about that same lingering at dawn after the
eleven-to-sevens, when she was tired and groggy and had a ninety-
minute drive home. And I knew she'd persist until she brought this
dog in or something else happened.

On a Monday night after work I headed out to where she was,
slip lead and beef jerky in hand. There was plenty of time to think during the long drive to a hospital well south of town. As our relation-

ship was clouded and too often strained, it had been awhile since we'd rescued an animal together—an albino kitten up a tree by the lake near her house, I remembered, just after my divorce. February 1993. I recalled the tiny pinkish creature, her claws barely able to retract, dazzled by the sunlight on water and, it seemed, deaf. And I remembered Mom waving her infallible can of tuna while I shimmied up the tree to teach that kitten how to back down. No need to teach her. As soon as I got a hand on her, the little cat clung to me. We came down together, her claws digging into my neck and her baby squall loud in my ear. Mom loved her on sight. She planned to keep that fairylike, half-blind and deaf kitten. She named her Valentine and bought her a little pink collar and a bed. Then she saw a LOST flyer in a grocery store and took Valentine back to her original home, where a young father with two little girls cried. *The little love letter from God,* Mom described Valentine afterward.

Mom had since brought in other cats without my help—pregnant females who gave birth in the bathtub and battle-scarred, spitting tomcats she deftly spun up into towels to get to the vet for neutering. She was a one-woman trap, neuter, release outfit, without the release. Indoors or out, she maintained every cat she found. Mom's file folder at the vet clinic was fat with names. Feather: a white cat with a gray blaze like an ostrich feather across her forehead. Little Black Kitty: a very small black tomcat with delusions of grandeur who took on—and bested—every stray dog that tried to take him out. Cinder, a beautiful gray cat with a water obsession who drank from cupped paws at the sink and loved to chase streams from the hose. Dozens of others across time. She was no cat hoarder, but she lived right on the edge of it—eight at one time, then ten, then twelve. Mom brought them all in, comforted and wrestled and was owned by them, sacrificing time and money, often giving them care she denied herself. While her compassion extended to all animals, she always understood cats best, respecting their independence and introspection.

Mom had not rescued a loose dog nor lived with a recovered one, that I knew of, since Hercules, who had left the apartment with Bob as abruptly as he'd gone into it more than twenty years before. This dog at the hospital must have thrown a long shadow for her to notice him on her way into and out of work. Her description is muddied by the poor light in which she sees him and her eyesight, blurred by growing cataracts she takes pains to deny.

I got to the hospital just as she was supposed to come off shift. I was surprised to find her in her gray Ford truck when I parked next to it. She had the engine on and her coat draped over her and was half asleep, sitting with her head tilted back. She didn't stir when I pulled up in my car or when the door clunked after I got out of it. Even in the dim light I could see that the truck's interior was strewn, from the floorboard across the seats, with hamburger wrappers and what looked like open mail.

"Mom," I said at her window, not wanting to startle her with a knock, and up from the floorboards beside her boiled a dog, frightened and furious, his forepaws on the front seat and his bark loud in her ear. Mom jumped awake, shouting an oath. She recoiled for a moment and then shook off the scare.

Holding up a hand as though to silence the dog, she turned to look directly at me without recognition. Two beats, three, before she squinted through the window and said, "Susie?" as though she still wasn't sure. The dog wasn't sure either, roaring across the seat right beside her with such force that he bounced hard against her right side. I saw her wince as her coat fell away, and then I saw the cast on her arm. My sixty-three-year-old mother had brought in a stray dog on the back end of an ice storm with her right arm in a cast, an injury she hadn't told me about.

"Bunny," she said to him. "Bunny, sshh-shhh-shh." She had already named him, this oddly bearded dog that raged like a caged lion and looked like an underfed mountain goat. He was a right mix:

golden retriever, maybe, mixed with some sort of curly terrier some-thing and maybe Australian shepherd. It was difficult to tell in the shadows, his body poised to jump again at the window, the white rims of his eyes showing on his wary face. I could hear his faint, con-tinuing growl.

With her good left arm, Mom rolled down the window slightly, releasing the funk of hamburger grease, stale cigarette smoke, and damp, dirty dog. She caught me up pretty quickly. She had broken her arm a week ago — slipped on the ice — and had been out on medical leave since then. But she couldn't stop worrying about the dog she'd been trying to befriend before she got hurt, so she drove out here with hamburgers late at night or early in the mornings, the times she regularly saw him. He had come to expect her, she said. She said he was so glad to see her after she'd been gone for a couple of days that she almost cried. At first she didn't see him anywhere, and then he heard her truck and came bounding across the field to the curbside, his head up and his tail waving slightly, as if he were asking, was it really her? When she got out of the truck to throw him a hamburger, it was tough with only one good hand, and she said he backed away a little, uncertain about her changed appearance and her clumsiness. But he took the burger. He figured it out and he took it, and every day he came closer, and then tonight he came wagging up and got right in the truck.

"Bunny," I said, because this dog still stared at me, growl ticking, stiff with dislike.

"He was chasing rabbits first time I saw him." Mom shrugged. She reached for her pack of cigarettes with the Bic lighter tucked tight into the cellophane, expert already at tapping a smoke free and light-ing it with one hand. The dog watched curiously, wrinkling his nose at the brief scent of lighter fluid.

"And now . . . what?" I sidestepped as Mom exhaled out the win-dow.

Mom looked at the dog. "I need to get him home and then tomorrow to the vet. You see how it is," she said. "He's okay with me, but I think he'll run from everyone else."

"He doesn't like strangers." The dog had ceased growling, but I saw him stiffen with every move I made outside the truck's window.

"He's just scared. Say Bunny! Bunneeeeeey-Bunny-Bunny-boy-eeee!" The dog's ears came up and he grinned at her. "Say it just like that," Mom said. "Bunnneeeey—"

I cleared my throat. "Bunneeeeeee," I croaked.

"Bunny, Buneeeeeeey," my mother corrected.

I mimicked: "Bunny! Bunneeeeeeey-Bunny-Bunny . . ."

". . . Boyeeee." Mom joined the big finish.

The dog tilted his head, confused by the twin howl of us. *Two of them.* He furrowed his brow. *What the hell?*

Bunny was a nicer dog than he seemed.

No chip, the vet told my mother, but he wasn't surprised. Micro-chips hadn't really made it to that part of town yet. Cruising one-armed in her truck, Mom made the rounds of grocery stores and checked shelters and the newspaper classifieds, but no one had reported a lost dog that looked anything like this one and no one responded to the flyers she had made at a print shop. She was conflicted, not re-ally wanting or needing a dog, but she was already fond of Bunny. He snuggled against her at just the right times, she said. He gave her kisses while the cats stayed aloof.

But she was beginning to be overwhelmed. A few days of kind-ness had brought a shift in the young dog, his cold fearfulness already replaced by something more like his true nature. Caution gave way to friendly curiosity, and then, within days, Bunny became buoyant, inclined to jump on friends he had accepted in greeting. He was a lot of dog for my mother, whose cast had another month left on it, and he was a lot of dog for her cats, who were appalled by his size and smell and speed. He was like them in some ways, leaping onto couch backs and scattering tablescapes, making everyday objects into toys. After tearing up a six-pack of toilet paper, he shredded it across every room of the house. Mom found him headfirst down a bag of cat food on the kitchen counter, a row of cat eyes glittering up at him from beneath a bookcase in the adjoining room.

The cats hated that dog. He ate their food, plundered their litter boxes, and chased them, unprovoked. He disrupted their entire existence. Some of the outdoor cats decamped. All of the indoor ones now spent most of their time in hiding. Mom called me to brainstorm about it. Determined to keep the peace, we made a sort of suite for the cats in her master bedroom and bath. She had stopped sleeping back there by then, the sunlight from its bay window too bright for her day-sleeping ways. She had begun to sleep in the darker living room on the couch. The cats could have the master bedroom and welcome to it, she said. She and Bunny would live everywhere else. Mom regretted that this new isolation would keep the cats from her. We planned on buying her a recliner, where she could daily sit with them and read.

Bunny had lived with my mother for just a few weeks when, late one night, a man kicked open her back door and stepped into the house. Mom was sleeping on the living room couch about twenty feet away. She jumped awake with the first crash of the door frame, rolled over, and saw him outlined by her back porch light—a big man with a reddish burr haircut. She tried to rise but couldn't, her cast tangled up in her nightgown. Bunny was nimble where she was not. The dog leaped from her side and charged the man, hitting him at chest level and catching the man's upper arm with such force that he fell backward over stacked bags of kitty litter and writhed on the ground as the dog took purchase on his upper arm and shook it.

"Get the hell out of here!" my mother screamed at the intruder.

"Okay!" shouted the man, now scrabbling on all fours, his voice breaking. "Jesus, lady, Jesus. Call off your dog."

Somehow he got out of there, closing the shattered door behind him. Bunny, the part-lion goat dog, returned to my mother's side. Mom later said she found a bloody trail leading across her patio into the backyard. Drips, not puddles, she described, a nurse used to looking at blood fall. One-armed, she hosed down the patio the next morning and brought in a contractor to replace the back door with a steel one and install new, heavy locks.

It would be weeks before she told me about this misadventure, and even then it was mostly to celebrate heroic Bunny. When I encouraged her to truly consider selling the house and moving closer to me, Mom said no, with an oath—the first in a chain of refusals that would span another broken arm, open-heart surgery, and two bouts of cancer. My fierce mother remembered the loss of her own mother. My grandmother had died shortly after Mom moved Nannie in with her. Uprooted from her hometown and miserable, she'd diminished quickly. Mom never got over the misplaced guilt she carried, even while doing her best for fragile Nannie, and she was convinced that the light went out on my grandmother when she was forced to move.

"Sus, I'm safer here than anywhere," Mom said gently. "I know every corner of this town." She loved the long drive home over bridges, the sun on the lake, and the sound of passing trains. "Besides," she said, "bet word got around that the crazy old lady has a kickass dog."

Bunny had a plaid collar, an engraved tag, and a microchip by the time one of my mother's fellow nurses called. The woman worked a different shift and saw Mom rarely, but she'd seen the flyer about a lost dog in the breakroom and later the same flyer in the grocery store, and she called Mom's number, because she was pretty sure she'd found the owner of the dog. Owned by a retired couple, if Bunny was the same dog, he'd come to the hospital in the backseat of the family car when the wife had come to retrieve her husband from outpatient care in late October. The woman had put her husband in the car and, unthinking, opened the back door to put in his walker. The dog bolted out of the car. Excitable, untrained, and very fast, he ignored her calls or failed to hear them. He was gone from sight quickly. He did not come back. The couple was heartbroken. Despite the husband's frailty, they'd driven through neighborhoods and come back to the hospital every day for several weeks. By Christmastime, with no sign of their dog, they'd given up.

My mother's colleague said she'd just overheard the two telling the story to another patient. "Anyway . . ." The woman stopped. Mom said the nurse let the story dangle with the longest pause. It was a cue where Mom could cut in and say the description was off or the time-line was wrong or otherwise sidestep giving up the dog she'd taken in. And Mom said it was a hole she almost fell into. She loved Bunny. She was already deeply attached. She'd grown accustomed to the smile and the wag through the window when she rounded the corner, the thump of his paws against the door to the garage when the truck pulled inside. She was grateful for the laughter he brought her, *haha-hagoddamnit*, as he reconfigured the house.

"Give me their number," Mom said. She later told me her fingers went numb pushing the buttons on the telephone, it hurt so much. She had never expected to have a dog so late in life. She made the call and transferred the microchip, and Bunny returned to his life as Rowdy, a shelter puppy the couple had adopted after the soldier husband had come home injured from the Gulf War.

Mom didn't mention him again for a long time, and then it was only through the haze of anesthesia after heart surgery. "I had a dog once. Bet you didn't know that," she said to me from the gurney. "I still have his collar on the knob of the back door."

Dogs test their boundaries.

22

GOOD FENCES

WE UNDERESTIMATE DOGS. I say we, because I'm no less guilty of it than anyone else sometimes. A new rescue dog stretches up and grabs my toast off the kitchen counter, and the next day I push the toast back a little farther, hoping to dissuade him, rather than acknowledging straight up that the dog learned something when he got that first slice of rye bread with Parmesan, and it was a tasty something, and now he knows counter surfing comes with reward. I can push the toast all the way to the backsplash, but he's got goals, this dog, he has tasted heaven, and he can smell the cheese. Even if he has to work a little harder, he will find a way to bag that toast. And he'll be reinforced when he gets it, again.

The same is true when a dog conquers fences and gates. A dog that learns it can dig under a weathered wooden fence or flip the latch on a chain-link gate has learned something, and it is no good putting the dog back in that same situation without any kind of change to the structures. I think of Bella, the lost beagle mix in Conroe, whose family could never get ahead of her digging, but the father admitted he should have installed the chicken wire he'd bought for the bottom of the fence and never did. *I thought he wouldn't do it a second time* is a phrase I hear often from searching owners, who didn't make improvements to the fence or put a lock on the gate after the first time. These things lost dogs have taught me: they will do it a second time, and a third, and a fourth. Make your fix quickly and make it substantial, because if there's a weakness an escaping dog can exploit, it will.

This last point is brought home to me by a spindly tan Chihua-hua. Coming back from breakfast at a local restaurant, I spot the little dog aimlessly crisscrossing a busy street. High-strung and nervous, she is wary of me when I get out of the car. She begins to move away just at the sight of me, even though I am not approaching her at all. But I can see she's uneasy with the direction she travels. She pauses on the sidewalk and looks back at me, steps forward and looks back at me again. She doesn't really want to go the way she was headed. If we give them a chance, loose dogs will often show us where they live. I get the sense that if I move from where I stand, she'll turn around and come back the other way. So I move across the street, carrying a take-home box of hash browns from breakfast, and I sit on the grass and pretend to eat. This is Puzzle's nonchalance translated to human actions: *I am not interested in you, dog. I am all about the hash browns.*

The dog seems relieved that she can head south rather than north. She is also interested in the hash browns. I watch her little nose bob now and then with the pleasure of their smell. I can see she has on a collar and tags, and I hope she might trust me and get close enough that I can at least see a phone number. Two big spotted dogs bay across the street. One is behind a fence, the other chained outside it. They aren't unfriendly, but they are interested in barking at the Chihuahua, and they are interested in the hash browns, too.

The Chihuahua creeps closer to me on knobby, arthritic little legs. Every few steps she pauses. In my periphery I can see her with one forepaw raised, poised for flight. We will be ten minutes together on that grass while her desire for hash browns overcomes her timidity. She finally takes some from my extended hand, and then another bite and another, but when I twitch a forefinger to turn over her tag, she screams as though she is being tortured, porpoises up from the grass, and dashes straight into the path of the two big dogs roaring from the fence.

"No!" I react a split second before I realize she is running toward them because she knows them. Both dogs are more interested in me than in her. Then I see a gap between the chain-link fence and the back porch it borders. The winter ground has shifted, separating the side of the house and the fence post into a V. No big dog could get out of that, but it is the perfect escape size for a Chihuahua. She must have shimmied through that spot before, too, because someone has stuck a tennis shoe in the gap, trying to plug the hole. The Chihuahua is still screaming as she runs for the hole and the safety of her yard. She scales the tennis-shoe blockade like a ninja at the same moment her family—two boys and their mother—come out. They have heard their little dog screaming. They see me with a handful of hash browns at the edge of their yard.

Yes, she is their dog, they say, when I tell them I found her in the middle of the busiest street on the block, that I was trying to see the owner contact on her tag. I hope they believe me, because I suppose it could look awfully like this stranger with a food lure was trying to steal their Chihuahua. But they are good-natured and unsuspicious. And she is a little reprobate. They laugh and shake their heads. "She got out again!" says one of them. The other one adds, "She gets out all the time." And then he adds proudly, "That's my shoe."

I mention that she's learned how to work the shoe now and that they'll need something else to keep her safe. It is my mother's move, telling neighbors what they need to do, but I don't want to find this old girl dead on the side of the road. This family takes no offense. The woman cradles the Chihuahua and assures me that they've got something in mind. As I'm leaving, I turn around, and the woman waves the dog's little paw at me. I hope her fix will be substantial. This dog is intelligent and ambitious and not streetwise at all.

I pass that house again not long afterward. The woman meant what she said. Both chain-link and shoe have been replaced by a beautiful six-foot privacy fence. I imagine those big dogs and that scrappy little senior on the other side of it. The big dogs are quavering and slavering at the universe, but I can picture the Chihuahua's sly form on the grass, considering the fence, looking up.

A hot Saturday morning, May's humidity meeting the promise of a scorching June, and local drivers seem angry about it, pushing residential speed limits, tailgating, taking corners so tightly I hear the squeal of rubber on curbs. If I didn't have errands to run, I wouldn't be out here on these border streets that divide quiet neighborhoods from strip malls and the freeway. Today, folks on the road seem to think they're on the highway blocks before they get there. I see a runner wisely step off the road and chug across sloping lawn borders, preferring, I guess, the risk of sprained ankles to getting flattened by a car.

This is no place for a lost dog, but when I turn a corner toward the post office, I see one — a pretty sand-colored cocker spaniel in the middle of a four-lane road. She is turning every which way, bewildered by the noise and proximity of passing cars, some of which honk and none of which are slowing down at all. Another lost dog with no street skills. Every close call makes her recoil into the opposite line of traffic, and from where I am, a half-block away, I can see her panic rising. She wheels blindly from a motorcycle and steps right into the path of an approaching car, which narrowly misses her, gives a long blat of the horn, and does not stop.

Chasing her in a car is the last thing that will help this cocker spaniel, so I pull over and get out of mine, perhaps fifty yards away. All the recent behavior study has coached me on the range of a frightened dog's responses, and I can tell that this one, obviously somebody's pet, has reached the point of blind reaction. She's doing all the wrong things, ping-ponging across lanes rather than running for quiet stretches of neighborhood grass. I've also learned that approaching or calling a dog in that mindset can be fatal. I think of my father's call across a rain-swept parking lot: *Don't move. He's still able to run.* It's hard to resist reaching out to her, but I know it's better to attract the stray dog to you if possible. Since that dramatic little Chihuahua, I've brought in a handful of lost dogs by seeming to ignore them. Again I flop down on the grass casually and pretend to eat something. I can see the cocker spaniel from the corner of my eye, and I can tell I have her attention, but I don't look toward her at all, smacking my mouth over imaginary corn chips.

It works. I can see her thinking shift and her erratic behavior stop. Focused on me now, she leaves the street for the sidewalk, then watches me from the opposite edge of the church lawn where I'm sitting. Crunching and smacking, I continue to ignore her until she's crept well away from the busy street she just escaped. I don't want to turn my head and send her skittering back into it. She comes closer, moving into my sightline—a beautiful, well-groomed cocker spaniel with a collar and tags on, obviously lost and unfamiliar with the neighborhood. It is tough not to look directly at her. Gregarious dogs might respond to direct eye contact, but frightened ones can read even good intention as an aggressor's cold stare, so I keep my eyes lowered and, along with the smacking, absently make the kind of kissy/smooching sound many owners use to call their dogs.

Including this dog's owner, apparently. The spaniel's demeanor completely changes at the sound, as though at last something seems familiar. She trots hesitantly toward me, creeping low as she gets closer, almost belly-crawling to me for the last few feet, trembling, tail stub wagging. She has been overwhelmed by this freedom. She is all regret and petition for comfort. Not sand-colored at all—recently groomed and coat trimmed down, she is white with tan spots. She nuzzles into my hand and accepts a stroke over her head, which gives me the chance to gently hook fingers under her collar. I have her.

I must have been holding my breath, because I exhale in relief, and she sighs, too, beaming up at me. We are fast friends now. Without letting go of her collar, I stroke her pretty head and down her back, massaging her shoulders and hips and finding the scratching places she likes best. She is very clean. She has not been out long. JOSIE, her tag reads. There is a vet clinic tag, too, but it's from several towns away.

Josie seems glad to let someone else make her choices. She doesn't protest when I lift her up to carry her to the car. She's comfortable in vehicles, too, settling down on the seat while I put a leash on her and at last give her the treat I'd been faking on the grass. I'll take her to my house for rest and water and then get to the business of finding her owner. It's not a long trip. I live less than a mile away from the place where Josie had been wandering. Unfazed by the bark, yap, and squeak of the home dogs, she settles into my bedroom—a strong little dog, surprisingly athletic, who leaps easily from the floor to my high bed, where she curls up as if she owns it.

I want to move quickly for her. For her owner, too. The temperature is no kind of heat for someone searching on foot, and there's something about Josie's ways that remind me a bit of Ace, an etiquette from an earlier day, as though she lives with someone older. One phone number on Josie's tag is out of service. The other rolls to a featureless voicemail.

The receptionist at the vet clinic confirms she knows Josie, and while she can confirm the last name I have from the voicemail, she's sorry, very sorry, but for security and privacy reasons she is not able to give out any address information at all. The vet clinic isn't close, so I wonder if Josie is visiting this weekend, or has she moved or found a new home—or escaped after a theft? The receptionist's voice is regretful. She knows I'm trying hard for this dog. What she can tell me is that the dog was last in the clinic six weeks ago, brought by the owner and the owner's son. As far as she knows, Josie still belongs to the same person. Then she whispers, very low, that the address they have for Josie is not in the city where she was found. She promises to call the microchip company to see if it has a record of change and to let me know if it does.

A last name, a dead phone number, and another number that could belong to anybody. It's time to turn to the Internet. I post about

Josie on our neighborhood social media page, asking if anyone recognizes the dog or her owner's last name. While I wait for neighbors to see the post and possibly respond, I begin digging online to see if I can get a match of name and phone number to an address or any kind of useful lead. Josie is undisturbed by all of it. She's having a pretty good time with a house shoe she found, flipping it and nudging it across the hardwood, then leaping back onto the bed to lie with it, gazing proudly at me.

I have searched online for less than five minutes when the neighborhood app lights up with a response. No one has recognized Josie so far, but a neighbor found someone with her owner's last name on the tax appraisal rolls, and from that she got a street address—four blocks from where Josie had wandered into the road. The tax appraisal rolls! I never would have thought of that. Our neighbor's lead is too good to pass up. I leash pretty Josie and load her back into the car. She's a compliant creature: cheerful, eager, interested in everything. Like Ace, she seems completely confident in the car. Also like Ace, she prefers to sit in the passenger's seat.

We are a few blocks away from the house in question when the phone rings. The man on the other end of the line knows Josie. She escaped from his house.

When we arrive, the dog pummels the car door with the force of her wiggling. She leaps from my car into the yard, on the end of my lead, strutting and circling and wagging up at the man, who scratches his head, bemused. He is surprised by her escape. Not that kind of dog, he would have thought. Josie is his mother's dog, and something of a stranger. His mother recently moved here to live with him and his family. The dog is kind of a featherbrain who has never tried to leave the yard before, and this morning he had let her out in the fenced backyard as usual. But he had recently found a hole in the fence that he had blocked with a bag of topsoil. This morning he'd been working in the yard, used the bag of topsoil, and forgotten to block the hole again. He is surprised that Josie found that hole so quickly and that she'd even try to slip out of it. He'd nearly not blocked it in the first place, because she was so not that kind of dog. But maybe she was. Clearly she was that kind of dog, because she'd been found . . . where?

When I tell him, the man goes a little pale beneath his tan. He knows that road. He knows how dangerous that road is on a Saturday.

"Well, thank you," he says, as he gestures for Josie to come to him. "Losing this dog would have wrecked my mother." He shakes his head, looking down at the wavy-coated dog as if she were a sunny, clueless little alien he could never take for granted again.

Some reunions leave me a little breathless, they are so completely co-incidental. One Saturday evening I have come in from working the dogs and am sitting with my feet up, Ace stretched across my shins, when I decide to randomly scan the Dallas-area lost-and-found pet pages on Facebook. It is my mother's service to animals and their owners, and I think of her as I scan the postings. I can't always do this. In north Texas alone there are many lost-pet pages, reflecting regions, counties, cities, and individual neighborhoods. Catching up on even one day's worth of posts on all of them could take hours. I check the pages for my area most often, but for some reason this night I scan more widely and come across a post from a young woman in Grand Prairie, five cities away across the DFW metroplex. She has lost a shih tzu and has been searching hard, posting widely about her on social media and lost-dog websites, with no luck. Today, however, some-one in the town where I live has contacted her. That person found a pretty, bewildered shih tzu beside a busy highway, and she wonders if it might be the lost dog of the woman five cities away.

It is not her dog, but the compassionate Grand Prairie woman posts the picture on the Dallas-area lost-and-found page anyway, hoping perhaps that someone else looking for their shih tzu will rec-ognize and claim her. I don't recognize the found dog either, but the photo shows her clean and bright—in great shape. She hasn't been lost long. I'm betting the shih tzu was lost locally. I live less than a mile away from the place where she was found. Copying the finder's photo of the dog from the Facebook post, I turn to our local Next-Door group to see if someone nearby is missing the dog. Within an hour I get a response:

OH PLEASE! PLEASE! CALL THIS NUMBER _____.
MY NAME IS _____ AND WE LOST OUR SHUTZU [sic]
THURSDAY NIGHT. HER NAME IS CHLOE PLEASE CALL
I AM AT THE PSA AT MY SONS BASKETBALL GAME
PLEASE.

A second post underscores the urgency: *That's my baby please call me. [phone number]*

And a third: *She got away on Thursday night, please please call. She will definitely be put on a leash from now on. We miss her so much!*

And a fourth from the owner's mother, who adds, *I have been looking everywhere for her dog! If you can please contact her at [phone number]. We have proof of ownership.*

The dog, who had never wandered before, had slipped away during an off-leash outing in front of their home. This is another thing the search for lost dogs has taught me: they don't wander until they do. Or as a fellow trainer says to her clients, *Your dog hasn't wandered . . . yet.*

I message the Grand Prairie woman. She is cautious, and appropriately so. A beautiful dog like this shih tzu could be so easily and quickly appropriated by the unscrupulous. The family claiming her has correctly identified the dog's gender. The Grand Prairie woman tells me she will reach out to the finder to say a possible owner has been located.

But it's a loss that will not resolve quickly. Whoever found Chloe has offered a work phone number and has mentioned that she might not get any phone messages until the following Monday. For the owner of the lost dog, I can imagine how painful a weekend it might be—grief of loss, followed by recognition and certainty, and then hope of a reunion that cannot be rushed. By now our neighbors have been following the online story, too, and my post on NextDoor lights up with questions about why the finder hasn't called back. People want the good word now.

It takes thirty-six hours for Chloe to go home. The finder goes to work and hears the necessary phone message. The connections are made, proof of ownership is given, and an overjoyed little dog, who has been sheltered and treated kindly, is returned. It's a feel-good story from every angle — the owner who has foot-searched for three days, the finder who did the right thing and reached out online, a distant owner of a different lost dog who knew the found shih tzu was not hers but forwarded information so that someone else might find their missing dog anyway, and I, who came across the story and boosted the signal to the happy, lucky right place. We all felt lighter when Chloe went home, but looking back later, I remember how casual my decision was to scan Facebook lost-dog pages that night, a place where Chloe's owners did not know to look. That random choice made the difference. Some outcomes turn on just this small a thing.

The dog in the road two blocks south of my house is another pretty, silky creature, obviously an escapee and not a long-time stray. Like so many wanderers, she seems to have sniffed her way across the sidewalk and from phone pole to phone pole until she gravitated into the middle of the busiest street in the neighborhood. Why do they choose it? I don't know, but I find so many lost dogs on it, unaware of its dangers of speed and driver sightline. Ellen is driving me home from the airport when we first spot her, nose down to the street and heedless of the approach of Ellen's car. Something tasty must have flattened there this time, because the exquisite dog is lapping at the grubby asphalt with fierce attention. When we pull over and get out, her head comes up, and she gives us a long, appraising look without moving. There is nothing soft in her posture. She is a cautious dog about to make a choice.

It's a moment's standoff. And I can tell already that this is not a dog that will come to two humans miming a food lure. The dog is in the center of the road, and a wrong move from us could keep her in it, running away. This is a Sunday, and so the road is quieter than at other times, but people tend to speed here, and there are dips in the road that block a driver's ability to see too far ahead. After a quick discussion Ellen and I walk north on our side of the road, which will take us past the dog, but with our heads slightly turned away and down, we feign disregard. If we stared as we moved toward her, we might provoke her to flee ahead of us on the street, as though she were being chased. It's critical not to stare. I've learned that loose dogs that are wary rather than spooked will often move perpendicularly to my direction of travel instead of running ahead. A perpendicular move helps them better keep an eye on the stranger.

Ellen is a pilot, as I am, and we laugh a little grimly as we walk, comparing this moment with a skittish dog to intercepting an instrument approach for the airport when the clouds are coming down. There is not a lot of room for error. But—fingers crossed—if we move this way, this dog should move . . . that way. Not north ahead of us. Not east toward us. Probably not south, past us, either, but more likely west, away from us, still able to keep us in sight. So we walk north, intensely casual, hoping our movement will send her out of the street and into the grass on the other side. After a cautious moment, she crosses out of the street to the west sidewalk, and we both exhale.

We stop. I bend down, as though to tie my shoelaces. This dog is a flighty little creature but no real runner. When I kneel to my shoe, she scrambles south down the sidewalk past one house, then up a slight rise into the yard of another, where she stands, turns her face back to us, and stares. This yard seems familiar to her. She is confident there. *Maybe get a picture of her,* I murmur to Ellen, in case we'll need to make a sighting report on social media.

It's a gamble, but we turn and head south, which sends her

deeper into that yard. She is not going to let us get close to her, but this is her home, I think, or at least one that she knows very well. What I'd love to see is a move onto the front porch, but she doesn't do it. As we pass south on the opposite side of the street, she runs around the side of the house instead, and from there I can see her acting urgent at a closed gate. She couldn't be clearer. This is her house. This is her gate. She must feel a little cornered by my approach and the position of the garage. She really, really wants nothing to do with me, but instead of running, she paws at the gate more desperately as I amble near. Our shifting relationship is funny. She really wants to get away from me, but oh . . . would I mind opening this gate?

I pop the latch, and the dog bolts into the yard, where she keens at a screened-in porch and wants that door open, too.

Wondering how this dog got out past a closed gate and really hoping I'm not about to be charged with some weird, dog-assisted trespass, I let her into the screened porch. I would love to spend some time in this beautiful backyard garden, but I head out the back gate, latching it carefully. When I round the corner of the house, I see that Ellen has wisely knocked on the door and is now talking to the owner, asking if that is indeed her dog we found in the street. I see a flash of uncertainty in the woman's expression, because the dog we found sounds very like hers, but her dog is standing at her feet, right here, inside the house. By this time I've caught up with them and tell the lady how the little dog showed me her house, her gate, her backyard, her screened-in porch. After I let her into that screened porch, she'd dashed through the house to emerge beside her owner at the front door now — the very picture of innocence, like a dog that would never, ever think of skipping the joint.

Her name is Pookie. But how did Pookie get out in the first place? The owner thinks back to an hour or so earlier, when she'd gone out the front door to turn on the sprinkler system. She had thought Pookie was asleep upstairs, but the little dog must have slipped past her and down the steps when the woman's attention was turned to her garden. Who would imagine that a dog you thought you knew could be so sneaky?

That neighbor and her husband pass my house on a walk months later. When they spot me in my yard, they thank me again for saving Pookie from the street that time, and they describe her further exploits. Having learned that she could shimmy through doors like a phantom, Pookie had built on her success and gotten bolder. She had slipped from the house a handful of other times. Front door, back door, gate, garage. They were lucky to have caught her. But they've learned. I pass their house and see their front-porch fortifications. A metal puppy gate now blocks Pookie's getaway path down the steps.

It's so easy to overlook the keen senses of dogs and their changing take on what are, to us, subtle differences in their world. Contractors leave a yard, and a dog dashing outside not only traces the space those strangers walked through but runs to the gate, the last place a departing worker touched. If that gate is ajar, the dog will quickly find it. And then he is out. A storm blows over a weakened section of fence, and another dog, out after supper, smells the change in her baseline scent of the environment. Here is dirt turned over. Here is old wood, freshly splintered. Here is a hole that was not there before. And then she is out. And then she is gone. An aging little senior has never strayed from the side of his loving owner. For years and years they have taken his nighttime constitutional off-leash, but this one night, in the gathering dusk, distant rabbits in the grass tease that old dog's young drive. The owner gazes down at her cell phone. When she looks up, the dog she thought she knew has disappeared.

To love our dogs and protect them, we must understand the power of their intelligence, curiosity, resourcefulness, and awareness of their changing world — awareness we do not necessarily share. On their behalf, we need to pay attention. I should get a tattoo: DOGS DON'T WANDER UNTIL THEY DO.

It's never a dull search when
chickens get involved.

23

THE LITTLE STRANGER

WE ARE ON an evening walk in a nearby town, Ace peppered with pecan shards and squirrel poop from a patch of grass where he dropped and rolled. It's a pleasure that will take some cleanup, but I couldn't deny him. Like Puzzle, Ace is never happier than when he wears a little of the world. He trots ahead of me, prickly and speckly, and when he pauses at the sound of voices from a yard in front of us, I start picking bits from his curly coat. The voices rise. We spot a young man and woman circling their house on the corner. They are whistling and clapping their hands. *Oreo, Oreo, Oreo,* they call through the wails of a little boy, who chugs across the unmown grass beside them, his face shiny with tears. Ace perks at the sight of the toddler, stretching the lead taut for a moment as he extends his nose to catch the scent of strangers.

Oreo the puppy, who was just in the backyard, *just* in the backyard, they tell me, has been missing for ten, maybe fifteen minutes, and they have looked everywhere. He went out the back door and then maybe squeezed through the fence. I haven't seen a fat ten-week-old black-and-white bull terrier puppy in the blocks we just walked along, but I offer to help them search. The father declines at first. *No, we've got this.* But when his wife lifts their wiggling, starfished, dirty-diapered toddler and hisses, *Do we? Do we?* the young man changes his mind and shrugs. *Help,* he mouths to me, grinning, as his wife takes their boy into the house. He gestures me around one side of the house while he silently takes the other, playfully pointing two fingers at his eyes and then outward, like SWAT teams on a crime show do. A character.

We meet in the back. Ace noses across a pebble-and-grass driveway, and the young man shows me the place they last saw Oreo. *Right there,* he says, and points hard at the space, as though he could conjure the puppy back. His voice is tight. They've had this little guy only since yesterday. He says they've been calling for a puppy who doesn't even know his name.

Their wood-frame house is broken up into two apartments, surrounded by a battered privacy fence divided by lattice into separate little yards. Behind that house, a series of garage build-overs and single-story homes painted in identical colors appear to be other apartments in the same group. The young man knows some of his neighbors. Others he doesn't know at all. He and his wife and son haven't lived here long.

Maybe one of the neighbors saw Oreo. With luck, maybe one of them took the puppy in. I suggest he start knocking on doors while Ace and I walk the line of houses. It's not the best situation. We're not in a place I know well. I don't have my search vest with me, and Ace is on a short, off-duty leash. If the young man can let the neighbors know we're out here helping, that would be good. I explain to him that Ace is still in early training and that he doesn't trail a traveling animal. He searches by airborne scent. If we find Oreo, great, but I want to make sure this family doesn't rule out an area Ace and I have searched. Even if Ace clears this set of yards right now, two hours from now a moving puppy could walk into the space. At the very least we can give the man an extra set of eyes and a nose for the job. If none of us find Oreo, I do know a couple of handlers with experienced dogs a few cities over. *Search dog,* the young man says dubiously, looking down at the grit-speckled Maltipoo. At the sound of his voice, Ace looks up and wags, a twig sprouting from his tail.

The young man is watching when I give Ace the *find dog* cue, which means find any dog in the immediate area, and Ace scrambles forward. Nose high, nose low, nose high, he skitters in little bursts, hopscotching through the grass like a child. It is an odd gait for a searching dog, but he somehow makes it work. Short-legged Ace, with his compromised hip, will never be a trailing dog for long distances. I have focused his training on small search areas, confined spaces, debris, and rubble. It's the kind of search he is suited for. Ace is happy weasling into tight spaces for any strong scent of dog or cat, and he's good at it. A few weeks ago, on a *find kitty* cue, he located a six-week-old kitten wedged in a tin downspout—a kitten whose echoing cries misled searchers because her mews seemed to be coming from the roof, funneled by the network of storm gutters on the two-story home.

We will search house by house. Ace and I work our way around the clutch of unfenced garage apartments that share a common lawn. A squirrel dashes across the gravel. Sparrows flush from overgrown bushes. Ace ignores both. He bobs his head but does not alert on a pretty calico cat crouched at the edge of the garage roof. The cat doesn't budge. Ace skips forward. Some of these pier-and-beam houses have rusted gaps in the skirting around their foundations, and Ace puts his nose to the ragged holes in the sheet metal, then turns away. Then he stops, raises his head again, and quivers a little, signaling a dog behind chain link on a neighboring property, a dark creature with a lowered head that stares hard at both of us. Ace turns sideways and refuses eye contact. Even from this distance, he does not want to challenge the dog's gaze.

We have worked our way across the compound of matching homes when we hear an uproar in the nearby alley—frantic squawks, shrieks, and the rapid beating of heavy wings. I recognize the noise. Those are backyard chickens squawking their alarm, and one angry, strident note sounds like a rooster defending his flock. Bird activity can be significant to any search—for humans or animals—and bird behavior will sometimes mark the location of a find. I'm not sure what all this sound means, but this is a lot of bird.

We enter the alley, Ace still ahead of me but cautious, his head stretched forward and tilted slightly, his tail lowered. The leash is slack between us. I will not force him ahead. He steps slowly across the alley's gravel toward the sound of chicken scolding and the *thup-thup-thup* of beating wings. Ace is choosing to explore this, but every hair seems alert. He has seen chickens, but we have never worked among them.

That rooster is the first thing I see when we get to a yard edged with small trees and tumbled chicken wire. A forbidden rooster in town, against ordinance, he is a huge red fellow with a proud tail that's spotted at the base and curves red and green up and away. At once athletic and outraged, he is hackles up and rushing at the base of the chicken run in short attacks, sniping and jumping and flapping his wings—the kind of dance I witnessed as a child when another rooster set upon a snake. The hens, now safely behind the chicken-run screen, seem to be egging the big guy on. They have flustered up onto roost bars and are peering down at the conflict, squawking encouragement as if they're at a prize fight.

Ace is dazzled by the display. Sidestepping a little anxiously, he also seems stymied by it—we have never searched through adversaries. Nor can we. But he is stretching earnestly toward the chicken yard when the rooster catches sight of us. The bird lifts his proud head and cocks it at Ace. He is clearly choosing battles. And in that moment of calm I can see what the rooster has cornered. One black ear and a white forehead patch peek out. That must be a dog. If this isn't Oreo, then his twin must be on the lam. Curiosity might have brought the puppy here, but now he clearly regrets it. He is cowering between the side of the chicken run and a rubber water tub. We can hear his frightened cries, trilling honks that sound like they're made by tiny geese.

The rooster is speeding his way toward us, his eyes on Ace, hackles fluffed and wings flapping, when an older man steps out of the back door. *Situation size-up* is the first thing I think when I see him. Tall, laconic, he is unfazed by the calamity. Seeing an unfamiliar woman with a leashed dog in the alley, he steps firmly across the grass to where the rooster challenges us at the coil of chicken wire. *Shup!* he barks to the rooster, and in a single motion swoops down to grab the bird by the legs. In seconds the man is dangling the rooster upside down. The frustrated bird screams, flaps a couple of times, and settles, craning his neck to give us a cold eye.

"Can I help you, miss?" the man says.

"I think that's the lost puppy we're searching for," I answer, pointing. The man looks, shrugs. He tugs back the chicken wire with his free hand and wordlessly nods us into the yard.

Oreo squeaks at Ace's gentle approach, and he squeaks at the sight of me, and he squeaks again when I lift him to my shoulder. Too plump to move quickly or hide well, the puppy had been no match for that rooster. There are little patches of fur missing from his shoulders and back where the big bird got to him. Oreo ducks into my neck, shuddering chicken dust. He still has puppy breath. It smells like spoiled milk and coffee.

"Thanks so much," I say to the man on my way out.

"Y'bet," he answers. Still holding the illegal rooster upended, he lifts it a little higher, then puts a free fingertip to his lips, like it's a secret we share.

Rescued from the rubble following a tornado and fed and groomed by volunteers at the Rowlett Animal Shelter, this Pomeranian was reunited with his family, who lost their home.

The tornado's path, visible from my mother's house.

24

A WINTER STORM

WHEN THE FIRST STORM roars up from south of the city, I am at dinner with friends in a Dallas tapas restaurant. Susan and Ellen and I have come through a rough year and are comparing notes, celebrating the animal saves we've been a part of and the fact that we got through the year relatively intact. The restaurant where we sit shines like a little jewel as the sky around us dims. Dallas–Fort Worth has seen its share of violent weather in December. We've had winter tornadoes before. Forecasters have warned us about the risk of storms, some possibly severe, for days. Tornado Alley gets a lot of warnings like that, but so many don't pan out that it's easy to disregard them, a risk folks are willing to take. Though the winds were fitful and the air seemed a little unstable this afternoon, my friends and I have come to the tapas restaurant anyway. Now the place, with its wide windows, is full of people lifting glasses, wearing Santa hats askew. We are not alone.

We notice when the sky goes dark early, and we notice when the trees outside begin to whip. The room tenses. People eat a little faster; a few think better about a second bottle of wine. When I take out my iPad and bring up live weather radar, heads turn from other tables. Dessert or no dessert? The radar shows us the dark band of the storm that approaches, but its track appears to lead well south of where we sit. Reasoning that we'd be more at risk in a vehicle than we would be in the windowless back of the restaurant, if necessary, most of us stay put. We eat our goat-cheese-stuffed peppers and our patatas bravas and our ice cream with sherry poured over the top.

We all look a little thoughtful when the civil defense sirens go off, a countywide alert, and at just about the time I am looking toward the protected hallway with the bathrooms, the sirens stop. The storm has passed, clipping our southern edge as the radar had suggested, and people who'd been half out the door, leaving their dinners on the table, turn back. We make Texas weather jokes and laugh a little. But the tone of the room has changed.

I leave the radar running, face up next to the olives. Another storm cell is growing from the same area that spawned the first. My father is in a hospital near it, and I want to keep an eye on the swelling green, yellow, and red of that storm's signature as it moves. Nightfall approaches, and now it is difficult to tell what is dusk and what is storm sky. When the up-lit trees begin whipping again, our table neighbors turn to ask me what the radar shows.

This second storm seems to bloom as we watch. It looks shifty and angry, its hook echoes potentially vicious. Word goes around the restaurant quickly, and a waiter asks if I'll hold up the radar so that others can see. Patrons and waitstaff alike watch the radar as the storm morphs rapidly into a monster. A double handful of guests pay their checks hastily and flee. They are heading home, out of range of what is coming or ahead of it in time to duck and cover beneath their own stairs — that's what they're saying. They barely clear the door when the civil defense sirens go off again. Instead of turning back, they run in suits and high heels and party hats for the false safety of their cars.

The sirens stop. They start up again almost immediately.

We stay put, watching the radar and eyeing the internal hallway of the restaurant, just steps away. Susan, Ellen, and I finish our fried ice cream and sherry with forced merriment, our teeth a little clenched. Two waiters peer over our shoulders to see the radar. The second storm boils red just a few miles south of us, and its alarming hook makes a sweep along a freeway three exits away.

That storm is heading for my mother. I kept the radar open with my hospitalized father in mind, south of Dallas, but now the full force of the storm is heading for Rowlett, a northeastern suburb, a city built on a peninsula between the arms of Lake Ray Hubbard. As we watch what is no doubt a tornado roil along the I-30 corridor, I reach for my phone and call her, hoping she'll hear the phone over wind and sirens, hoping she'll answer or take cover, or both. Mom has a love-hate relationship with the telephone. She slept through a lost roof once during another storm. I can never be sure. Four rings, and it rolls to a decade-old voice message: *Hi. Sorry I can't come to the phone right now. Please leave a message. I check voicemail twice a day.* It is a pleasant fiction. My reclusive mother, struggling against paranoia and telemarketers, rarely answers her phone. She hasn't checked phone messages in years. Every now and then she hits the Delete All button, but that's it.

I leave a message anyway: *Mom, there's a tornado heading for Rowlett. Please hide with the cats in the laundry room until the sirens stop. I'll be there as soon as I can.*

We sit where we are until the Dallas sirens fall quiet. Susan heads for home, five minutes away, and Ellen and I load up in my car. I've got search gear in the back if we need it. We head northeast along I-30 toward my mother's house in Rowlett, just twenty minutes or so behind the storm. Not much traffic heading where we're going, but the opposite lanes are full of panicked, fractious traffic. Then we see the first popcorn flash of emergency vehicles, and the cars ahead of us begin to waver and slow.

Our first sight of the tornado's aftermath is I-30 peppered with debris. This isn't the roadside trash you might expect, either. Among shining fragments of car we see a wide scattering of clothing, a shredded motorcycle, a twin mattress wrapped around a sign. As we make way for more emergency vehicles, their flash strobes an apartment complex just south of the freeway. We can see survivors milling aimlessly. Second floors have crumbled, roofs have blown free. The walls of several buildings have been completely debrided, exposing a honeycomb of apartments.

Jesus, I say, like a prayer. People must have died in this. Ten minutes from my mother's house, in the thrown lights of vehicles, we can see the path the tornado plowed across housing, the high overpasses of freeway, and from there to the lake separating Garland from Rowlett. With search-and-rescue gear in the back of my car, we have a moment's question about whether we should stop and offer aid or move along. We've been plucked off the street to help before. A policeman with a flashlight gestures the cars on I-30 forward. I count police cars, fire trucks, and ambulances. Help is here and more is coming. I can see the urgent flicker of lights approaching from the south.

We drive on, across the I-30 bridge over Lake Ray Hubbard. I stare toward the place where my mother lives, in the first row of housing to meet that tornado's track. It is a black void at the edge of the water. Rowlett has been blown completely dark.

My cell phone rings. I jump for it unreasonably, slow to remember that Mom's phone doesn't work without power. It is my father. He had watched the storm track past his window and had turned the TV on. "Is your mother okay?" he asks. "And her cats?"

They've been divorced for thirty-nine years.

We creep toward her, picking our way along roads strewn with debris. "Are you okay?" we call out to people we pass. Thumbs up, they're okay, they nod or gesture or shake their heads yes and no at once. They are translucent in the headlights, gutted with loss. I've worked the aftermath of plenty of tornadoes, but the nature of that violence strikes me fresh every time. No wonder the ancients described these storms with a monster's random malice: it's a rampage we are seeing. With all the twisting and tearing, we can imagine great claws.

Block after block of houses are mostly leveled. Ellen and I agree:

we'll check on my mother, then go back to help where we can. We make a turn and find that her immediate neighbors have been spared. Some big trees are down and fences blown flat. But at least from what I can see in the dark, my mother's house is weirdly, miraculously intact. I jump out of the car and find excited rabbits chasing each other across her sodden lawn.

I bang on her front door. My mother is a little deaf. Years ago, when her paranoia met germophobia, she had her locks changed and refused me a key. Ever since then she's peeked out of the house at me from a distance, pointing to a place in the doorway where I can leave things she's asked for or gifts I've brought. She's had two rounds of chemo for cancer and says she lets no one in because she's immuno-suppressed. That phobia covers a deeper reclusiveness, and I know it, and she knows I know it, but I've learned not to push. The same mother who shouted from the darkness at a burglar who kicked in her back door once had a small stroke when a neighbor made too many demands through her bedroom window about a shared tree. Mom can handle love only from a safe distance. This is what we've got.

"Susie?" I hear her frail voice ring out from the living room, just steps away from the front door.

"Mom! Are you okay?" I shout. "There was a tornado. Garland and Rowlett have been hit very hard."

"Susie, I don't have any power."

"I know. We've come to get you out of here. I can take you to a hotel while the recovery is going on. A hotel by me. You may be without power for days — weeks, even."

"My cats."

"We can bring your cats."

"No," she says. "They got scared. They're gone. I can't find them."

"We've got flashlights. Let us in, and we'll find them."

"I'm doing okay. The cats will come out when they've calmed down. I just need a few things."

She shouts a short list of practical things she will need — snacks that will keep without a refrigerator, cat food and litter, camp lights with batteries so she can make her way through the house.

"Mom, please. This isn't safe. We could have you all out of here in an hour and in a safe place with power — and Wi-Fi — in two hours. That way your Facebook friends won't worry."

There is a longer pause. My mother lives on social media. That Wi-Fi is bait where hot food and lights are not.

"You are *not* coming in this house," my mother says. "And I'm not leaving without the cats."

The tornado that struck Garland and Rowlett the day after Christmas 2015 was one of nine spawned by the same storm. The Garland-Rowlett twister killed thirteen people, some immediately and some who died of their injuries after time. Most of the fatalities were in vehicles at the critical intersection of two freeways when the storm hit. In Rowlett, more than 450 homes were damaged or destroyed, leaving many homeless. *It could have been so much worse,* residents murmured where they stood in shelters. Many people had been away for the holiday weekend and missed the storm entirely.

Many animals did not. Some had been left behind for the long Christmas weekend and were now also homeless, cut off from dog sitters, wandering injured and hungry. Pamela Reid, an animal behaviorist who specializes in disaster work with the ASPCA, notes that "pets are much more likely to try and make an escape during stressful situations." Many dogs become storm-phobic and cats hyperanimated even before the worst arrives, and human fear can escalate that. Both cats and dogs may have an increased urge to escape. While cats often make a point-to-point dash for safe hiding places, dogs may run as far as stamina allows. Even after violent weather has passed, they may be slow to calm. The torn terrain is now disrupted, confusing for those who would circle back to places they know by sight and scent.

Even gregarious dogs can become xenophobic in these situations. The friendly black Lab on the corner, overwhelmed by change and strangers, flees.

Helping my mother and her neighbors in Rowlett in the following days, we see some of those dogs running in the distance, kiting at full speed across ravaged neighborhoods, frantic because of the sounds of backhoes and excavators pulling the rubble apart. Pets from intact houses are also roaming at large, having found their way through damaged fences. We take pictures of those loose animals when we can and post the sightings online. Some days after the storm I extract a spitting white cat from a gutter. His owner has come back to their roofless house for three nights and has been calling for the old fellow.

A few of the dogs with collars and tags we manage to get home again. Other Rowlett residents are doing the same with a grim ferocity, a community of survivors determined to pull life out of loss. They are assisted by a well-known animal rescue and recovery team out of Dallas, Duck Team 6, which helps work pets out of the rubble. Friends of Rowlett Animals, a volunteer group associated with the shelter there, mounts a multitiered rescue effort that shelters storm-found animals, publicizes them on social media, reconnects them with owners, and runs a donation drive for food and supplies for owners who need them. It is a time of great generosity.

And it is a time of scams. Within twenty-four hours after the tornado, a few unscrupulous groups emerge, often headed by someone with multiple identities and suspect truths about his or her rescue credentials. They come from parts of Texas and nearby states with claims of crates and warehouses for safe harbor, asking for superstore gift cards and PayPal donations to private accounts. In that freefall period after the storm, many compassionate people are duped by these scams before word shuts them down. There are troubling stories that a few of the so-called rescuers took Garland and Rowlett animals out of town and out of state despite the city shelters' media-wide pleas for those pets to remain where their owners could easily find them. It is an ugly trick but a common one, an animal disaster specialist tells me, when shady groups take animals and essentially hold them for ransom miles away, demanding money for the cost of their rescue.

Several friends and I work in Rowlett and the damaged small towns surrounding it for the next two weeks—a different job every day. Once human loss and injuries have been accounted for, the work shifts to recovery, a need that goes on long after the search teams and media have left. Sometimes we clear debris from roadsides and farmers' fields. Sometimes we help people sift through the rubble to find whatever valuables they can shove into a cousin's car before the long drive to a new life somewhere else. We unload donated supplies at the animal shelter, where volunteer groomers have come in to tidy up animal survivors and volunteer photographers take pictures of them to share online. Sometimes we help residents who are bringing in an animal, and sometimes we comfort those who've lost one. *My dog,* we hear more than once. *If I could just find my dog.* Or, *You have to understand what this cat means to me.* We witness powerful moments of reunion. A teenaged driver brings in his grandparents. Their home is gone, but he thinks he saw their cat's picture online. Another older couple cry when they find their five-pound Pomeranian alive and in good health. *Surely not,* they had said when they first saw their flattened home. *Surely he would not have survived.* But here he is, as overjoyed as they are.

My mother persists by lamplight. Through the door of her house she tells me that she has found her two indoor kitties, Butterfly and Patch. Or rather, they found her. They had crawled up into the underbelly of her overstuffed sofa and stayed there for almost seventy-two hours. She woke up on that couch to find them plastered on either side of her, ha ha ha. She's been without power for days now, cut off from news of the outside world. Even so, she will not open the door to me. So I sit on a milk crate she has beside her front door for fast-food deliveries, and I lean against it and tell her what I've seen. The Rowlett tornado skipped right across the water and took out houses two streets away from her. This neighbor's house is gone. That neighbor's crepe myrtles were crushed by a flying car. One family's trampoline flew right across the street and wedged in someone else's tree.

My mother hasn't driven in a few years. I describe a road she used to take daily, how the tornado wiped out a whole row of houses along it and, across the street, left a balsa-wood nativity scene untouched. Someone had a field with a big handmade NO DUMPING sign on it —the sign had been there for years—and nature had dumped half of Rowlett in that field, it seemed.

Mom knows she was lucky. She says she's worried now about four feral cats she's been feeding for months at her front door. I don't know these cats. A few times when I've visited, one cat or another has slunk away from me, a murky, low-bellied shape around the corner of her house, but I haven't been able to make out anything more than suspicious eyes and stripes. Mom describes them: Bojangles, Freddy, ShyKitty, and LucyLou. She's never petted one of them, but she's watched them through the window and knows their ways. They will come to the fence at the sound of her voice, waiting for food. But since the storm she's been coughing, and she doesn't have much voice for calling, and they haven't come.

I tell her about my studies in lost-pet behavior. In shouts through her locked door, we reminisce a little. We talk about the things we did right on those searches for lost dogs and cats years ago, the things I've recently learned about missing animals that sure would have been helpful to know back then. "Remember the kitties, Sus," my mother says. She believes—and she is right—that lost cats are often under-served. We talk about cats and territory and what it takes to displace them. I tell her that two streets away, where the tornado plowed up the neighborhood, I've seen some very spooked cats, but my mother's street and the area behind it were relatively untouched.

I think Mom's ferals will come back. I put cat food on the front porch and promise I will keep an eye out for them. Bojangles is red, and Freddy is black with a tattered left ear. ShyKitty is a gray tabby, and LucyLou has a black spot on her side like a clover. Before Christmas, Mom says, she had made some real progress with LucyLou, got her all the way to the back door.

"LucyLou squeaks likes a mouse, and she'll come to that," my mother says. "Remember, when you look for her, don't get pushy. If you see her, sit down and go *eek-eek. Eek-eek-eek.*"

Two weeks after the storm, it is old news for those who are not still living it. A wide swath of Rowlett is covered in tarps; debris is slowly moved out of the rubble to curbside, waiting for the big trucks to come haul it off. Some volunteer groups are still bringing food trucks to storm-riddled neighborhoods; the Friends of Rowlett Animals are suiting up in something like rubble gear to deliver pet food and supplies to those who have no vehicle left to come get them. There are some miracle stories that have helped sustain everyone. A man found his neighbor's dog in the rubble days after the tornado. An urgent and enterprising cat dropped a New Year's litter of kittens in an overturned car.

My mother has had her power back for a little while now. She returned to social media and received virtual hugs, high fives, and some scolding because she would not let me evacuate her. She sidesteps the scolding and posts about her experiences: how she heard a couple of funnels overhead, how she wasn't really scared, how her indoor cats, Butterfly and Patch, are doing. She was in better shape to weather the storm than most, she says, because she has long lived so sparely, by choice.

Mom's insomnia is still a part of her, and she jokes a bit about it online now, poking fun at friends who sleep the night away while she's howling at the midnight moon. What my mother doesn't say is that she's spending a lot of time on the lost-pet sites associated with the north Texas storms of December 26. Stoked on moon pies and instant coffee, she's making matches—this tornado-lost pet photo to that found-pet post. She emails me when she can remember her own email address and mine. Otherwise she messages me on Facebook. She needs new glasses and can't see so great, she says. So she's been leaning close to the computer screen. Could this missing brown Chihuahua be the same dog as that found one shown with an injured front leg? Are these two bull terriers the same? There is a cat missing in Garland that sure looks like this one brought to the shelter in Rowlett. She asks me to take a look and tell her what I think. Some of the matches I can't be sure about; the found photos are notoriously poor. But some images are clearly the same dog or cat, or in one case a lop-eared rabbit. Mom is responsible for a few people getting their pets back. She connects found notices to lost-dog posts and vice versa and reads me owner thank-you messages from behind the front door. From where she sits in a fragile state, my mother jokes that she is lost-pet mission control. She is overjoyed to be of some service to a city she has come to love and fiercely refuses to leave.

Mom has not seen her missing feral cats, but during almost daily visits to her house I have seen three of them at the fence around dusk. A red cat, a black cat, and a gray cat—Bojangles, Fred, and Shy-Kitty, just as my mother described them. I try cooing my mother's cat song to them, in my voice which is very like her own, but they are not fooled. They stare at me, unblinking, waiting for me to drop some food on the porch and go.

Hoping to search wisely in terms of cat behavior, and needing in this uneasy time not to appear like I'm any kind of looter to other humans, I wear my reflective vest and shine a flashlight at ground level around Mom's neighborhood. I find no sign of LucyLou. Neighbors furrow their brows, shaking their heads. They do not recall ever seeing such a cat. My mother frets about that. LucyLou is very petite, Mom says. The cats all come from somewhere east of her and cross the railroad tracks right behind her house when it's time for supper.

LucyLou comes with them, but she alone will jump the fence when my mother calls her, an easy cat to see at twilight, with that white body and clover spot.

Maybe she was killed in the storm. Maybe she was hit by a train. Mom knows I've seen plenty of death. She asks me to walk the roads and the railroad tracks looking for LucyLou's little body. I do, feeling the pull of old family urgency from my childhood, when this animal or that one went missing and we foot-searched for their bodies until we dropped. No sign of LucyLou in Mother's neighborhood or anywhere along the railroad tracks.

Okay, Susie, Mom says when I come back to the door and check out each night. No LucyLou. She sounds more resigned every time. I tell her I'll try again tomorrow. *Okay, Susie,* she repeats. And she is done talking. When she wants me to go away, she says *Bye-bye now* and stops speaking altogether.

Miles away, my father has been sick. He never really recovered from surgeries last year, and he's now battling lymphoma. Between chemotherapy and unchecked infection, he has been constantly assailed. I got bronchitis working in Rowlett and a cough that will not go away, so when I visit him, I scrub up, glove up, and wear a mask. Dad tells me the doctors thought that maybe they'd caught the lymphoma early enough, that they can cure this, but he doesn't know. He doesn't know. Dad sounds exhausted from the fight. There is leavetaking in the sound of him when he calls from yet another hospital room to ask how my mother is doing. In all the years they've been apart, I've never known him so concerned. I tell him that Mom is stubborn but safe. He laughs a little at that. I tell him about her indoor cats that came out from under the couch and the outdoor strays who've mostly reported back for their meals. I tell him Bojangles, Fred, and ShyKitty are accounted for, but she's worried about a stray she hasn't seen since the day of the storm. I've been searching for this cat for some days—a little white cat named LucyLou, with a spot on her side like a clover.

There is so long a pause after I tell him this that at first I think my father has fallen asleep on the other end of the phone.

Dad says, "LucyLou. With a clover."

"Yes."

"Sus," he says gently, "take care of your mom. LucyLou was a cat we had before you were born."

Some lost dogs leave clues.

25

BRING EGG HOME

To tell you the truth," says the lady at the cash register, "I'm not crazy about that dog." Though there's no one else in the store, she drops her voice low. She touches a sky-blue fingernail to the LOST sign in the window over the register. It is a neighbor's sign for a neighbor's dog, a sign the cashier put up because she loves her friend more than she dislikes the friend's fat little pug mix, named Egg.

The cashier needs to vent. That dog does nothing but snort and snipe and shit, the woman says. He'll come at you and nip a little if you get too close to his owner. And then he doesn't keep all his crap at home. Egg knows what he's doing. He knows. She has seen him hop out of the car with his owner, who moves slowly on a prosthetic limb, and Egg knows she can't catch up, and he races around the back of the car to poop not in his own yard but in the neighbors'—in this case, the cashier's. And he just stares at you with little pig eyes when he's doing it, she says, then he turns around and scratches his back feet at the steaming lump, his head up all proud, like *Check this shit out.*

"Nice of you to put out the LOST sign, then," I say while the cashier taps in my debit card, which for whatever reason won't read at the gas pump.

The woman sighs. She doesn't miss the dog, but she doesn't wish him harm either. Her friend is heartbroken over Egg's disappearance. He's slipped through the backyard fence before a few times, usually to chase cats, but this is the first time he's been gone this long. Egg went missing a couple, maybe three days ago, and everyone on the street is thinking coyotes or that the little dog drowned in the flash flood of a summer storm they had night before last.

"Is he scared of storms at all?" I ask, pocketing my debit card and wondering if Egg got stuck somewhere hiding from bad weather.

The woman says he isn't scared of anything she knows of. He leads a quiet life with his owner, but on his own Egg gets a little wanderlust. He busts the fence and chases cats and cars. She paints a picture of a round little dog with a snub nose and a pig tail and legs like cigar stubs that can somehow, surprisingly, haul ass.

No one has exactly searched on foot for him, she says, though everyone on their road knows that Egg is gone. With all the rain lately, no one has put out any signs. Egg's owner is disabled. She can't really search or put out signs or anything like that. But maybe the neighbors should get a few out—at least at the junction with the farm-to-market road that leads to the freeway, just in case Egg got that far. A few of them have gone so far as to drive along the highway a ways, looking for his body.

Egg has on a collar and two noisy tags. A microchip? The woman looks blank. She has no idea what that even is. Her cell phone rings, and the cashier jumps, looks at me, and mouths *Maybe?* She picks up the phone and shakes her head at me. She keeps hoping she'll get a phone call from her friend that Egg has been found.

On my way back from a conference in a distant town, I don't live anywhere near here. But there is something about Egg's story —and his owner's situation—that makes me offer to help. I've got some time, I tell the cashier. I'd be glad to talk to Egg's owner and walk the area looking for evidence of Egg. Sometimes we call it *cutting sign*. The woman is curious about what I'd look for out there. Spoor: fresh tracks and poop, I tell her, because if he survived that storm and is in the area, he'll probably have left both. I'd look for trampled vegetation, signs of bedding down, discarded food remnants. And pugs shed quite a bit. I'd look for fur fall and snag. There are worse things I'd look for, but I don't tell the cashier that.

She gives me a long look, as though she's sizing up my offer. She turns away and gazes out the window a minute. Perhaps it's the license plate on my car, with its message of rescue, that changes her mind. Without a word further, she picks up the phone and punches in a number. "Deb," she says after an interim, "there is a woman here at the store that might can help you find Egg."

I hear a buzz on the other end, and the cashier's face changes.

"No, no," she says, "it's free." Her body tenses as she says this, and she shoots me a look, mouthing something I can't make out. After another buzz and a few *uh-huhs*, she hangs up the phone. "How much does this really cost?" she asks me. "Because Deb couldn't pay it, but I—"

"No charge," I tell her. "Really."

The cashier relaxes. She was going to try to pay for this, but payday isn't until Friday, and until then any check she wrote me would be hot.

She prints her friend's address on a napkin and slides it across the counter. Then she warns me again about the coyotes and about a couple at the end of the road who I'd want to talk to before I spent too much time anywhere near their house. They're sort of shoot-first-ask-questions-later kind of people, she tells me, suspicious of strangers but nice enough in their own way.

Egg and his owner live in the country on a long road that must have had development prospects at one point, and then its fortunes changed. After a few brick-and-siding tract homes from the '80s, there is a stretch of raw field. Then I pass more houses. Some are elderly ranch homes from the '50s; a few are even older—farmhouses in their day, with what's left of their stables still tilting in back. There's a row of mobile homes close to the road, and a silver Airstream trailer is set way back from it, shining like a huddling bug in the tall grass fifty or sixty yards away. The road starts with pitted asphalt and turns to gravel for a stretch, then hooks, as sharp and unforgiving as a frozen elbow. It ends in a kind of cul-de-sac that seems to have been made by numerous people turning around at the dead end and clipping the brush. I can see what appear to be four-wheeler tracks scudding off the road into the wilder terrain beyond.

I've missed Deb's house. I also have to turn in that makeshift space and make my way back past the elbow crook. When I find her home, Egg's owner is sitting on the front porch, her right leg extended and a walker at her side. She waves a green dish towel fiercely at me until I stop, and when I get out of my car, she calls that she saw me pass the first time, that I shouldn't feel bad, because everyone misses her house after the guy who used to live across the street took out her mailbox when he was backing out wildly. That duck-shaped mailbox was her signature. She hopes to get another one soon.

She should rise to greet a visitor, she says as I come up the steps, but she shakes her head. *Can't. Can't.* Then she thanks me for coming all the way out here for Egg. It's been three days now without a sign of him. All the cheer goes out of her face when she says this, and she drops her head. It's all her fault, because she could see that the fence was bad, and all it took was one good wind to make a loose section into another gap he could get through. *The things you are always going to do,* she says.

When I ask, she points the way he went last time and the time before that. He has his little tendencies, she says. He likes to bark at other dogs through fences, and he really likes chasing cats. She thought she heard some fence-line barking deep in that first night that he disappeared, but she hasn't since. Egg has on a collar that was tan plaid once, and he has his rabies and his name tags on. Or did. She points around the side of the house to the gap in her fence that Egg must have slipped through.

I check it out. It's a small hole for a pudgy dog. Egg has some enterprise. Sure enough, the splintered cedar has caught fur from his side and his belly and maybe the back of his neck. Some of the fur is buff, some black, and some appears to be ticked with white. I carry plastic zip bags on human and animal searches, and they come in handy now. I bag each bit of fur separately and label it according to the part of the dog I think it must have come from, assuming that the dog didn't squeeze out of the hole upside down like a dolphin.

When I go back to Deb, she shows me a framed Christmas picture of her dog. The church did Santa pictures with kids and pets, and there is Egg on the narrow knees of a skinny teenage Santa. Egg looks sly, his chin lifted, grin wide, tongue out, his dark eyes narrowed in the black crinkles of his face. He is wearing an elf hat, but it's slipped defiantly way back on his head.

When I ask whether Egg likes to forage—eat trash and cat food and the like, maybe catch something wilder—Deb's eyes widen. She's never seen her dog say no to anything, but she doesn't think he's in any kind of shape to catch, like, a creature to eat. As I move to search for his prints in the muddy stretches away from the hole in the fence, she calls out that he really likes eating bugs. He'll snap a butterfly off a flower faster than you can say *Don't*. Can a dog live on bugs?

After a long silence, Deb calls around the house, *Please tell Egg his mama wants him home.*

All the neighborhood dogs are interested in this stranger walking past them. Some are behind fences; others are on tie-outs that they run taut, baying at me from the ends of straining chains. A few leap onto couch backs and yap at me through windows. There's a kind of vague territoriality about all this, as though the dogs have put me on notice that they are there and paying attention, but none of them seem particularly hostile. After a bark or two, a few are ready to be friends. One young chocolate Lab with soft eyes wags her entire backside fiercely, crabbing sideways toward me on her tie-out the second time I pass.

It's thoughtful, slippery work making my way through the spaces Egg might have traveled. I've always enjoyed this kind of work and was fortunate that my first SAR team had an experienced man-tracker to teach us. Cutting sign was an important adjunct to K9 search. The process is similar for wandering animals, perhaps even more curious because of its surprises where habitats collide. I admire the experienced wildlife trackers who can walk around a space and tell the recent story of a given acre—who's fighting, mating, killing, eating, and hiding there. Even the gentlest landscape can reveal to them something not far from Jack the Ripper's London.

I'm not yet that experienced. But I do know a dog's print from a raccoon's, possum's, cat's, or coyote's, and I know something about Egg and his temptations. For a long stretch I find no clear evidence of pug, no scrapes of dog fur along underbrush, no prints in the muddy runoff toward ravines (which would suggest that Egg had been that way after the storm)—only some remnants of rabbit and clumps of coyote scat, peppered with hair, feathers, and bone, one clump chillingly close to a child's plastic playhouse in an unfenced backyard.

But across the street from Deb's house, two or three houses down, I find *transfer*: three diminishing prints where a small dog stepped out of mud onto pavement and walked his feet clean. A few feet away there's a fur-fuzzy edge of a flattened box under a car that's dripping oil, where some light-colored animal has crawled. That fur looks a lot like the fur I've collected. I turn my head. Deb's front porch is visible from this spot. If this fur is Egg's, he's been here since the rain two nights ago, and he could see home from where he lay. In an area with witnessed coyote kills, this daft wandering dog seems to be out having a good time.

When I stand, a woman in the adjoining house is looking at me through the window. She must have seen the LOST PET SEARCH vest I'm wearing, because she meets me from across the grass as I step off the driveway, a petite woman wearing jeans and a LAISSEZ LES BON TEMPS ROULER T-shirt.

"Have you seen a—"

"You're looking for Egg," the woman says.

She must see the surprise on my face. She says Deb has paved the way for me. She's called up and down the street. Everyone knows everyone around here. She says they'd do anything for Deb. I show her the three prints leading from behind her yard onto her neighbor's parking pad.

"I haven't seen him, but you go on and look where you need to," the woman says. "He acts tough, but Egg needs to go home. Coyotes have already taken a few cats this spring." She points in the direction of the kills.

Two hours later, three round prints, some fur scud on the edge of a box, and one small mound of dog poop are the only maybe signs of Egg I've found. I've knocked on a few doors, and those who answered all knew about him. *My God,* the conclusion seems to be, *that dog leads Deb a dance.*

I ask one neighbor, an elderly man so like my dad's brother, my Uncle Davy, that I keep doing double takes, is there any chance someone around here would have been annoyed enough to do something with Egg? He shakes his head. Not lately. There was a guy lived here for a few years that some folks wondered about when another dog went missing. That guy didn't like anybody, really didn't like that other dog's noise, made it pretty clear he didn't like him. Dog's name was Barker. Enough said. But they never had any proof. He points to the house where the man who took out Deb's mailbox once lived. Same guy, he says. Gone awhile.

This would probably be a good wildlife-camera-and-humane-trap situation, I say to him, thinking of a good friend who leads one such team in Minnesota. The man brightens. Uncle Davy's doppelganger has a humane trap for possums (*No offense,* he says, *but they eat my chickens' eggs*). But we both shake our heads when he gets it out. The trap seems too small for chubby Egg, who would have to squeeze into it as if it were a corset. We are talking about other traps that neighbors up and down the road might have, and I'm thinking about my friend five states away, who might be able to send equipment that I could drive back out here, when we both see Deb waving her dish towel from the front porch. She shouts something as we approach. Neither of us can make it out.

"What's she saying?" I ask the man.

"*Pfffft.*" He shrugs, pointing to his hearing aid.

"He really likes June bugs!" Deb says as we come up the steps. "He eats so many that it makes him sick. I can't leave my porch light on when he's out."

June bugs. So willful, fractious, trash-foraging little Egg is also piggish for June bugs, those fat, brown, buzzy creatures that throw themselves against light and fall backward onto the ground, spinning and wiggling helplessly there, unable to right themselves. Some summers they are so thick you crunch your way to the door just to get inside.

June-bug gluttony is how we lure a lost pug home. Attraction. Leave the porch light on, I suggest to Deb, who asks her immediate neighbors to pull in their outdoor cat food and leave their lights on, too. It takes a little while, but it works. I've been home a few days when I get good news. Deb's neighbor found Egg curled up on a doormat, fat, sleepy, unrepentant—and safe—surrounded by bug legs and a few filmy wings.

On a training search, Puzzle poises over a buried scent artifact.

In the company of Puzzle, this pair of lost dogs, Nala and Tanner, turned up in my living room.

26

BIG DOG, LITTLE SHADOW

B ENEATH A LOWERING SKY and pouring rain, Puzzle and I work across the gloom. It is a SAR training day, like hundreds of others before it, which began an hour or so after dawn. Two pierced vials of bone chips and teeth could be tucked deep in this three-acre space, and together we are charged to find them. Any of the three acres could have just one or both vials. The entire search area could have nothing at all. Despite my rain gear and the golden retriever's water-repellent vest, we are both soaked to the skin. Rain has even made its way down through the tops of my snake gaiters, penetrating the lacing area of my boots. Every step brings a double squelch of water in the boot and water out of the boot.

Another handler runs behind us, monitoring the search.

Moving at a steady trot back and forth across the space, her nose low and up again and low and up, Puzzle thrives in this. She has always loved working in the very worst weather best. I jog fifteen feet or so behind her and at times almost lose sight of her in the downpour, seeing only the light blur of her form and the moving double pulse of the LED light on her vest: *I'm here. I'm here. I'm here.* Sometimes I can just see the sodden, happy swing of her tail as she steadily clears the first acre.

When it's time to move along the side of a building to the next space, she pauses, shooting me a glance over her shoulder, checking in before moving on. She rounds a corner of the building bordered in heavy boxwood and, after a strong gust of wind that blows the rain sideways, disappears. Moments later I see her braiding back and forth against a dumpster, hear her bark, and see the double bounce on her front paws before she stands up on her back legs, her alert signal. She will pop up and down on those back legs until I get to her, and then she'll sit, point her nose to the scent source, and bark again. It is an alert even a child would notice. Somewhere in the course of our career together, Puzzle decided to make her alerts big production numbers. Miss Big Finish, one search friend calls her. Sure enough, a vial is taped to the back of an open dumpster door.

"A find!" I call to the monitor. "Good girl!" I praise the dog. "Good recover!" She beams at me and chatters a low grumble-woof, amiably stretching her nose for the inch of beef jerky she's about to get as a reward.

Another cue to search forward, and we move on, threading our way around signs and gas meters and vehicles. This acre does not allow for the easy sweeps of the earlier area. There are many crevices to check, and scent, borne on the shifting wind and tangled in the downpour, requires a different engagement from Puzzle, who may have to belly-crawl under structures to suss the source. It takes twice as long to work this part of the sector, and when Puzzle does not alert in any corner of it — indeed, does not even show interest in any corner of it — I hold my breath. No SAR K9 team wants a *miss*, having a live or deceased victim in their sector go unfound, and though Puzzle has proven herself reliable and these training samples are very small, any dog can sidestep a corner where scent coils, and any handler can fail to see the small nonverbal behaviors that suggest the dog is onto something very faint. Handlers have nightmares about misses. It means that much.

But in her way, Puzzle says that nothing is here. I tell the monitoring handler she's cleared the area, and we move on to the third and last acre. Part gravel and part untended grassy field, with potholes that could sprain an ankle, the field looks like a good time for Puzzle and a harder trudge for me. Even the monitor elects to stay behind on the gravel. I can't help but grin at the sight of my dog's ears flashing through the grass as she bounds. And then, just a minute or so into the new space, she quickens. I hear a bark, and maybe ten yards away from me, Puzzle rises up on her back legs and her blond head periscopes over the blowing grass.

"We've got a find!" I shout to the monitor as I slosh toward Puzzle. "A find!" I confirm again as I reach the spot where the vial is tucked deep in a hummock of grass.

"Praise your dog," the monitor calls, then "Praise your dog!" again, because he can't hear me. But I am already praising my dog. A treat and a tight whisper, a cup of her sweet face in my hands; I bow my forehead to this beautiful dog.

Puzzle has just turned twelve. This is her retirement search.

Anything good that I do beside a dog I owe in some way to Puzzle. The willful, high-drive puppy that came into my life in 2004, bound for a potential search-and-rescue career, taught me how much she knew that I did not. My God, Puzzle was an instruction—curious about everything and ready to launch herself into anything if there was a find and praise at the end of it. We were fortunate in our early trainers, who encouraged me even as they laughed at the cocky golden adolescent who liked to carry her own lead and prance her way back to base after a find. Ours was an education taken at a run— beside Puzzle, there was no other way. Our work together taught me to experience the world in new ways, to pay attention the way a dog does, with a whole-body focus. Puz still teaches me to assess with all my senses, to give up human preconceptions and trust the reality of scent I cannot see.

At home she has also made a difference to my relationship with other dogs. Spending all that time watching her shifts of demeanor in the search field and learning to translate her messages has shown me how much any dog communicates, reliably, if we take the time to learn its language. Now I better understand dogs' individual moods, the alliances and territories and points of discord between them, and the affection and attachment one dog will form with another. More importantly, when I slow down and turn my gaze to the house dogs, I can see important changes earlier—especially small shifts in health, which are important with the hospice seniors. I once heard an art historian explain that when you study the close work of a master painter long enough, lean in to learn how a single twist of a paintbrush creates a figure, it informs everything you see in the larger painting when you step back. And so I have learned from Puzzle.

Her lessons carry across local neighborhoods and fields. When I began to work formally at reuniting lost pets, I didn't realize how often my search would begin with a found animal and an unknown owner. How many lost pets have I discovered quivering behind alley trashcans or crisscrossing busy roads, bewildered and afraid? Too many to count. Puzzle certainly still brings them in. She is checking out the base of a phone pole one evening when a fierce little West Highland white terrier comes boiling out from under a bush straight for us, tail in motion. That little guy is of two minds about us, happy to meet the golden but disliking me, the company she keeps. He chooses to stand beneath Puzzle like a sentinel, looking left and right, alternately nuzzling her with affection and growling at me with a side eye. Fortunately the Westie has on a tag, and it's a new one, white letters on black. He is not going to let me reach for it. The phone number shimmies when he growls. *Angus,* says his owner on the other end of my call—*Angus,* like a sigh, with a gust of relief. She was just starting to panic. The dog had slipped out when she was bringing in groceries, and *Let me tell you,* she says, *even these short dogs can move fast.* She can't believe he's already three blocks away. When he sees his owner, stiff little Angus becomes a puppy again. The lady apologizes with her arms full of wiggling Westie. She offers me reward money. She says

Angus acts tough but is just a big chicken. The last we see of him is his paws on the dashboard. He is done with us. A traveling man, just passing through; his head is already turned for home.

Not long afterward I'm busy cleaning house. The other dogs are out back, but Puzzle is with me, and she is good company while I clean. She is half napping, half supervising from the couch, from which she can see into the depths of the house. For a high-drive dog, Puzzle enjoys lazing during someone else's work. I vacuum around her, marking the couch to catch later. I've already swept and mopped and thrown open doors and windows to air out the house. I leave her to spend a good half hour in the back bathroom scrubbing rust stains, and when I come back through, gloved to the elbows and with a mask against the fumes, I find three dogs where there had been just one. Puzzle has company. A very old golden and a Rhodesian ridgeback are stretched out on the couch beside her. Did they just walk into the house, or did she find them in the yard and they followed her inside? I'll never know exactly what happened, but the canine strangers give me a *Yo!* bob of their heads when I approach. They accept a friendly shoulder scratch and let me check their tags. Tanner and Nala. These dogs slipped through a gate five houses away. Just another day in Puzzleland. After a glance at them and an almost human shrug, she grins at me affably: *The door was open and they wanted to come in, and what's a girl gonna do?*

Though she has officially retired from missions, in summer 2016 Puzzle continues to train almost daily—short detection searches over lesser distances, often involving very small samples of bone, tissue, or blood. We are contributing to some research, using a variety of human scent artifacts across a wide range of conditions. I carefully log every search, a painstaking record that details the scent artifact (what kind, size, how old, how contained) and the conditions searched, including weather specifics, type of environment, and how that space is maintained—a splintered wooden floor with fifty-year-old varnish, for example, versus an urban greenbelt shrouded in car exhaust from a nearby freeway. Puzzle enjoys the challenge, and I am happy to see her still eager to search. There are some days when she hears the familiar sounds of my gear in motion that she rushes to the door with such excitement that I wonder if I retired her too soon.

Puzzle thrives on this work and on long walks around the neighborhood, where she drops and rolls in every patch of desirable grass. Just after her twelfth birthday, her annual wellness exam suggests that she is in fine health. We found what appeared to be a benign, unchanging mass on her adrenal gland four years ago, and we've been monitoring it since then, but apart from the stiff shoulder and hips from time to time, everything seems very good. Puzzle is trim. Other than having occasional thoughtfully remote periods, she is happy and engaged. She and the big dogs still play tug-of-war, and she and Ace commune together across the backyard, ferreting creatures and noting fresh, spaded dirt in the garden. They put their noses to earth and scent its secrets.

In July we head to the vet for a teeth cleaning and the removal of some small skin lumps on Puzzle's head. The lumps are probably insignificant, but she's a senior dog that has seen a lot of sun, and some of these lumps are in spots likely to be rubbed by a collar or scraped by her own back foot when she's scratching, so we're going to have them removed. It is a procedure involving sedation, and a blood test to make sure sedation is appropriate, and even though her bloodwork is great and this is one of the least invasive procedures Puzzle has ever had, I grit my teeth the whole day of her appointment. I never take even a grooming for granted.

I get a call early in the afternoon. Great news! Puzzle has done very well. She is awake, eating and drinking, alert. She is still a little wobbly when I get there, but she pushes through the door of the examining area, pulling on the lead to get to me, more than ready to go home. Puzzle doesn't have balance enough yet to jump. It takes help to get her into the car and the second help of a kind, passing neighbor to get her out of the car and into the house. Puz settles on the floor beneath the ceiling fan, a little drowsy but content.

Puzzle hasn't had many surgical procedures. The last was five years ago. This time she is slower to shake off the anesthesia than I remember. I have to remind myself that she's twelve now and that she has a slower metabolic rate than she used to. I can't expect her to let go of the drugs in her system the way she once did and the way the younger dogs still do, acting as though nothing happened just hours after they get home.

The golden hates fuss. As outgoing as she's always been in the search field, Puzzle has always disliked scrutiny and stares. She tolerates being the object of attention in presentations, because she's gracious and has a willing heart, but the laissez-faire attitude that makes her a good magnet dog, the casual, low-stress demeanor, is the very thing she wants from the humans around her. Knowing this, I keep an eye on her but give her space. She rests quietly, moving from room to room occasionally, finally choosing her favorite spot on my bedroom floor, where she stretches out in a relaxed, familiar pose.

I have kept the other dogs away from her. Their curiosity and kindly but tactless sniffing of the vet smell is an annoyance she just doesn't need. A few hours after we get home, she's resting easily. She seems tired but comfortable. She sleeps just steps away from my bed, and I only half sleep through the night beside her. Familiar sounds: I'm glad to hear her get up a few times and move for the water bowl I've put out, her tags jingling against its metal side as she deeply drinks.

By dawn Puzzle is upright again and on her chest, but she wants no part of breakfast. I see in her face the withdrawn expression I have noted a few times before. I can't place it. I don't understand it. I call the vet's office. Though she's ticking all the boxes with regard to movement and water and bodily functions, there is something amiss that I can see but cannot name. It's frightening, this inability to read a dog whose language I've come to think of as an extension of my own. The clinic staff confirms that Puzzle's doing all the right things. I should see improvement soon, they tell me, and I do. Just after I hang up, Puzzle rises again, takes a casual drink, and then looks at the door.

Maybe I've worried unnecessarily. Usually surrounded by her dog friends, perhaps Puz doesn't understand this isolation. Maybe she's lonely for the others or thinks in some way she's being punished. I open the bedroom door to let in Jake, Gambit, and Ace. At the sight of them, her head raises and her expression brightens. Ace comes forward to exchange nose sniffs, and she flops down beside him. He paws her forefeet softly. Her tail thumps the floor. Puzzle washes his face, and Ace returns the kindness, a single lap in the soft spot between her beautiful eyes. This is so much better, and my heart lifts.

I give Ace a scritch and Puzzle a kiss before I leave them together. "Sweetheart," I tell Puzzle on my way out the door, "I'm glad you're doing so much better. I'm going to get you some steak for a treat, and tomorrow maybe we'll do a little searching." Though she cannot follow the words, she seems to understand the affection in my voice and nuzzles my neck. With Ace beside her, Puzzle stretches flat beneath the ceiling fan, extending her back feet luxuriously, and yawns.

When I come home from the store an hour and a half later, Jake and Gambit meet me at the back door. They are verbal and anxious. Ace, who would normally be in the thick of them, isn't. Where is Ace? He is in my bedroom, pressed against Puzzle's chest. When I enter the room, there is something in his stricken face that tells me before I kneel to her and know. Puzzle is gone.

Making signs at the kitchen table.

27

LOVE, FIND US

THE LIGHT IS OUT in our house. Shades still drawn against the morning sun I'd thought might disturb Puzzle earlier, the walls lean in, and the house seems to fold on itself. I sit beside her on my bedroom floor. I call the vet's office and a pet crematorium, and while waiting for help to arrive, I message several people who knew and loved Puzzle best — friends and search team members and neighbors whose lost dogs she calmed enough to bring home. Search work and flying have made me relentlessly practical in a crisis, and perhaps these tasks save me, but my heart thuds in my ears anyway.

We meet kindness. Though this is not a standard service, two sweet young techs come from the vet clinic to take Puzzle. They must see death often. Even so, I am struck by their gentleness. One tech strokes her soft ear while the other covers her with a blanket. They carry her out on a little stretcher, and I walk beside her out of my room, through the house, and down the steps, Puzzle's forepaw in my hand all the way to the van that bears her away.

A woman at the crematorium is professional during my wooden phone call, telling me there is a discount for police and search dogs. But then this stranger, who realizes she once read a book I wrote about Puzzle, weeps when she recognizes her name. A neighbor ties a bouquet of roses on the fence. Another leaves a bowl of pasta on the porch. Later, others text me: they've made a donation to a search team in Puzzle's honor.

But what do I do, now that death's tasks are managed? A few

months earlier this dog had consoled me when I lost my father and in the following days when my confused mother could sometimes not remember my name. Now there is a hole in my vision, a traveling absence in the house in the places where Puzzle was. I am alone, and I can't stop moving; I pace the place, trying to find my lost dog. Outside, Ellen, who has known Puzzle since she was a puppy, wrestles with her own grief and keeps the other dogs occupied in the backyard. They are subdued out there, perhaps reading Ellen's sadness or processing their own. I am not sure what sense the dogs make of Puzzle's death. But they know.

At bedtime we are a family of strangers, the big dogs and I. We've been years together with our rituals, Jake and Gambit and Puzzle at the foot of my bed, and in this last year Ace, the little big dog, wedged between them. Tonight the survivors jump on the bed cautiously and settle in their spots without the usual grunts and scruffs and wagging. They are here and not here. We are us and not us. We avoid the place that was Puzzle's, a space we do not take.

I turn out the light. All day I've been dreading the darkness, and rightfully so. My divided mind races across three planes of despair: why this might have happened, how she might or might not have suffered, and an overwhelming sense that I failed Puzzle in her most urgent hour. In the language of search, I had missed, and she had died alone. I have never cried easily, and I haven't cried all day, but now in the darkness I don't have any fight left. I roll on my side, press hot tears into my pillow, and wail. I feel the shift of dogs at my feet. Jake and Gambit stiffen and cautiously drape their heads across my knees.

But it's Ace who comes up from the foot of the bed. He is small and strong and sure. Ace pads to the place where my heart hurts, where nothing answers, and he settles, pressing next to me in the way he had earlier cradled his dying friend.

"Hey," I whisper to him. Ace stretches forward and washes my face.

The sun rises. I explode into wakefulness when a cat lands in the middle of my belly at dawn. Thistle has food in her dish, but she always resents seeing any hint of the bottom of the bowl. Right now she can see the bottom of the bowl. The dogs roar with me down the hall to fill it, and I stumble to the coffeepot and drink with one hand and feed them all with the other — *Wolfen, appeased,* I call it. The dogs go to their feeding spots. I put one bowl fewer on the floor. Today I will drink more coffee than is sensible, clean the house fiercely, and throw a ball in the backyard until even young Gambit flops down in the grass, bemused and exhausted with play.

We continue.

Work will distract us, and there's plenty of lost-pet work to do in the coming days. It's vacation season, and that means more dogs and cats slipping through open doors and gates, straying from home, escaping from house sitters, or bolting from well-meaning friends who offered to pet sit without any clue that the uprooted dog would climb their low fence or that the displaced kitty would leave a speed streak across their faces between the car and the house. Kids, contractors, brand-new rescue fosters — pets escape from all of these, year-round, but more often in summer.

It's also very hot outside, and while most of the able-bodied dogs and cats are physically able to duck out of the heat, plenty of lost and panicked senior pets aren't. And the littlest ones don't know how to. Search for the very young and the very old is especially time-critical when temperatures soar to one hundred and above. And often the worried owners who contact me are just as fragile as the animals that have gone missing, if not more so. They meet me on their porches with their heads ducked against the sun. *I don't know. I don't know,* they tell me. *She has never gone missing before.*

On their behalf, I try to help in whatever way is needed. Some have no stamina for foot-canvassing. Some need help making signs. More than a few have no Internet connection or any idea how to use social media for their missing pet. Others need help searching shelters. Most need encouragement when they're at the edge of giving up.

It is a wider world of search that Ace has shown me. As a K9 handler working search and rescue for missing persons, my role beside a dog is singular. The terrain changes, the situation changes, but the job remains essentially the same: follow the dog. In the main, law enforcement interacts with the family and directs the search. Lost-pet response requires a different flexibility. You may make a hundred flyers for a lost Yorkie one day, walk through shelters for a poodle the next day, and the day after that run a search dog for a kitten trapped somewhere beneath an abandoned house. Lost-pet response also requires that double foundation in behavior and psychology, an investigator's sense of what might have happened in the friction between animal impulse and human choice. Objectivity, compassion, stamina, strategy: lost-pet work requires it all.

I am aware that even as I help others move through their losses, I am working through my own. Mom wavers, sometimes aware that Dad has died and Puzzle has followed him and sometimes blanketed from that grief. *Give Puz a hug for me,* she messages a couple of times, and I do not correct her.

I fill the first days after Puzzle by making more signs to loan out. The Fast Five loaner packet of yard signs I made a while ago sees a lot of use, and now more people ask to borrow them than there are signs to lend. With the dogs in attendance and the cats pawing at scraps of poster board, we listen to Sinatra, and I bend over the kitchen table, a marker dangling from my lip the way my mother's cigarette once did.

LOST DOG, I letter carefully across each sign. LOST DOG, LOST DOG, LOST DOG.

My mother's portrait
of Smokey and me.

This image stays with me:
Puzzle holding a stay next
to a detection find.

A HOT WIND blows across the scorched grass. Hot even at seven in the morning, yet there is an edge to it sometimes where we stand. A sliver of coolness gusts across us, promising change. The dogs turn their noses into the new air. Gambit sparks and Ace capers. They are ready, again, to run.

All the home dogs are grateful to get back to their jobs. This is the life they know and the activity they most want beside me. They need a challenge reinforced with interaction and affection. They've seemed worried by the upset rhythm and changed routines of the house, and if they could understand, I would apologize to them. I know I've been sluggish, short-tempered, and unresponsive. With the search dogs, at least, I've been holding out, avoiding K9 search training of any kind, unable to give any dog the *find* cues that were part of my life with Puzzle for so long. As useful as those LOST DOG signs I made will undoubtedly be, they were a sidestep, too, a way to avoid a routine I knew would hurt.

I know this about the dog I've loved and lost. Puzzle was intelligent and headstrong and bossy and willing and dear. But she was never self-indulgent. The golden retriever is a working dog, and she was a golden to her bones. I remember most how she soldiered through discomfort when I needed her to get the job done. Puzzle wakes me with her going. Whatever it takes, get back to work.

So I have put on my search boots to train with young Gambit on human scent and human finds. Not even dawn when we start, it is sultry already, the air humid and thick. I expect the sight of Gambit's sunny, eager face and his leap away—so like Puzzle's—to rip right through me, but when I shout that first "Find!" and see the boy take the space at a bound, head up, snagging scent and joyful, it is relief I feel, and a sense of Puzzle so near that I could almost touch her. Gambit and I have a good morning of hard searches and challenging finds. We are both better for it. The young golden returns home with a bounce in his step.

Ace also goes back to training. He has seen my get-ready motions and knows what's up, rising on his back legs to bat at me playfully with his paws. The day's heat makes his work even harder in the late afternoon. That parched wind has risen, funneling air through the spent summer underbrush. Everything is in motion, including scent, and I feel for little Ace working across the dust eddies and scattering pollen. We are searching for fur from border collie Dutch today. Dutch's owner is the one who'd generously provided two big bags of Dutch clippings, and I've tucked open tins and mesh sacks of black-and-white fur across today's half-acre space. I used tiny toddler ponytail holders to tie some tufts of fur together; otherwise one good gust of wind would send every bit of Dutch aloft. Ace is a talented little dog, but finding a Dutch tuft on a roof four houses away might be too much to ask of him.

With his long, low-slung build and centuries of ratters scrambling through his DNA, Ace's search style still has quirks. That hitch in his step, where the muscles didn't knit after the dog attack, still slides into a sideways shimmy when he's narrowing scent. Sometimes his backside still tries to outrun his nose. I can read that signal now. When Ace skitters sideways, he's close to his find. He'll pop out of it at the last minute when he gets to the source. It's like watching a kid driver pull skids in an icy parking lot.

Ace's search vocabulary is a new physical language for me, and I am beginning to make sense of his moves that mark scent snagged, scent intensified, scent found. Ace is always eager. Today he shows me how eager. Some training dogs are happy to make one find, get a reward, and be done with it, but the especially high-drive dogs are excited when charged to *find more*. Crazy little Ace is one of those dogs. Rather than flagging, he winds up with each added cue. Ace finds a first tin of Dutch fur wedged beneath an overturned planter, and then another and another, working his way across rock, grass, and rubble. The last tin of Dutch's coat is hidden deep in underbrush, and when Ace narrows that scent to its source, he dives into it so eagerly that he emerges wearing a beard of border collie fur. He is successful, and he knows it. Ace sits, beaming. He sneezes, and a cloud of Dutch rises, lifting over the fence and beyond.

After a crisis of confusion in which she cannot remember my name, my mother opens her door to me at last. It takes the presence of a social worker and the insistence of a police officer to get her to agree. Mom knows she has a daughter; she has the shape of me without the details. The storm has done more damage to the house than even the insurance company had caught, and black mold has bloomed along one wall at the far end of the house, a danger to anyone but especially to my mother, who has been breathing it since the first false all-clear. It is time to go — and she knows and doesn't know it as she sits winking in the sunlight from the front seat of my car. We are masked up and hustling her away from here as fast as we can. Tiny, frail, her gaze uncertain, my mother carries her head high nonetheless, and tells the police officer that he needn't hover. *I am not a flight risk,* she says to him firmly. Then she extends her hand in the way of '50s debutantes and says, *You've been very kind.* I pack up her most-needed items and her two beloved cats. We are headed to medical attention and then to a pretty, pet-friendly apartment in an assisted living facility not far from my house. Exhausted and overwhelmed, I'm fueled by relief.

My mother watches me wrest boxes across the lawn. Does she feel the same sense of déjà vu that I do, revisiting our years of hasty moves? Does she remember the peculiar waddle humans make with a cat carrier full of shifting, unhappy feline? Because I am making it now, swaying drunkenly to the music of Butterfly's and Patches's angry yowls. They are last to be captured and loaded into the car, their bewildered faces relaxing slightly when they catch sight and scent of Mom in the seat ahead.

"Susie," she says—and she has my name back, just like that— "get that picture from the living room of you and Smokey." In a house crowded with clutter and eighty years' worth of possessions, this is the only memento she has asked for.

I know the photograph she means, taken not long after the little cat's escape from the neighbor's shed, a few days after we buried her kitty doppelganger in the backyard. Mom cradles the framed picture in her arms, tracing the outline of her first-grade daughter and the cat across the dusty glass. She is silent as we drive, sometimes gazing out the window at the place she is leaving, at the shorebirds and the winter-silver lake, sometimes looking down at the picture of Smokey and me. Then she begins to tell Smokey stories—how the kitten would play fetch with the crumpled cellophane of a cigarette pack, how she would head-bump the door when she needed to go out. She remembers our elaborate, misguided funeral for her. She says, "Your father saved her. She would have died without your dad."

While my mother's short-term and recent memory falters and there are cold, long moments when she looks at me without recognition, that picture, propped up in her little apartment, seems to be a gateway to her past. With a little prompting, she connects. Mom knew a lot of tragedy when very young. I might have expected shadows in her stories, but there are none. For weeks she speaks of a loved puppy named Pokey and a later family dog named Chief, before she married, and sometimes she progresses right through to the sequence of cats and dogs that found us or were themselves found. LucyLou is there, and Tiger, Rosie, Smokey, Archy and Mehitabel, and Bertie. Buddy and Bunny, the kitten Valentine. Muddy Wiggles is there, too, and Mom laughs rather wickedly, telling me, *Your grandmother was pissed!* Through their names, sometimes she finds my own.

My mother's verbs are fluid—from *is* to *was* and back again—and time has lost its order. In the final months of her life, she forgets what we have lost. *Ask your dad,* she says to me sometimes, or *Give Puz a good scratch for me.* She asks about Ace's latest search adventures in the same breath that she reminds me to feed Rosie only chicken kibble, never fish. Living or dead, we are all very much present to my mother and need tending. I do not correct her. And so we laugh across that seamless ocean, old blows softened, old grievances forgotten, where only the best of love and memory remain.

Not every lost-pet search needs a search dog, and even as the man on the phone is asking if I can bring in a K9, I'm sidelining Ace from the job. The man is an acquaintance I have passed in the hallway outside my office. I'm not sure how he knew to ask or got my number, but his rapid-fire first words—*Hiwe'vemetmyniecelostagerbilweneedasearchdog*—are not at all what I expected on the one day I've given myself to get a pedicure. I cup my ear to hear the phone over the nail salon's meditation music with waterfalls, my feet wrapped in paraffin and mango-coconut-banana moisturizer. What was I thinking? I smell like the buffet table at a Jack Tar Village.

The niece—and the man's brother, sister-in-law, nephew—are here in a motel, visiting. They brought their pets with them: a cat and a gerbil. The gerbil has slipped from his cage somehow. He disappeared this morning before they got back from breakfast. They returned to an open cage door and no gerbil, and the cat is at large in the room. The caller has his suspicions. *You would have to know that cat,* he says. *Can you help us? Can you bring your search dog?*

I'm glad to help search, but this is no mission for rat-catching Ace, who might have a conflict of interest. The man is disappointed. He hoped a search dog would be faster. Certainly a search dog might be faster, and maybe too fast, I think. But it's a small room in a new building, and unless this gerbil shot out the door when the family opened it—*Or the cat got him*, says the man, already pretty certain—he's in there somewhere. With five of us searching the space, I think there's a good chance we can flush the gerbil into view.

I've driven past this pet-friendly motel often but have never visited. It is pretty and functional, and I imagine that any gerbil that slipped out the door would briefly live the high life in the pool area, bordered by blooming crepe myrtles and crumbed with dropped food from the vending machines not far away. The family, when they open the door to me, swear that Nutmeg couldn't have slipped out the door. They tell me they came in being supercareful, afraid that the cat might shoot out.

In an overturned motel room that now looks like a crime scene, that cat is a presence. She's a stunner, an exquisite seal-point Siamese with a triangular face and tip-tilted blue eyes, wearing a black velvet collar and a pair of tags. She sits on a small table and acknowledges me with a graceful lift of her chin, the tip of her tail flicking where it is wrapped around her dark front paws. Her name is Elsa, the young son tells me, and at home she likes to catch birds.

Elsa shifts a little, watching, as the family and I briefly sit to make a plan. I have an idea that we work the room like a tiny grid search, a line made up of three of us on our hands and knees looking in and under and up into everything we encounter, and the other two watching from the opposite side of the room to spot the gerbil if he's flushed. The family has already done something like that, the father tells me—well, not as systematic, more like random banging things and shaking them and turning them upside down.

And so, while the parents crouch like catchers at home base against the wall to the bathroom, the two kids and I crawl around the motel room, peering into every crevice and fold with my SAR flashlights, hoping to catch sight of Nutmeg or a flash of eyeshine. The young girl who lost him is remarkably stoic about the whole thing.

She can't be more than six, but she's more interested in the search than she is bereft, and the possibility of seeing Nutmeg's sparkling eyes is more exciting to her still. She and her brother scoot and crawl and slither like old search pros while the cat turns and watches us from her spot on high. It is a thorough grid search, too, with every blanket and pillowcase stripped again, every suitcase upended, and every shoe shaken. We find other treasures, including a dime, a quarter, and a tiny brass earring on a French hook braided into the carpet under the bed, but no gerbil. The little girl says, "I smell coconut!" and I wince.

Nutmeg is not in the bathroom, I'm told. The parents say that the door to the bathroom was shut while they were gone. They had a look already anyway, a quick sweep of the tiny tiled space, but they open the door and invite me to go ahead and look again. Then we hear a sound: *ch-ch-ch-ch-ch-ch-ch, ch-ch-ch-ch-ch-ch*. All of us hear it at the same time, including Elsa, whose eyes darken with interest. The cat leaps from the table and stalks low across the floor. Elsa freezes, intent on the bathroom door.

Ch-ch-ch-ch-ch-ch-ch, ch-ch-ch-ch-ch-ch.

"What the—?" says the father at the same time I say, "Shut the door."

We've got him. Much to Elsa the cat's disappointment, we send the little girl into the bathroom for Nutmeg, who must have scaled the shower curtain and then slid into the bathtub. Maybe he's been there the whole time. Maybe he just now slid in. But he's not been able to get out again, and it's Nutmeg's little feet we hear scrambling across the smooth acrylic, a lost gerbil in a bathtub getting nowhere on the run.

Ace has found a dog that from a distance looks so much like Puzzle it is as if we are seeing a ghost.

I've been wistful today. We've been walking her old neighborhood route, Ace and I, when we round a corner and the little dog's head pops. He's not on a search cue, but—perhaps a carryover from his lost days evading attack—he physically remarks the dogs and cats he picks up. What has Ace caught? A scent? A sight? A sound? I don't know, but he's intent on an odd space for a family pet. When we turn down the utility alley, a light golden retriever stands at the shadowed bend of it, head lowered to the bordering weeds. A beautiful senior golden, moving a little stiffly. My unreasoning heart leaps, and even Ace makes a squeak of recognition, straining hard on his lead before he raises his nose and shivers and pauses, confused.

Not Puzzle, but a dog very like her, and alone.

We hold still for a moment, cautious. I cue Ace forward again, and it must be the scent of him that the old golden picks up first. Now I can see the retriever better: he is a very old male who does not appear to hear our approach. He raises his silvered head thoughtfully. I see his nose working, and his tail swishes a little. He is disoriented, loose from somewhere, strayed and stuck in the bend of an alley he can't quite negotiate. The dog takes a few uncertain steps toward us, turning his head a little, as though he sees better from the sides of his eyes.

And now I recognize him. It's Tanner, one of the dogs I found on the couch visiting Puzzle months ago. That gracious old boy has slipped through his gate again. You couldn't quite call him a runner, but he is a critical wanderer. Just a few houses from home, he is lost, bewildered by the overgrown alley. Standing in the blind bend of it, he risks getting hit by a turning car, too.

Nose to nose, Tanner greets Ace. We lead the old boy home gently, and he is glad to be led, his pace increasing slightly with every step toward the scent he knows. In the yard he nuzzles his best friend, Nala, the younger dog who this time preferred the cool grass to wandering. We leave them to their family, and that golden swoosh of tail, familiar and endearing, is the last thing we see before the gate latches firmly behind them.

❦

Having worked search and rescue for almost twenty years, I recognize one day that almost any car trip I make crosses ground I once searched. Local geography is overlaid with the names and faces of those reunited, and shadowed sometimes by those who were never found. This is no less true with the search for lost pets, but here the challenge is often much closer to home, a search that begins with a neighbor's frantic cry or the flash of a dog caught in someone's headlights as they turn down my street.

I stand in my front yard one evening and realize that in our immediate neighborhood, with Puzzle, with Ace, or alone, I've brought home at least one dog from eight houses in my sightline and three just beyond, some fifteen dogs in a handful of years. I can no longer count the lost dogs from farther away. And the cats. (The gerbils, at least, are in the single digits.) Every search is a story of what can go wrong when we think all is well. Sometimes it was the owner that asked for help. Sometimes it was the displaced pet, bewildered and anxious, I met first. Nothing has changed since then.

Owners who ask for search help are often apologetic: *He's only a dog, but . . . I know she's just a cat, but . . .* I need no persuading. Research bears out what animal lovers have known for a long time. The pets we bring into our families can make a difference to our lives, our health, and our happiness. Making a difference to them improves us, too. The love matters. Their fates matter. And when they go missing and the potential for their suffering is real, our faithfulness to them also matters.

Missing-pet response is a service that I'm proud to be a part of. I am not the only soul out here doing this, certainly. In my area alone, there are at least five other trained lost-pet search specialists on the ground — some paid, some volunteer — a couple of skilled humane-trap capture teams, and a dozen or so more volunteers running social media lost-pet pages, plus any number of shelter volunteers and paid staff members who reach out to us about this dog or that cat that may be the one we seek. Extrapolate those numbers nationwide and the workforce for lost pets is impressive, particularly in urban areas. There are a lot of us out here making signs, running search dogs, mapping sighting reports, rigging humane traps and wildlife cameras, and sweeping the darkness with flashlights for eyeshine. There are many important, informed ways to serve. The need for meaningful help is great.

Here, a few friends and neighbors have stepped forward to volunteer. Often the owner we worked with on the last search joins the team for the next. We make signs, post online, visit shelters, canvass neighbors, and I run Ace, the little found dog, now a search K9, on behalf of the lost. There is more we can offer. With Ace for tight spaces and rubble, I hope to train a direction-of-travel dog to show us which way a lost pet wandered. We've got a practice drone to crash with and a better one to fly across the search spaces that need a big-picture view. That friend in Minnesota who leads a humane trapping team has offered to make us one of their gentle traps, tripped by a laser, its video fed straight to a cell phone. Somewhere my father leans forward, fascinated and certain that this is not at all over the top.

My parents are with me in some way on every lost-pet search. They taught me respect for animals at an early age, giving me my first lessons in thinking like a dog or a cat. Where do the lost dogs go? Mom and Dad paid attention. So many of the things I learned as a child are echoed in modern strategy for lost pets. My troubled parents, searching for something just out of reach between them, had better success with the animals they saved. They showed me how to read a dog in motion and a dog poised with indecision. They taught me how to reassure a panicked cat from thirty paces. My parents knew all about living at the edge of wilderness. They were made for the kind of stillness that brought the wanderers in.

A dog whose mission was always reunion, off-duty Puzzle also attracted animals from their hiding places, and much of what I understand now I learned beside her. *Soft posture. No fuss. Don't stare.* None of this was intentional on her part. Puzzle simply was what she was. One way or another, she could bring a frightened dog to trust.

Now, when it's the lost dog I meet first, I try to become a magnet human, or at least not someone to fear. Is it possible? I think so. I recover dogs best when I have the patience of my parents and the softness of my golden retriever. It is counter to every human impulse, but it works. In many cases the loose dog freezes to make sense of the figure in his sightline. If they aren't spooked from their experiences, the gregarious dogs will often trot right to me. But the aloof dogs pause before they approach and retreat, freeze and approach, head down and tails trembling. The xenophobic dogs, reactive to so many things, are the most difficult to bring in by hand. When Puz was with me, it was easier. Even the most skittish sometimes ducked their way to her, and thus to me. Without her, I sit down on the grass and try to channel that sweet serenity. I hear my mother's wisdom — *Let them think it's their idea* — and my father's words, *Don't give them a reason to run.* So I toy with the weeds and scratch my head and yawn and look away. Calming signals, behaviorists call these. Dogs give them to each other and share them with us. It's a bittersweet moment, full of memory, waiting there on the grass. But it's a heart-lifting moment, too, when those lost pets find an ally. I gaze up at the clouds and hold my breath a little, sensing a frightened animal's approach. First a twitch at the edge of my vision, he is a shadow, then a dog, crouch-crawling toward me over hard ground.

Love comes full circle.

AFTERWORD

FOUR YEARS AFTER Ace wandered alone, I still look for some hint of his lost owners, online and off-. Having traveled the spaces where he was purportedly seen—and found—I've shown his face to area vets, groomers, boarding facilities, mail persons, delivery drivers, and neighbors. How hard will people try for a lost pet and an owner they do not know? I've been encouraged by the kindness of many strangers who have taken their time to consider this dog lost one, two, three, four years ago. (Because Ace was born with a significant telltale trait, a vet clinic near where he was found reviewed every Maltese, poodle, and Maltipoo the clinic had on record to see if a dog with that trait showed up there—a hero's effort.) I am grateful to the people who stopped to help the search when they did not have to. While I may never learn where he came from, every moment spent reaching back to Ace's history has been an instruction on how dogs get lost and stay lost and what must happen for them to come home. One dog's past in Conroe has informed how I search for other lost pets, and for the found pets, how I search for their owners.

Ace brought with him a plot twist. In unexpected ways, the scruffy dog from Conroe reunited me with my parents. My father was the first to hear about Ace and his troubles. My mother would spend days searching online leads on his behalf. At our own eleventh hour,

Ace was a point of focus for the three of us. The little dog that had known love and lost it recalled us to our own.

My father died just months after his eightieth birthday. My mother followed him the next year. They had last seen each other in some parking lot in the early '90s, I think, Dad handing over old photos that included their wedding pictures, my mother's family album, and a succession of sepia images of beloved dogs and cats. It was the last of our family, in a box, that my father handed over, but having moved on to other lives and other loves, in some part my parents never let each other go. When my father said, "Take care of your mother," he had recognized her emerging frailty of mind. At the end of her life, my mother often said how glad she was that my father had found happiness at last. *"Tell him,"* she would say with such urgency, forgetting that he was gone.

Both parents were figures in my earlier works—the hazard of having a daughter who writes memoir!—and both knew I was writing this book. My father heard some of the stories that would be included here before they were written. I owe Dad for some of these specifics. Occasionally he'd flash out a snippet of old memory that wasn't always comfortable. Dad couldn't exactly remember the name of the hitchhiking dog in Wichita Falls, but he recalled my disastrous finger-painting of the rent-house wallpaper in Technicolor detail. My mother, who survived the Rowlett tornado of 2015 and eventually did agree to move to an assisted living facility closer to me, read some of these chapters or heard me read them to her. Mom was a champion for animals, for mental health care, for resilience, and for love, and she encouraged me to write the truth we shared.

My mother was a woman of intelligence and humor. With advanced COPD, even on oxygen she was increasingly confused. Once, when she realized that she'd just asked me to read her a chapter we'd finished moments before, she said to me smugly, "But I'm the very best audience. I can be fascinated again and again." Hard-edged as some of our early life together was, in these chapters my mother recognized the beauty I found there, the tenderness and respect I hold for both my parents. Mom enjoyed the Wiggles chapter especially, where the small dog and the child were reunited through her own enterprise. The day before she died, my mother had me write the dedication to this book on the whiteboard at the foot of her hospital bed. And she asked me to read the Wiggles chapter to her again. "Swoosh," she said about her ingenuity in that story. Miming her basketball shot, she said with a grin, "Nothin' but net."

At the time of this writing, Ace is eight, maybe nine years old. He still works confined spaces and rubble—most often for cats, whose lost behaviors include a lot of silent tucking and hiding, and sometimes for orphaned litters of kittens or puppies whose birthplaces are uncertain. Ace is now joined in our MAR work by Paisley, a Shetland sheepdog puppy in training who lives to trail, my direction-of-travel dog at last. We mix formal exercises with motivational searches most days—short, high-energy finds that earn big joy and praise. Heading out to the same space where Puzzle trained, we pass a stream made of river rock that I had built in her memory. FIND MORE, PUZ, reads a stone in that small rush of water. We head out to do the same.

ACKNOWLEDGMENTS

No book is published without the help of good people, and it's my fortune to have been encouraged, challenged, and supported by a whole host of them while writing this one. First, many thanks to the dog trainers, animal behaviorists, veterinarians, and lost-pet specialists whose work has informed my own. Some of you I have met, some I have interviewed, some I have trained with, some I've run dogs beside, and some I've simply followed workshop to workshop, book to book. I would particularly like to acknowledge the work of Dr. Patricia McConnell, Dr. Stanley Coren, Dr. Risë Van Fleet, Dr. Sophia Yin, Dr. Ian Dunbar, Elizabeth Marshall Thomas, Jennifer Arnold, Alexandra Horowitz, Sarah Kalnajs, Victoria Stillwell, and Cat Warren. Many thanks go to Kat Albrecht, certainly among the first to develop and formalize lost-pet recovery strategy, and her colleagues and associates with the Missing Animal Response Network. I must also acknowledge the following lost-pet response individuals, teams, and organizations, whose fieldwork I have had the opportunity to follow online or off-line: Bonnie McCririe Hale of Texas Pet Detectives Association, Kimberley Freeman of LostCatFinder.com, The Retrievers Lost Pet Recovery Team, Granite State Lost Dog and Cat Recovery, Buddha Dog Rescue and Recovery, Duck Team 6, Landa Coldiron, James Branson and Three Retrievers, Mutts & Mayhem Search and Rescue Team, and the ongoing work of Lost Pets of America and Mission Reunite. Special thanks to the Animal Shelter Volunteers of Texas, whose outreach efforts saved Ace. I am also grateful to owners-turned-search-strategists Stormy Brock, Drew and Laura Evans, Jim Hill, and Jennifer Doerflinger Hill, whose searches provided so much insight. Their love, strategy, and perseverance made all the difference to their lost dogs, and their choices informed the advice I give owners now.

I am grateful for the ongoing support and encouragement of my agent, Jim Hornfischer of Hornfischer Literary Management, and my editor, Susan Canavan, at Houghton Mifflin Harcourt. Also at HMH, I would like to thank these good people for their patience and expertise: Jenny Xu, Mary Cait Miliff, Martha Kennedy, Lisa Glover, Liz Duvall, Taryn Roeder, Liz Anderson, Emily Snyder, Crystal Paquette, and Katie Kimmerer. Many thanks to Kennedy Rhoades at Layered for her support and encouragement on a twelve-hour day with this manuscript.

The following friends were beside me through the loss of my parents and Puzzle in the span of a year—at the same time I was writing this book. So much love to Marina Hsieh, Ellen Sanchez, Susan Blatz, Jon and Suzan Morris, Kim Cain, Devon Thomas Treadwell, Carolyn Zagami, Paige Whittingham, Robin Hopes, Christa Bellows, Rob M. Seaborn, Cindi and Johnny MacPherson, Terry and Michele Benjamin.

Lost-Pet Checklists

Before your pet has a chance to go missing, here are some important ways to prepare:

1. Make sure your pet always wears a collar or harness with current contact information attached. Replacing tags, some modern collars have names and numbers printed on the collar itself. Breakaway collars or harnesses are possible alternatives for owners who worry about pets snagging and strangling on their collars.

2. Microchip your pet and make sure that contact and address information are updated. A useful tip: when you move, change your dog's microchip and tag information on the same day you change your address with the post office.

3. Keep a snippet of your pet's fur in a freezer bag for use by a search K9, if needed. If you replace your dog's or cat's collar, the old collar can also be useful as a scent article for the search dog. Place it in a sealed freezer bag, where the scent should remain viable for six months.

4. Using a nontoxic inkpad for rubber stamps, make a pawprint impression. Prints of all four paws are ideal, but at least one paw can give searchers an artifact to compare to any found tracks.

5. Consider a GPS or radio-frequency pet-tracking device attached to your pet's collar.

6. Become familiar with and bookmark lost-pet pages for your area on Facebook and connect with your neighborhood on NextDoor.

7. Store a few quick sign-making materials. A good starter sign kit could include five full-sized pieces of neon posterboard, five out-dated campaign signs with stakes, a roll of clear packing tape, and a wide-nibbed black permanent marker. With these on hand, you can make five bright signs for ground staking in about twenty minutes.

8. Keep two or three current pictures of your pet that include at least one whole body shot and a face shot against a plain background. In the event you need to post photos of your pet, shots with busy backgrounds make your pet more difficult to see from a moving vehicle. Also store a photo of at least one vet record of your pet and a clear photo of you with your pet to help prove you are the owner of the lost animal. Savvy finders are now wary of false claims using photos lifted from social media posts, so have additional proof on hand to reassure them.

If your pet goes missing, here are critical search strategies to consider. **When possible, divide the search tasks below with reliable family or friends.**

Creating Awareness

1. Make an immediate visual canvass of the area where the pet was lost; talk to neighbors and passersby. Make a point to connect with those walking their own dogs. Many take the same routes once or twice a day and are excellent resources for sightings. Talk

also with your mail carrier, delivery drivers, and utility workers. If there is ongoing construction work in your area, ask crew members to keep an eye out for your pet as well.

2. Build, copy, and post flyers and signs in your neighborhood and with nearby businesses — especially vet clinics, pet supply stores, groomers, gas stations, convenience and grocery stores. Post one below your own mailbox. Some city ordinances or HOA policies restrict where signs can be placed along streets or how long such signs can be there. Placing signs on parked car windows, asking neighbors to "host" signs in their yards, and deploying volunteers to hold signs at intersections are often successful workarounds.

3. Post on social media, particularly area Craigslist and Facebook lost-pet pages and NextDoor. On NextDoor, select the widest posting area possible. Consider also using email lost-pet distribution platforms like HelpingLostPets, PawBoost, etc. Some of these platforms are free, while others have an associated charge. Make sure to have notifications pushed to your email or phone if possible. Once you post on social media, check those resources at least once or twice a day. Not only monitor your own post but watch others that come in. Often finders post a pet they have found without necessarily checking for a lost-pet post that matches.

4. Canvass your area by foot or vehicle repeatedly with flyers at different times. While you may encounter some of the same people, you will more than likely meet new ones on every canvass. Hand flyers and personal interaction help people invest in your search.

5. Make sure that local signage is easy to read, is reasonably weatherproof, and includes a prompt method of contact — a phone number or email address that can be answered quickly and reliably, day or night, is best. Excellent tips for LOST or FOUND PET signs can

be found at missinganimalresponse.com and missingpetpartner ship.org.

6. Notify the microchip company that your pet is lost or stolen. This is an important flag to put on your pet's record, so that any finder becomes aware that the pet is lost and an owner is actively searching for it.

7. Remind others (on signs and in conversation) not to chase or call to your pet. An anxious animal processes strangers — and even its owners — differently, and calling or chasing can actually push an animal back into flight mode.

8. Tag your vehicle. Using wide-tipped markers made for writing on glass, put critical information on the back window. Missinganimal response.com has excellent tips for car tagging.

Search Strategies

9. Consider the use of a K9 lost-pet search promptly (within twenty-four hours is advantageous , though experienced K9 teams may be effective after more time has passed). Fresh scent is always optimal for trailing dog success. Area search in situations where an animal may be trapped or down with injuries is equally time-critical for the lost pet's sake.

10. Check area shelters. Beginning with shelters closest to the place where your pet was last seen, make a physical check at least every two or three days, and when possible provide information to staff about your missing pet. Working outward from the area where the animal was lost, check shelters incrementally farther away. Sometimes drivers will encounter a wandering or hurt animal and will take that animal to a shelter near where they are going rather

than the shelter closest to where they found the animal. Keep in mind that your animal may wander awhile before ending up in a shelter, so shelter checks should be maintained for the duration of the search.

11. If you receive sighting information that suggests your animal has been seen near wilderness, work with a lost-pet consultant or humane trapping specialist to set up a feeding station/wildlife camera/humane trap in the area. This is thoughtful, strategic business that requires expertise, but many strategists offer consulting services by phone or online. Missinganimalresponse.com offers a state-by-state list of trained lost-pet consultants.

The Search over Time

12. Once you have the search established, keep information refreshed with new signs and photos periodically. This reinforces awareness and indicates that the search is ongoing. Updated wording on signs might say STILL MISSING or STILL SEARCHING FOR plus the critical information. Think creatively: some pets have been reunited owing to flyers attached to Halloween treats, placed near GPS-based gaming sites, or taped to items at garage sales.

13. In addition to shelter outreach, check Petfinder.com at least once a week. That platform is commonly used by both shelters and rescue groups to promote animals available for adoption, and it allows you to plug in information that narrows the search. Thus it is possible to search for every listed male senior Chihuahua in a hundred-mile area if you choose to. Consider searching with fewer discriminators and a wide general area, as sometimes breeds, gender, and age are incorrectly listed and dogs lost in one city can easily end up in another.

14. Revisit your social media posts with updates. Encourage readers to invest in your search by keeping the narrative fresh and adding new photos. A *still searching* post may not be as effective as *Joey has been missing two weeks. On this kind of hot day, he liked a taste of my ice cream* — and add a new photo. Some searching owners create standalone *Bring (name of pet) Home* pages on social media, which are easily shared.

When You Find a Pet

1. Do not chase. Cats in place, unless injured, should be noted and photographed, if possible, but not pursued. Many outdoor cats are "rescued" from their own homes with good intentions but are not actually lost at all. Wandering dogs should be contained and brought into safety, if safely possible. If you are unable to hold on to the pet while you search for an owner, the animal should be taken to the shelter closest to where it is found.

2. For a loose animal that is not in your possession, a quick cell-phone photograph and a social media post on a page relevant to the area can yield important sighting information. Include location, day, time, and the direction the animal was traveling in.

3. If the animal is in your possession and is wearing a tag, use the contact methods listed. Most rabies tags also include the name of the vet clinic where the vaccination was given, and in the absence of an owner tag, that clinic can research the rabies tag and may be able to contact the owner. If the pet is not wearing any tag with current information, have it scanned for a microchip. Veterinarians, shelters, lost-pet teams, and some rescues usually do this free of charge.

4. Make and post FOUND signs local to the place where found. Consider the closest busy intersections along routes people must take

to commute to work or buy groceries or get gas. Often searchers are also cruising neighborhoods, so if you found the animal near your home, a sign in your own front yard can be an excellent way to connect.

5. Post online. Craigslist, Facebook, and NextDoor are excellent resources. Make sure to check those resources for *Lost* notices that match the animal you have found. Deep checks—that is, back-searching across time on those platforms—are especially helpful, as the pet found today may have been lost weeks ago.

6. Touch base with care providers, including veterinarians, shelters, and local rescue groups.

7. If you transport an animal out of the area where it was found (to your distant home or shelter, for example), keep in mind that owners may be searching much closer to their own homes. It is important to spread word in the area where the found animal originated.

8. Please remember that a found pet may be muddy, hungry, and in distress, but this does not necessarily mean that that pet has been abandoned or abused. A dog lost even one day after a rainstorm can emerge unkempt and anxious. A cat that has been stuck in a shed for a week may be thin and sunken-eyed. Though compassion moves us on behalf of such animals and we may become quickly attached, it is important to consider the pet's owner, who may also be searching. A found pet should not be immediately adopted or given a new home before you make a meaningful attempt at reunion. This is reinforced by law in most states, which consider pets property rightfully and legally owned.

SOURCES

Albrecht, Kat. *Dog Detectives: How to Train Your Dog to Find Lost Pets.* Dogwise Publishing, 2007.

"Alleviating Concerns." *Alleviating Concerns about Microchips | HomeAgain Pet Microchip,* HomeAgain, 2018, microchip.homeagain.com/alleviating-concerns.html.

Arnold, Carrie. "Pictures of Rescued Pets: How They Are Coping with Harvey." *National Geographic,* August 28, 2017. https://news.nationalgeographic.com/2017/08/dogs-harvey-hurricane-pets-cats/. Accessed 19 February 2018.

ASPCA. *How Many Pets Are Lost? How Many Find Their Way Home? ASPCA Survey Has Answers.* Press release. New York: ASPCA, 28 June 2012. Online.

Blow, Stanley III. "After 559 Days, Murphy's Home at Last." *Waterbury Record,* 14 January 2016.

Brown, Ali. *Scaredy Dog! Understanding and Rehabilitating Your Reactive Dog.* Allentown, PA: Tanacacia Press, 2004.

"Dogs, Dogs, Dogs." *The Andy Griffith Show,* written by Everett Greenbaum, James Fritzell, directed by Bob Sweeney, CBS/Mayberry Enterprises, 1963.

"'Every Day Is Tag Day™'—Is Your Pet Protected?" *American Humane,* American Humane, 7 April 2018, www.americanhumane.org/blog/every-day-is-tag-day-is-your-pet-protected/.

McConnell, Patricia. "Caution: Your Dog Is Watching." *The Bark,* Issue 14: Spring 2001 (6 March 2018), reprinted in *The Other End of the Leash* by Patricia McConnell, PhD, http://www.patriciamcconnell.com/finding-a-lost-dog.

"More Than Ever, Pets Are Members of the Family," Harris Poll, 6 July, 2015, https://theharrispoll.com/whether-furry-feathered-or-flippers-a-flapping-americans-continue-to-display-close-relationships-with-their-pets-2015-is-expected-to-continue-the-pet-industrys-more-than-two-decades-strong/.